MANAGING FOR PROFIT
IN THE NONPROFIT WORLD

PAUL B. FIRSTENBERG

THE FOUNDATION CENTER

1986

The excerpts on pages 12, 32, 127, 216, 225–226 are from *In Search of Excellence* by Thomas J. Peters and Robert H. Waterman, Jr. Copyright © 1982 by Thomas J. Peters and Robert H. Waterman, Jr. Reprinted by permission of Harper & Row, Publishers, Inc.

The excerpts on pages 30, 48–50, 212 from *Marketing for Nonprofit Organizations*, 2nd Ed. by Philip Kotler, © 1982, are reprinted by permission of Prentice-Hall, Englewood Cliffs, NJ.

The excerpts on pages 31, 133, 134, 135, 139 from *Direct Marketing, Strategy, Planning, Execution* by Edward L. Nash, 1982, are reprinted by permission of McGraw-Hill Book Company.

The excerpts on pages 35, 36 are from *Widening Circles* by Elizabeth Sturz. Copyright © 1983 by Harper & Row Publishers, Inc. Reprinted by permission.

The excerpts on pages 46–47, 57–58 from "Helping Hands, Companies Change the Ways They Make Charitable Contributions," by Wendy L. Wall (June 21, 1984) are reprinted by permission of *The Wall Street Journal,* © Dow Jones & Co., Inc., 1984. All rights reserved.

The excerpts on pages 118–119, 131, 179, 205 from "The Business of Managing Arts Organizations," by Thomas J. C. Raymond and Stephen A. Greyser (July/August 1978) are reprinted by permission of the *Harvard Business Review.* Copyright © 1978 by the President and Fellows of Harvard College; all rights reserved.

The excerpt on page 144 is from *Management Control in Nonprofit Organizations,* rev. ed., by Robert N. Anthony and Regina E. Herzlinger. © Richard D. Irwin, Inc., 1980, Homewood, Illinois.

The excerpt on pages 145–146 from "Why Data Systems in Nonprofit Organizations Fail," by Regina E. Herzlinger (January/February 1977) is reprinted by permission of the *Harvard Business Review.* Copyright © 1977 by the President and Fellows of Harvard College; all rights reserved.

The excerpt on page 221 is from *Managing for Excellence,* by David L. Bradford and Allan R. Cohen. New York: John Wiley and Sons, © 1984. Reprinted by permission.

The table on page 242 is from *The Big Foundations,* by Waldemar A. Nielsen. New York: Twentieth Century Fund, 1972. Reprinted by permission.

The excerpts on pages 133, 138, 225 from "Broadening the Concept of Marketing," by Philip Kotler and Sidney J. Levy are reprinted by permission from the *Journal of Marketing,* January 1969, published by the American Marketing Association.

Printed and bound in the United States of America

Cover designed by Greg Apicella

Library of Congress Cataloging-in-Publication Data

Firstenberg, Paul B., 1933–
    Managing for profit in the nonprofit world.

    Bibliography: p.

    Includes index.
    1. Corporations, Nonprofit—Finance. 2. Corporations, Nonprofit—Management.   I. Title.
HG 4027.65.F55 1986   658'.048   86-80827
ISBN 0-87954-161-X

This book is dedicated to
Deborah Phillips and Ron Sherman —
for being there.

MANAGING FOR PROFIT IN THE NONPROFIT WORLD

Contents

Acknowledgments

This book grew out of a search for a text focused on the process of managing tax-exempt, nonprofit organizations. There are a number of volumes pertaining to specialized aspects of managing nonprofit organizations, such as budgeting, financial controls, accounting, marketing, and the like. But no one appears to have attempted the publication of an integrated overview of the business of managing exempt, nonprofit organizations.

In putting together a course for the Yale School of Management on nonprofit enterprises, I found that I had no choice but to tread on the dangerous ground of drawing generalizations about the art of managing such enterprises. This book, then, reflects the results of my efforts to develop a set of meaningful insights and observations about running nonprofit organizations.

The volume draws heavily on my fourteen years of experience as a professional in the nonprofit world: first as officer-in-charge of the Ford Foundation's program-related investments, then as financial vice-president of Princeton and executive vice-president of Children's Television Workshop, and most recently, as senior consultant to Tulane University. The writing also incorporates three years of research and investigation into a range of other nonprofit organizations in connection with my teaching at the Yale School of Management. The book reflects importantly the contributions to my course of guest lecturers Anthony J. Panepinto, Gail Harrity, and George Kaufman, as well as of my students, many of whom have had experience in nonprofit organizations.

It also reflects the particular contributions of students Joseph Seldner and his wife Peggy, who read the manuscript at various stages of its development, and especially Kim McCann, whose substantive assistance in organizing and editing the final text was invaluable.

I also express my appreciation to several experts and scholars who reviewed and made valuable suggestions for improving parts of the manuscript: Charles Cammack, George Kaufman, Donald Knab, Michael O'Neill, Sharon Oster, Stefen Permut, Carl Schafer, and Walter Slocumbe. The importance of their contributions, of course, in no way relieves me of full responsibility for this text.

I am very grateful to Thomas R. Buckman, Patricia Read, and Rick Schoff of The Foundation Center for their helpful and supportive assistance in the publication of this volume.

In addition to acknowledging these contributions, it is also appropriate to express my gratitude to my former colleagues at the Ford Foundation, Princeton University, and Children's Television Workshop for their professional insights and comraderie and, in particular, to Eamon Kelly, president of Tulane University. Each is a remarkable leader who has taught me a great deal, not only about management, but also about leadership.

To my two colleagues in most of the nonprofit ventures I have launched, Kenneth S. Sweet and Gibbs LaMotte, I also express my appreciation for their professional ingenuity and for their personal friendship.

I also acknowledge the enormous support given to my teaching and work on this book by the Dean of the Yale School of Organization and Management, Burton G. Malkiel. He has for many years been mentor, personal advisor, and friend.

To my unique friend, special confidant, and beautiful spouse Joanne, I express my profound joy for all the good things she brings into our life.

Paul B. Firstenberg
October 4, 1985
New York, New York

Introduction:
The Organizational Design
of the Book

THE CHALLENGE OF DELIVERING QUALITY SOCIAL PROGRAMS in the face of increasingly harsh economic realities and a constantly changing environment requires superior leadership of our tax-exempt organizations. Managing a university, foundation, symphony, museum, or health care facility is every bit as demanding as running a private business.

Nonprofit organizations thus need to be in the business of "business": they need to be able to avail themselves of state-of-the-art management techniques used by our most successful for-profit endeavors. Equally, they must fully understand in what ways their uniqueness as nonprofits can be tapped to render them excellent performers of their social mission.

The economic challenge confronting nonprofit organizations is in part a product of the shocks and volatility our national economy has experienced over the past several decades and of the special economics of service-based enterprises. This book focuses on how nonprofit organizations, faced with such difficulties and operating in a context of constant change, can improve their financial condition and administration. It asserts that professional management and the willingness to take risks to effect change lie at the core of improved finances and better administration. In times which test the viability of even our most venerable nonprofit institutions, professionalization of management—and the daring to be entrepreneurial—have become imperatives.

Observations about intangibles of leadership and the quality of organizational environment are deliberately combined with analysis of specific, substantive managerial functions and processes. This combination reflects the growing recognition that management must touch emotions as well as intelligence, that it must be inspiring as well as demanding, and intuitive as well as rational. This volume will maintain that the driving force of a nonprofit organization is its value system, and that sensitive concern for individuals' emotional affect, for their personal needs and feelings, is as important as setting rigorous performance standards and devising innovative strategies in enabling enterprises to master new challenges.

The term "not-for-profit" encompasses a wide variety of organizations with differing tax status. In this book, "nonprofit" or "not-for-profit" refers to only a part of the total not-for-profit world: organizations which meet the requirements of Section 501(c)(3) of the Federal Income Tax Code and are thus (1) exempt from federal income taxation, and (2) can receive tax deductible donations. Many nonprofit organizations qualify for income tax exemption, but contributions to only certain types of enterprises are deductible.

The book is divided into six sections.

Section I

The chapter entitled "The Nature of a Nonprofit Organization: Legal, Tax, and Economic Considerations" first profiles the scope of exempt organizations in the United States. Next, it reviews the basic legal and tax characteristics that must be met for an enterprise to qualify as a tax-exempt, not-for-profit organization and the public policy reasons for the special tax treatment accorded different classes of exempt institutions.

The text then defines the underlying economic dilemma of not-for-profits: as service-based enterprises, they enjoy only very limited opportunities for productivity gains to offset rising wages. Accordingly, regardless of how tightly costs are controlled, they will continue to rise in service organizations. The limited opportunity to offset wage increases through productivity gains makes this inevitable in institutions where the major expense is personnel costs. An overriding managerial challenge is to make revenues grow at least at the same rate as the inexorable increases in expenses. The range of processes for creating new revenues is explored in Section II and forms a basic focus of the book.

Section II

"Financing Growth" addresses the struggle of most nonprofit organizations to raise their revenues in the face of both the turbulent economic conditions of the 1970s and 1980s and the austerity of government social budgets in the present decade. The initial chapter, "Expanding the Revenue Base, Traditional Sources," explores ways to maximize revenue from government, foundations, corporations, and individuals. Serious concerns are expressed in the chapter about the dangers of excessive dependence on government funding.

The pressures to increase income have led to intensified interest in finding nontraditional sources of income—income earned from an organization's own business activities. This is the subject of the chapter entitled "Making a Profit for Your Nonprofit Organization." The chapter explores ways to identify opportunities to earn income and various options for organizing and financing different approaches for developing such nontraditional revenues. The policy objections which are often raised to such efforts are analyzed in the chapter "Changing the Nonprofit Mind-Set Toward Commercial Income."

The following chapter, "Endowment Management in the 1980s," examines the policies and procedures for maximizing returns from endowment funds. Such funds are a critical source of income for a good many nonprofit institutions. The chapter also explores the trade-offs in determining the amount of endowment income to be expended currently vs. the amount to be reinvested for the future. Finally, the chapter delves into the appropriate roles of professional staff and trustees in administering an endowment fund—a topic with implications beyond endowment management.

Section III

Opportunism, informed intuition, and plain old "gut instincts" are important in enabling management to lead an organization to find new revenues and to adapt its programs to new realities. However, in an increasingly competitive and complex universe, nonprofit management must also employ more deliberative processes of leadership. The section "A Planned Approach to Change" contains separate chapters on "Strategic Planning: Playing to Your Comparative Advantage," "Marketing: An Undervalued Art," "Budgeting: Quantifying Priorities," and "Tax Planning: Forethought Rather Than Afterthought."

Strategic planning, marketing, and budgeting constitute the critical managerial tools for charting and recharting the course of an enterprise. Although strategic planning, marketing planning, and budgeting are discrete managerial techniques, their integration into a coherent process is the primary means by which senior officials can set and reset the basic directions of an organization. They attune management to change and provide the procedural means for adapting its programs and operations to new realities.

Tax considerations are as central to a nonprofit organization as they are to a profit-making business. Advance consideration of tax consequences is especially critical to an exempt organization intent on increasing its revenues through its own business endeavors. The tax law also importantly affects the nature of the salary and benefits an exempt organization can offer its personnel. Finally, the tax law provides the central framework for federal oversight of exempt organizations. For all these reasons, tax planning is accorded special attention in this volume and is reviewed in the final chapter in this section, as well as in the book's first chapter on the nature of a nonprofit organization.

Section IV

In addition to utilization of planning processes, managing a modern nonprofit organization to cope with changes requires first-rate, full-time professional management in partnership with a strong board of trustees playing its appropriate role.

The fourth section, "Professionalization of Management," focuses on the kind of able personnel the modern nonprofit organization must seek to employ, how to recruit such personnel, and the compensation arrangements and management development efforts needed to attract, retain, and motivate talented personnel. This material is covered in the chapter entitled "Developing Human Resources."

The section also describes, in the chapter "Managing Your Board: Building a Partnership," how management and boards can best relate to each other and the functions trustees should and should not perform.

Section V

In this section, the book moves beyond the substantive elements of professional management to discuss the managerial style and outlook that characterize the "entrepreneurial nonprofit organization." Its premise is that adaptation to a constantly changing environment is a modern organizational imperative. This means a disposition for risk-taking—for confronting the uncertainty inherent in moving away from the status quo—is essential to the continued vitality of all nonprofit institutions.

Entrepreneurial management—or risk-taking management—is seen as the process of motivating an institution to grow as it encounters change and new opportunities. But in the nonprofit sector, as in organizations generally, there are obstacles to risk-taking and innovation. To overcome these, a climate for risk-taking must be deliberately fostered within the institution.

The fifth section of the book draws a portrait of an entrepreneurial organization, outlining the factors—substantive, emotional, and environmental—which can institutionalize within an organization the propensity for risk-taking and innovation.

Section VI

The final section of the book contains two profiles: one of Ruth Maxwell, founder of an innovative nonprofit organization dedicated to servicing chemical dependents, and one of MacGeorge Bundy, who radically changed the Ford Foundation's program goals during his tenure as its president. Both pieces are intended as models of entrepreneurship in different settings in the nonprofit world.

I.

The Basics of
the Exempt Organization

1

The Nature of a Nonprofit Organization: Legal, Tax, and Economic Considerations

AMERICA'S TAX-EXEMPT, NOT-FOR-PROFIT INSTITUTIONS play a critical role in the life of this country. They account for a vital part of our nation's educational system, scientific and social science research, health care, art and culture, public broadcasting, social services, and public advocacy. This reflects a peculiarly American tradition: in most other countries major social institutions are run and funded by the state. In the United States many public-service institutions are privately controlled. They are supported financially by private sources or a mix of private and government funds.[1]

PROFILE OF EXEMPT ORGANIZATIONS

An economic profile of the country's tax-exempt, not-for-profit institutions has been developed by Gabriel Rudney of the Institution for Social and Policy Studies Program on Non-Profit Organizations at Yale University. His work, *A Quantitative Profile of the Nonprofit Sector*, Working Paper-40, November 1981, offers the best quantitative picture of the philanthropic sector currently available. Rudney's analysis[2], centered around data for 1980, notes:

> The philanthropic sector spent $129.2 billion in 1980. The "philanthropic sector" is defined as organizations whose income is exempt under the federal income tax laws and to

---

[1] For a discussion of the various types of not-for-profit organizations, see *Giving in America: Toward a Stronger Voluntary Sector, Report of the Commission on Private Philanthropy and Public Needs*, (Washington, D.C., 1975, pp. 32–33, 36). (Referred to hereafter as *Filer Commission Report*, as the report is commonly called after its chairman, John H. Filer.)

[2] For an earlier profile of the nonprofit sector, see *Filer Commission Report*, pp. 34–36.

which contributions are deductible. (See pp. 13–15 for a further definition of this sector.) The expenditures consisted of $128.1 billion of actual outlays (i.e., $42.6 billion in purchases of goods and services and $75.4 billion in employee compensation) and $9.1 billion in the imputed rental value of buildings and equipment owned and used by such institutions. The expenditure of the sector exceeded the budget of all nations in the world except the United States, France, West Germany, the United Kingdom, Japan, and undoubtedly China and the U.S.S.R. as well.

The philanthropic sector employed 5.6 million workers in 1980, or about 5.7 percent of all U.S. employment. However, the sector employed nearly a seventh of all the country's professional workers and sector employment exceeded that of such critical for-profit industries as construction and automobile manufacturing.

Employment in the philanthropic sector grew faster between 1960 and 1980 than the total U.S. labor market—at the rate of 5.5 percent a year compared to 3.4 percent for employment as a whole.

The nonprofit sector's share of GNP in 1975 was only 3.2 percent compared to 81.6 percent for profit enterprises and 14.2 percent for the government. But the nonprofit sector's share of the GNP was the fastest growing between 1960 and 1975—nearly twice as fast as the government's share while the profit share actually declined during the period. Note, the classification "nonprofit" includes not only organizations to which donor contributions are deductible but also private nonprofit membership groups (social clubs, fraternal organizations and labor unions) that are organized largely to confer mutual benefits on their members. Although tax exempt under the federal income tax laws, donations to such organizations are not deductible. (See pp. 13–15 below.)

Sales of services by the philanthropic sector—$61.5 billion—covered less than half of the $129.2 billion of its costs in 1980. The shortfall was financed primarily by private and government donations and from investment earnings; very little of the cost of such services was financed by borrowing.

The philanthropic sector had a favorable "balance of trade" with the business world. The sector purchased goods and services from business totalling $42.6 billion in 1980 while business purchases of nonprofit services and its donations to nonprofits totalled but $6 billion.[3]

These figures, as well as the other data compiled by Rudney, point out the significance of the tax-exempt not-for-profit sector of the American economy.

THE TEXTURE OF THE NONPROFIT WORLD

Not-for-profit organizations are diverse in their aims and character. They vary from enterprises that cannot by the very nature of their mission make money (such as religious or "voluntary" organizations), to organizations that seek to make money, but for a variety of reasons, decide to operate within the limitations of the tax-exempt, not-for-

---

[3] These figures were drawn from Gabriel Rudney, "A Quantitative Profile of the Nonprofit Sector" (New Haven: Institution for Social and Policy Studies Program on Non-Profit Organizations, 1981).

profit form.[4] Some of these latter nonprofit organizations may even become profitable enough to convert to profit-making companies.[5] Hence, the term "nonprofit" actually covers a spectrum of organizations as different from each other as they are from profit-making organizations.

Equally, the working environment of the exempt not-for-profit world is diverse rather than uniform, as nonprofit organizations have their own varied cultures. The nonprofit universe is not simply a neat and tidy world of days filled only with lofty insights, dispassionate analysis, and people moved by high ideals. Pragmatic as well as altruistic motives often explain the behavior of people who work in nonprofit organizations. Powerful, frequently selfish emotions can be at play. You find in the not-for-profit world strong ambitions, powerful needs for personal approval, heightened desires for personal gain, power, and personal vindication. It is, in short, a very human world . . . no more or less so than the profit-making segment of our economy.

The not-for-profit world is also an intense, highly competitive universe in which marketing, public relations, economics, strategic planning, and other business considerations are as much in vogue as idealism and a sense of social mission.

The not-for-profit sector is a highly exposed and visible world. Tax-exempt nonprofit organizations solicit public support with the aid of tax incentives for many of their benefactors and enjoy tax exemption for most of their income. The justification for these special benefits is that such organizations are dedicated to providing a public benefit. But the special treatment and purpose of such organizations inevitably means they live in the potential glare of the media and under the scrutiny of governmental bodies often anxious to accrue power and influence at their expense. At the same time, the constituency which benefits from the nonprofit organization's services is not typically the same group which provides the financial support for the organization. Thus nonprofit organizations normally have multiple publics with which they must deal regularly.[6]

The leader of a modern nonprofit organization must reconcile and balance the dual objectives of such institutions: advancement of the public welfare and promotion of the well-being and survival of the enterprise. The mission of a nonprofit institution is the glue that holds the organization together, giving it the sense of purpose which motivates its staff and attracts financial and public support for its activities.

---

[4] For a description of the economic spectrum of not-for-profit entities, see Norman Waks, in *Strategic Planning in Private Non-Profit Organizations* (a collection of papers published by MITRE Corporation, Bedford, MA, December 1979, pp. 2–7).

[5] See the history of System Development Corporation in Claude Baum, *The System Builders: The History of SDC* (Santa Monica: System Development Corporation, 1981).

[6] Christopher H. Lovelock and Charles B. Weinberg, in "Public and Nonprofit Marketing Comes of Age" (*Review of Marketing 1978*, Zaltman and Bonoma, eds. Chicago: American Marketing Association, 1978, pp. 416–420), describe the four major characteristics of nonprofit organizations as: multiple publics, multiple objectives, provision of services rather than physical goods, and public scrutiny.

At the same time, every nonprofit organization engages in a series of business activities, it must perform a financial function, as money must be raised, managed, and budgeted. Every such organization must perform a production function in conceiving the best way of arranging inputs to produce the outputs of the organization. Every organization must perform a personnel function, as people must be hired, trained, assigned, and promoted in the course of the organization's work. Every organization must perform a purchasing function in acquiring materials. It also is clear that every organization performs marketing-like activities, whether or not they are recognized as such. Tax-exempt nonprofit organizations must also engage in careful tax planning to protect their exempt status and to minimize potential taxation of any unrelated income that they may earn. Thus, a nonprofit organization has many of the operational characteristics of a business organization, and, as this book will seek to show, many management techniques serve both profit-making and nonprofit enterprises.

Still, it would be a mistake to conclude that nonprofit entities can be run in precisely the same fashion as a business enterprise. Nonprofit organizations are not founded with the same motives and objectives as profit-making businesses.

By opting for the nonprofit form, one sacrifices a number of the most significant attributes of business entrepreneurship—the prerogatives of power incident to individual ownership and the potential extraordinary financial reward that ownership in a new venture can bring. There is a different impetus to creating a nonprofit institution. In choosing the not-for-profit form, a founder is in fact signaling that compensation and working conditions, important as they are, are not the only inducements for working in his or her enterprise. It's also a signal that commitment to its program and social goals is as crucial a motivator as any. In organizing the enterprise as a nonprofit entity, the founder is establishing the importance of its social mission as the dominant value of the organization.

Within the nonprofit form, it is the social mission which defines the goals of the organization, establishes the framework for the aspirations of its staff, and sets the tone for the everyday operation of the enterprise.

In business, survival on a profitable basis is the goal.[7] The specific goods or services the business delivers are only the means to this end. But in the not-for-profit world, even institutional survival is not a sufficient goal. Continued existence as an institution must be linked to continued service of a social purpose. The ability to perform a socially useful mission that is not being fulfilled by profit-making organizations is the justification for the existence of a tax-exempt nonprofit—it is what attracts people to work for the organization, and what attracts support from the outside world. If a nonprofit

---

[7] Peters and Waterman point out that the factors that motivate first-rate performance in business are far more subtle and complex than the desire for profits. But economic gain is still the most powerful reason that private businesses are formed. *In Search of Excellence* by Thomas J. Peters and Robert H. Waterman, Jr. Copyright © 1982 by Thomas J. Peters and Robert H. Waterman, Jr. Selected excerpts reprinted by permission of Harper & Row, Publishers, Inc.

organization loses sight of the overriding importance of its mission and offers only institutional survival as its highest value, it will lose both its internal strength and its external appeal.

Do these differences in purpose and aims between nonprofit and profit-making institutions make the need for professional management of the former any less urgent? In my view, the answer is plainly *no,* and a good part of this book is devoted to illustrating how professional management processes and techniques can provide material benefits for nonprofit organizations.

Does the absence of the prospect of "getting rich" mean that nonprofit institutions are inherently less energetic or entrepreneurial than business enterprises? The example of the Maxwell Institute (profiled later) and the other individuals and organizations referred to in this book suggest the answer is decidedly *no.* A risk-taking atmosphere can be as readily created within the not-for-profit structure as it can in a business environment. This is a crucial point to which we later devote the section "Superior Entrepreneurial Management."

DEFINING A NONPROFIT ORGANIZATION

Exactly what is a not-for-profit organization? A not-for-profit organization is defined by both state law, under which not-for-profit organizations are chartered, and the Federal Internal Revenue Code. The code exempts certain classes of not-for-profit organizations from taxation on the profits of their activities. It also establishes that gifts to specified types of not-for-profit organizations are deductible from the donor's taxable income.

Such organizations also often qualify under state and local government statutes for exemption from local property taxes, though the tests for local property tax and federal tax exemption are not always the same. For example, New York City has ruled that the Asia Society, an organization exempt from federal taxes because it is engaged in promoting understanding about Asian countries, is not exempt from city property taxes because it is not a teaching institution. The latter is not a test under federal law.

We will first examine the qualifications the code establishes for exemption, and then take note of the special treatment under the code of one class of exempt organizations—private foundations. Next we will look at how state law defines nonprofit institutions, and then review the nature of governmental oversight of such organizations. In the last part of this chapter, we will review the nature of the economic dilemma underlying most not-for-profit enterprises.

Federal Definition: A 501 (c)(3) Organization

Many kinds of organizations are set up on a not-for-profit basis, and the motives for establishing such organizations vary widely. All of the varieties of not-for-profit institutions recognized by the Internal Revenue Service are described in sections 501 (a) through 501 (h) of the tax code. This book is concerned only with those not-for-profit organizations which are organized to qualify for tax exemption under Section 501(c)(3) of the Federal Internal Revenue Code and are eligible under the code to receive tax-deductible contributions. Throughout this book the term "nonprofit" will refer to such exempt organizations.

Section 501(c)(3) of the Internal Revenue Code of the United States confers on not-for-profit organizations exemption from federal income taxation on certain but not all forms of income received by the organization. Equally, if not more importantly, Section 170 allows federal income tax deductions for gifts by individuals and companies to such organizations. It is this latter provision that makes organizations qualifying under Section 501(c)(3) unique among not-for-profit entities. As noted below, other classes of organizations are granted exemption from income taxation under the code, but donations to them do not entitle the donors to a tax deduction.

There are significant benefits to qualifying under Section 501(c)(3):

- Substantial wealth may be accumulated without the organization being subject to income taxes.
- Substantial property may be accumulated that is exempt from local property taxes.
- Individuals and companies can make gifts to the exempt entity and receive a tax deduction in the amount of the fair market value of the gift rather than its cost.

To obtain such benefits, an organization must meet three tests. They are:

- The organization is operated exclusively for the purpose of pursuing charitable, educational, religious, or scientific objectives, or certain other purposes enumerated in the code.
- No part of the net earnings of the organization may inure to the benefit of a private individual.
- No *substantial* part of its activities represents an attempt to influence legislation, and it does not intervene at all in public elections.

In essence, these statutory tests mean that, to qualify for the favored tax treatment, an organization must:

- be dedicated to furthering a public charitable purpose rather than private gain (some public purposes don't qualify—e.g., sports clubs).
- have its mission fall within the specific classifications of exempt charitable purpose established by the Internal Revenue Code.
- accept certain restraints on its political activities; namely, an organization will not qualify for, or will lose its exempt status if:

  1. a *substantial* part of its activities is attempting to influence legislation by propaganda or otherwise.

2. it participates or intervenes, directly or indirectly, in any political campaign on behalf of, or in opposition to, any candidate for public office.

3. its main objective can be obtained only by legislation or a defeat of proposed legislation, and it campaigns actively for such objective (as opposed to engaging in non-partisan analysis).

In the case of private foundations—as we will discuss below—the limitation on political activities was changed in 1969 to a flat prohibition on seeking to influence legislation.

How these tests are interpreted will be examined later in the book. Suffice it to say in this introductory chapter, organizations that meet the tests of Section 501(c)(3) of the code reflect the nation's long-standing public policy of encouraging, through tax exemption, nonprofit organizations dedicated to the support of education, religion, science, culture, and humanitarianism.

Non-501(c)(3) Organizations

Over the years, the types and number of organizations exempted from federal income taxation has proliferated well beyond religious, educational, scientific, and philanthropic institutions. Tax exemption also is accorded to:

- nonprofit business organizations such as trade and professional organizations.
- nonprofit social and fraternal groups.
- nonprofit welfare organizations such as labor unions, conservation associations, and the League of Women Voters.

These three classes of organizations and a half-dozen more are entitled to exemption from federal taxation, but in contrast to charitable, religious, educational, and scientific organizations that meet the tests of Section 501(c)(3), gifts to these organizations are not tax deductible to the donor.[8] Such deductible gifts are a major source of revenue to many exempt organizations. In this sense, these three classes of organizations are less favored by the tax code than groups that qualify under Section 501(c)(3). This is the critical difference between the 501(c)(3) and other forms of not-for-profits. It is worth noticing that in some respects, however, they are more favored—for instance, in the broader freedom of some of these organizations to seek to influence legislation or to participate in election campaigns.

Federal Tax Policy and the 501(c)(3) Organization

Why the favored tax treatment for 501(c)(3) organizations? There is no clear answer to this question, and many different speculations are offered.[9] In my own view, the

---

[8] Of course, many members of trade, professional, and union organizations can deduct their membership fees from their taxes as "business expenses."

[9] See, on this subject generally, Bittker and Rahdent, "The Exemption of Non Profit Organizations from Federal Income Taxation" (*The Yale Law Journal*, vol. 85, no. 3, January 1976).

basic thrust is to grant favored tax treatment to organizations that pursue a type of public purpose one would not expect to be served by an organization operated for the purpose of making a profit. In short, as I see it, the rationale for the favored tax treatment is to encourage the undertaking of activities that would not otherwise be pursued by the profit-making, tax-paying sector of the nation.

The underlying notion is that there is value in a pluralistic structure serving the public interest, and that there is a benefit in fostering a diversity of approaches to meeting public needs. The idea is that a richer mix of responses to public needs will be developed by encouraging both private and public initiatives, rather than by confining all responsibility for servicing such needs to politically responsive public agencies.

In a democratic society, governmental bodies inevitably must take political considerations into account. Ultimately, they must assess the impact of every action on the electorate or at least on the chosen representatives of the electorate.[10] This can limit the actions of governmental bodies in ways that nonprofit organizations are not constrained. Similarly, the need to make a profit and repay investors constrains a profit-making organization in ways that a nonprofit institution is not burdened.

Thus, there is a niche for the nonprofit enterprise. Whether, in fact, the tax subsidies provided for in the federal tax code—and in parallel state legislation—are indeed necessary to encourage the formation of nonprofit organizations is a matter of some debate. Moreover, it is often argued that even if the subsidies are required, it is inappropriate to use the tax code to subsidize and encourage the pursuit of certain social aims. The argument is made not only by conservative president Ronald Reagan, but by such liberal tax theorists as Stan Surrey, who served as President Kennedy's principal advisor on tax matters. Such theorists of the right and left both argue that the tax code should be used solely for the purpose of raising revenue and should not be an instrument for accomplishing social or economic ends.

Typically, the argument against granting tax exemptions and deductions for gifts to nonprofit entities is put this way: the grant of an exemption and deduction will cost the government revenue. In fact, the lost revenue properly should be regarded as "tax expenditures." In this light, the question becomes whether public monies should be spent for priorities set by self-perpetuating private groups or by the legislature elected to represent the public interest.

The question is not whether exempt institutions are "good" or "bad" organizations, but whether support of such organizations should retain priority over the other pressing needs of society. Continuation of tax benefits year after year to an exempt organization requires no appropriation or other action by Congress. This gives the activities of these organizations, whose agendas are set by private individuals, automatic

---

[10] Arguably, the judiciary is a governmental body that can act without regard to political considerations. Not many lawyers believe courts are indifferent to politics broadly defined, and in any case, the courts are limited in their ability to act on public matters by their nature as judicial tribunals, by the constitution and by the legislation that creates the courts.

priority over other social needs which are met, if at all, only by annual appropriations by the legislative body.

In considering these arguments, it is important to differentiate between the exemption granted to 501(c)(3) nonprofit organizations and the deductions granted to individuals and corporations for gifts to 501(c)(3) organizations. On one hand, the changing of prevailing policy to tax the profits of such organizations would not necessarily promise a large flow of new tax revenues. A good many such organizations barely earn enough to cover their costs, even without the benefits of depreciating their plants or tax loss carry-forwards from prior years. Both such tax benefits would be available if the organization's revenues were subject to taxation. (Moreover, would you tax the "capital" of charities, such as gifts, which are not given to schools to meet tuition expenses but to add to plant or endowment?) The revenue loss to the government from exempting nonprofit organizations from a tax on their "profits" may be quite minimal.

On the other hand, granting a tax deduction to individuals and to taxpaying organizations for gifts to 501(c)(3) enterprises does involve a substantial revenue loss to the treasury. This makes the charitable-giving deduction a real tax cost, and the appropriateness—and practical necessity—for such deduction is a matter of continuing, intense debate.

Having raised these policy issues—whether tax exemptions and deductions are necessary or appropriate to encourage the activities pursued by nonprofit organizations—I leave them on the table for your reflection. This book will take the tax code as given and focus its attention on how, within that framework, leaders and managers of nonprofit organizations most effectively can accomplish their aims.

Foundations

Within the general class of organizations that meet the tests of Section 501(c)(3), foundations have been split off and treated separately from other qualifying organizations by the Tax Reform Act of 1969. This separate treatment of foundations reflects both traditional populist congressional distrust of the wealth and influence of these institutions and the 1969 uncovering—in the eyes of critics of foundations—of specific abuses. These involved the alleged extensive involvement of foundations in business, the alleged manipulation of foundations to serve various private purposes of their donors (such as using foundations to control corporate or other property), and alleged undue delays in the flow of benefits to charity.

The behavior of foundations was the subject of intense focus in the hearings leading up to the Tax Reform Act of 1969, which is the basis of the current scheme for the regulation of foundations. Although some members of Congress had attacked foundations from time to time, nothing had come of these complaints until the special atmosphere for reform arose in 1969.

The atmosphere of the 1969 hearings was charged with the backlash against the Ford Foundation's movement in the late 1960s, under MacGeorge ("Mac") Bundy, into active support of the country's minority groups and of minority voter registration drives. For example, Ford's support of the Cleveland Core Chapter in 1967 led to an increase in registered black voters. When a black was elected mayor of the city in the next election, there was an outcry. Then, on the eve of the hearings came the disclosure that members of the late Robert F. Kennedy's staff had received grants totaling $131,000 to ease their transition to private life by providing a year of leisure. Bundy, who personally had approved of the grants, was accused of using foundation money for political favoritism.

About a month later, the press uncovered the relationship between Supreme Court Justice Abe Fortas and the Wolfson Foundation. While Wolfson was under indictment for stock manipulation, Fortas, as a sitting justice of the high court, agreed to accept a $20,000 annual fee from the Wolfson Foundation. Shortly after the Fortas fee disclosure, it was revealed in the press that Justice William O. Douglas was on the payroll of the Parvin Foundation, whose donor had extensive Las Vegas hotel and casino holdings. It was then brought out that Wolfson and Parvin once had been named co-conspirators in a stock manipulation case and that Fortas' wife, a private Washington lawyer, had been retained as an attorney for the Parvin Foundation. Fortas resigned from the court and a new charge against foundations was added to the list—that they had become instruments for the corruption of public officials.

A word of caution: one should not draw from this account of the events leading up to the Tax Reform Act of 1969 that the described "abuses" were widespread. I am describing the perceptions of the foundations' critics in 1969 without implying any personal judgment on how widespread the alleged abuses might have been. It was not the purpose of this book to evaluate these issues, and a lawyer's instincts compel me to say so.

As a result of these disclosures a significant portion of the 1969 act, as finally written, was devoted to the regulation of foundations.[10a] Under the act, private foundations are subjected to more extensive regulation and requirements than the other form of exempt organization. The view of Congress was that such organizations did not have sufficient accountability and responsiveness to the public. Hence, Congress created a regulatory scheme designed to ensure these ends.

Private foundations are defined [509(a)], when read in conjunction with 170(b)(1)(a)(i)–(vi), as *all* 501(c)(3) type organizations *except*:

1. churches.
2. educational institutions (schools, universities).

[10a] Waldemar A. Nielsen, author of several studies of foundations, offers this view of the impact on foundations of the 1969 legislation: "On the whole the abuses have been cleared up. The reform legislation has been remarkably effective." ("Foundations fail to live up to their potential critic says in new book," *The Chronicle of Higher Education*, November 20, 1985, p. 21).

3. hospitals, medical care institutions, medical research organizations.

4. organizations that support state universities.

5. governmental units and organizations which test for public safety.

6. organizations ("publicly supported organizations") that are supported by contributions from the general public, public charities, or governmental bodies (exclusive of receipts for exempt services).

7. organizations that are supported by contributions and receipts from exempt services, individuals, public charities, and governmental units, provided not more than one-third of their income is in the form of investment income.

8. organizations that are limited to supporting organizations described in (1) to (7).

All of the above eight categories are commonly referred to as "public charities" and are exempt entirely from the special rules that apply to private foundations. [The first six categories of public charities described above are defined in Section 170(a)(1)(A), while the last categories are defined in Section 509(a)(2) and (3).] The idea is that such organizations have a constituency that will oversee their charities, thereby obviating the necessity to comply with the special restrictions imposed on the behavior of private foundations.

Qualifying as a public charity involves meeting certain tests spelled out in the IRS regulations.[11] (See chapter "Tax Planning: Forethought Rather Than Afterthought.")

Qualifying as a public charity as a "support organization" under paragraph eight is also not as simple as it might seem from reading the above outline. The statute, Section 509(a)(3), spells out three tests which must be met to qualify, among which is that the supporting organization must be "operated, supervised, or controlled by or in connection with one or more [public charity] organizations."[12]

Private foundations are accorded markedly inferior tax treatment in comparison to public charities. For instance, in the case of private foundations:

- There are prohibitions on speculative investments and self-dealing (e.g., financial transactions between employees or directors and the foundation), limitations on business holdings, requirements for annual public reporting, and a requirement that the foundation disburse annually 5 percent of the market value of its assets. Violation of these prohibitions, limitations, and restrictions results in the imposition of taxes ranging from moderate to severe in amount, depending on the nature and continuing extent of the violation.

- Contributions are deductible to a lesser percent of the donor's taxable income (with no

---

[11] For the special requirements that must be met to qualify, see Paul E. Treusch and Norman A. Sugarman, *Tax-Exempt Charitable Organizations* (Philadelphia: American Law Institute, American Bar Association Committee on Continuing Education, 2nd ed., 1983, pp. 404–405).

[12] For an explanation, see Treusch and Sugarman, pp. 409–412.

carry-forward for excess contributions) than in the case of a public charity or operating foundation.

- The income of private non-operating or operating foundations is subject to an excise tax of 2 percent or 1 percent, with the amount of the tax depending on the amount of charitable expenditures ("qualifying distributions") made by such foundation. The income of exempt operating foundations (discussed below) is not subject to such excise tax.

- The prohibition on political activities on the part of foundations was changed from the test, first enacted in 1934, that "no substantial part" of a foundation's grants could be made for such purposes, to a flat prohibition against any "expenditure for attempting to influence legislation."

- Grants to individuals and voter registration programs must meet certain tests.

Operating foundations, as defined in the code, are a subcategory of private foundations—they are foundations that spend the bulk of their annual income and use the bulk of their assets to fund their exempt programs directly rather than make grants to organizations which administer such programs (e.g., a fully endowed museum that had minimal income from admission fees would be an example of an operating foundation. If the museum received enough income from admission fees, it could become a public charity and be exempt from the rules governing foundations). With certain exceptions, operating foundations are subject to all of the private foundation's rules; the principal exceptions are (1) they need to distribute annually only two-thirds as much a percentage of their assets as is required of a private foundation, (2) donors may deduct the same percentage for contributions as in the case of public charities, and (3) they are qualified, unlike a non-operating private foundation, to receive grants from other private foundations in the same manner as public charities. These exceptions reflect that by definition the income and assets of an operating foundation will be used to a substantial extent for the benefit of the public.[13]

The Tax Reform Act of 1984 [Sec. 4940(d)(2)] created a new class of private foundations, termed "exempt operating foundations," which receive even more favorable tax treatment than private operating foundations. To qualify as an exempt operating foundation, a foundation must:

- satisfy the existing private operating foundation requirements;

- have been publicly supported (as that term applies to public charities) for at least ten taxable years or have been qualified as an operating foundation as of January 1, 1983;

- have a governing body broadly representative of the general public, at least 75 percent of which must consist of non-disqualified individuals; and

---

[13] For an explanation of the treatment of operating foundations under the code, see Treusch and Sugarman, pp. 272, 289–291, 379–383.

- have no officer who is a "disqualified individual" at any time during the taxable year.[14]

A foundation making a grant to an exempt operating foundation will be exempt from expenditure responsibility requirements. In addition, exempt operating foundations are not subject to the two percent excise tax on investment income.

Whether the regulation of foundations is desirable has been debated. The appropriate degree of legislative regulation of foundations and the appropriate role of private foundations in a pluralistic society is interesting and controversial enough to warrant a book in itself. The primary aim of this text, however, is to explore how to operate institutions within existing policy.

Organizational Form

501(c)(3) not-for-profit organizations established under state law may take the form of corporations, unincorporated associations, or charitable trusts, or indeed any form available for the organization of either non-tax-exempt nonprofit institutions (e.g., trade associations and mutual benefit groups such as country clubs) or profit-making organizations.

Profit-making enterprises are owned by individuals who are intended to be the beneficiaries of the profit-producing activities of the enterprise. Nonexempt nonprofit entities are principally for the mutual benefit of their members. In contrast, the distinguishing characteristic of an exempt organization is its aim of benefiting society.

Thus, no individual may own an exempt nonprofit entity, and there is no legal manifestation of ownership that can be acquired in the marketplace. Hence, it is impossible for there to be an involuntary takeover of an exempt organization. However, this does not preclude voluntary mergers between not-for-profit organizations. That can be accomplished by one board of trustees voting to dissolve its organization and transfer its assets to an acquiring organization. The action must be voluntary on the part of the boards of both entities, and often the permission of the state is needed.

Typically, exempt nonprofit organizations are governed by a board of trustees, but in contrast to the board of directors of a profit-making corporation, the board of trustees of a nonprofit institution is responsible, as a practical matter, unto itself. It is a self-perpetuating board. In contrast, the directors of a private corporation are commonly elected by its owners or shareholders and can be removed by such shareholders

---

[14] With respect to a private foundation, the term "disqualified individual" means any individual who is:
  (i)   a substantial contributor to the foundation,
  (ii) an owner of more than 20 percent of:
      (I)   the total voting power of a corporation,
      (II) the profits interest of a partnership, or
      (III) the beneficial interest of a trust or unincorporated enterprise, which is a substantial contributor to the foundation, or
  (iii) a member of the family of any individual described in clause (i) or (ii). [Sec. 4940(d)(3)(B)]

at any time.[15] As there are no individual owners of a typical exempt organization, the trustees serve at their own pleasure and perpetuate themselves.

However, some exempt enterprises are organized as membership organizations. One example would be a university whose alumni elect the board of trustees. In such cases, the insulation of trustees is akin, in form at least, to a private stock corporation.

Governmental Oversight

In theory, exempt organizations are subject to oversight at the state level by the attorney general and at the federal level by the IRS. In practice, however, such oversight has not been especially vigorous at either level, at least until now. State attorneys general typically have not paid much attention to the activities of exempt groups (though the attorney general's offices in New York, Massachusetts, and California now are reasonably active). However, the IRS—under some periodic prodding in recent years by Congress—has been increasing its commitment of staff and resources to the oversight of exempt groups. There is evidence the IRS plans to be more vigorous in the 1980s in reviewing compliance by the exempt organization with the code, especially with respect to revenue-generating business activities.

Whether the IRS—as an agency constituted to collect tax revenues—is the most appropriate institution to review the appropriateness of an exempt organization's activities is another question.

THE ECONOMIC DILEMMA OF NOT-FOR-PROFIT ORGANIZATIONS

People still tend to think of not-for-profit organizations as objects of charity whose altruistic pursuits guarantee their survival. Important as such institutions may be, their future survival is by no means assured. The well-publicized hard times encountered in recent years by so many not-for-profit entities—from major private universities once thought to be economically invulnerable, to museums, dance companies, and health care organizations—are not simply by-products of the nation's economic difficulties in the early 1970s or 1980s. Even after the national economy improved, many nonprofit organizations continued to encounter severe financial problems. The harsh fact is that the nation's private, not-for-profit institutions face a financial dilemma that is related to the special economics of their own business, not just to the performance of the

---

[15] The degree of each shareholder's real influence in a large, publicly owned profit-making corporation long has been a subject of debate in this country. Undoubtedly, for many years the powers of shareholders of publicly traded profit-making corporations were more theoretical than real. Put another way, rarely were they exercised, especially in the case of public corporations whose shares are widely held. In such an environment, the boards of private corporations were as insulated from accountability as their counterparts in the nonprofit world. However, the proliferation of shareholders' suits against business directors in recent years, as well as take-over maneuvers, has the practical effect of making directors of most publicly owned corporations at least glance over their shoulders at the company's owners.

general economy. They can expect to continue to be hard-pressed even if the general economy performs well. To understand why, it is necessary to examine the special economics of the not-for-profit organization.[16]

In 1966, two Princeton economists, William Baumol and William G. Bowen, the latter now president of the university, published their pioneering study, *Performing Arts: The Economic Dilemma* (New York: Twentieth Century Fund, 1966). Two years later Bowen published an analysis of the economics of private higher education, *The Economics of Major Private Universities* (Carnegie Commission on Higher Education, 1968). The analysis of both industries was essentially the same—the more rapid rise in their costs than in the economy generally stems from the relatively static productivity that characterizes service industries. The import for the general nonprofit world follows from the fact that most nonprofit organizations are service businesses with relatively constant or "static" productivity.

The Baumol and Bowen thesis is simply that over the course of the twentieth century, productivity (measured by output per man-hour) in the private sector went up at a remarkably steady rate, at least until the mid-1960s. But as the two Princeton economists observed, the factors primarily responsible for productivity gains—new technology, the investment of capital in this new technology, and the economics of large-scale production—simply have not affected the education or arts industries to anywhere near the extent they have affected most manufacturing industries. Education and the arts are inherently labor-intensive businesses. In education there is no substitute for personal interaction between student and teacher, and as yet, no technological substitute for this human relationship. Equally, as Baumol and Bowen observed, the efficiency of a symphony orchestra or string quartet does not increase from year to year—you can't simply ask the orchestra to play faster or the quartet to perform with three players.

In essence, education, the performing arts, and other service industries are wage-driven. To attract and hold people, they must increase their wages more or less in line with the rise in the general wage level in the economy. Insofar as productivity is not increased, wage increases will be fully translated into higher-unit labor costs that must be passed on to purchasers of the service, or must be otherwise funded by the organization increasing its revenue.

To illustrate, suppose the average salary of a university professor in 1983 is $30,000 and he or she teaches two courses a year with a total of 100 students. The cost of teaching per student is $300. Say in 1984, wages rise 7 percent in the economy and the professor is given a 6 percent increase, or an average of $1,800. But the professor will not be more productive in 1984—thus the cost per student will rise to $318. That

---

[16] For a good summary of the economics of not-for-profit enterprises, see *Filer Commission Report*, pp. 79–88.

$18 increase in costs has to be paid for by an increase in tuition or by increased fund-raising.

Baumol and Bowen summed up the implications of the state of productivity in the service sector:

> The faster the overall pace of technological progress and capital accumulation, the greater will be the upward pressure on costs in any industry that does not enjoy increased productivity.[17]

The relatively higher costs of certain not-for-profit enterprises was obscured for many years because increases in support generally were able to keep pace with increases in costs. For example, a great upsurge in private giving in the mid-1950s, followed by a major increase in government support in the mid-1960s—just as private giving was peaking—disguised the problem for higher education. But the national inflationary spiral that began with the Vietnam War finally exposed the basic financial vulnerability of the nonprofit sector.

Inflation only exacerbates the general tendency of costs in service industries with static productivity to rise more rapidly than costs in the economy.[18]

The labor-intensive nature of service industries (i.e., usually more than 50 percent of the organization's budget will be devoted to personnel costs[19]) makes their costs more vulnerable to inflation-driven wage increases than industries with a lower ratio of wages to total costs.[20]

At the same time, as costs skyrocket, the incomes of nonprofit organizations suffer as inflation, especially when compounded by a recession, adversely affects the flow of

---

[17] William Baumol and William G. Bowen, *The Performing Arts: The Economic Dilemma* (New York: Twentieth Century Fund, 1966, p. 171).

[18] See William G. Bowen, "The Effects of Inflation/Recession on Higher Education" (*Educational Record*, Summer 1975, p. 151). For instance, studies have shown that the inflation in the costs of higher education has risen more rapidly over the past decade than costs in the economy. Whereas prices in general had risen through 1975 by about 50 percent over the prior decade, the costs of higher education had risen by over 75 percent during the same period. (See also *Filer Commission Report*, pp. 13, 82.) But as Baumol and Bowen noted in *The Performing Arts: The Economic Dilemma*, p. 170, the costs of an industry with static productivity will rise more rapidly than the economy whether or not the price level is changing.

[19] The Filer Commission estimates that up to 85 percent of the budget of institutions of higher learning goes to wages, and that arts organizations typically devote over half their budgets to personnel costs; for theatre, the ratio is 62 percent, symphonies 77 percent, opera 66 percent. (*Filer Commission Report*, p. 83)

[20] As Leonard Silk noted in "The Origins of Stagflation" (*The New York Times*, June 20, 1978, p. D2), there is evidence that, compared to service businesses, the relatively greater ability of manufacturing industries to increase productivity to offset costs may have narrowed a good deal over the past decade. Recent economic studies show that since the mid-1960s—when the country began to suffer from a simultaneous economic decline and inflation—we have experienced a dramatic drop in the rate of annual productivity gains in manufacturing industries. As a consequence, the productivity gap between service and manufacturing industries may indeed have narrowed. However, even if this is the case, the demand for nonprofit sector services is generally more elastic than that for manufacturing output. Therefore, nonprofit institutions find it more difficult than industry to pass along costs.

support from private sources, public funders, and endowment income.[21]

The economic lesson of the 1970s and 1980s for nonprofit enterprises is that inflation does not impact revenues and expenses equally. Contrary to what we once thought, income doesn't rise at the same rate as the price level. Inflation, especially in combination with a recession, tends to hold down the rate of growth of nonprofit income relative to growth in expenses . For instance, a study of 32 nonprofit theaters over the last five years shows that while their cumulative income rose by 56 percent since 1979, their expenses in the same period grew by 61 percent.[22]

Accordingly, the blunt fact of life is that unless an organization's real (after inflation) revenues are in fact expanding, it will be faced with having to curtail its programs. The dilemma of static productivity is thus one of the central vulnerabilities of almost all not-for-profit organizations and a compelling imperative for them to change their goals and mode of operation. It has placed most of them in a financial vise for over a decade and compelled managements to slash budgets and search desperately for new revenue sources.

In this book, how nonprofit organizations can expand revenue bases to offset cost pressures will be examined. The point is that you cannot hope to chart a new course for an organization or to give it a lift and energize it if its *real* resources are shrinking. And if you want to expand programs, that means finding a way to increase the organization's real revenues at a faster rate than the inflation of its expenses. The challenge to the leadership of nonprofit enterprise is to find ways of doing this.

---

[21] The analysis of the Filer Commission indicates that "the purchasing power of giving did not keep pace with the growth of the economy through the 1960s and early 1970s and that in recent years, it has fallen off absolutely when discounted for inflation." (*Filer Commission Report*, p. 15) It can be speculated that the decline in private giving stems from the fact that the real value of financial assets has fallen under the pressure of persistent inflation. For instance, the stock market in 1974 suffered its worst decline since the 1930s. A large part of private giving is in the form of appreciated securities (*An Analysis of Voluntary Support of American Colleges and Universities, 1973–1974*, Julian H. Levi and Sheldon Elliot Steinbach for the American Council on Education), and when appreciation has been wrung out of the market, so to speak, giving is likely to decline. Similarly, during a period of inflation, governments will be under greater pressure to hold budget growth in check, and in real terms there may be little if any increase in such resources.

[22] Freedman, "Financial Problems are Compromising Nonprofit Theatres," (*The New York Times*, March 14, 1984, p. 1).

II.

Financing Growth

2

Expanding The Revenue Base: Traditional Sources

PERHAPS THE SINGLE MOST IMPORTANT CHALLENGE to the leadership of nonprofit businesses today is to find innovative ways of expanding their *real* revenues. This is the point I stressed so much in the introduction and in the first chapter, "The Nature of a Nonprofit Organization: Legal, Tax, and Economic Considerations."

This chapter explores the potential for increasing traditional sources of funding for nonprofit entities through:

- government contracts and grants.
- grants by foundations.
- gifts and grants by private corporations.
- gifts from individuals.

In a later chapter, the potential of profit-making activities as a means of generating new revenue sources will be explored. (See chapter "Making a Profit for Your Nonprofit Organization.")

FUND-RAISING AS DONOR-MARKETING

Some nonprofit institutions still leave the raising of funds largely to chance, in the belief that they have such a good cause that people will support it, or that there are always a lot of people out there looking to give money to charities, and one simply needs to contact them. But in the face of today's competition for funds, an organization cannot hope to be effective in raising money simply by proclaiming its good works. Funding for nonprofit organizations is a scarce resource. Potential funding sources are typically inundated with all kinds of appeals for support, and getting their attention takes skilled planning and execution.

In fact, there is such a profusion of messages unleashed on the public today that it is hard for any single enterprise to be heard. A torrent of advertisements for commercial products and services, campaigns for political candidates and issues, and appeals for worthy causes clog communications channels. To be noticed at all, you have to cut through this clutter with a sharply differentiated and powerfully delivered message.

A laissez-faire approach to fund-raising also fails to take into account that the actual raising of funds from individuals or institutions involves a quid pro quo: value is given by a donor in exchange for value received from the fund-seeking organization. For instance: government agencies are looking to advance a program which furthers their political interests; foundations seek organizations which can implement their objectives; corporations want to advance their public relations goals; private donors tend to seek enhancement of their self-esteem.

Philip Kotler, in his *Marketing for Nonprofit Organizations,* maintains:

> Why do individuals give to charity? Nonprofit organizations need a good understanding of giving motives in order to be effective at fund raising. The answer called "altruism" tends to mask the complex motives that underlie giving or helping behavior. The best working hypothesis is that the individuals "give" in order to "get" something back. In other words, donations should not be viewed as a *transfer* but as a *transaction.*[1]

The key to mounting an effective fund-raising effort in such an environment is *marketing.* The best targets for an organization's fund-raising efforts, as well as the tactics for reaching such prospects, will emerge naturally from a "marketing approach" to fund-raising.

The driving force of any marketing approach to fund-raising is the recognition that donors are not so much altruistic benefactors as intelligent and pragmatic financial providers whose specific needs and interests must be met by an organization seeking their support. Kotler points out in *Marketing for Nonprofit Organizations:*

> Exchange is the central concept underlying marketing. It calls for the offering of value to another party in exchange for value. . . . The marketer knows how to research and understand the needs of the other party, to design a valued offering to meet these needs; to communicate the offer effectively; and to present it at the right time and place.[2]

A marketing approach begins with a conscious calculation of an organization's potential appeal to different possible funding groups. The analysis will take into account

---

[1] Philip Kotler, *Marketing for Nonprofit Organizations,* 2nd Ed., ©1982, p. 427. Excerpts from this work are reprinted by permission of Prentice-Hall, Englewood Cliffs, NJ.

[2] Kotler, *Marketing for Nonprofit Organizations,* p. 6.

the intense competition that exists for financial support of exempt organizations, and seek to identify a particular segment of fund providers to whom the organization may have a stronger appeal than those of other fund-seekers. The single most important decision in devising a marketing campaign is positioning.

That's how marketing professional and author Edward L. Nash argues. In his book, *Direct Marketing, Strategy, Planning, Execution,* he defines positioning as "the portrayal of product in its proper status vis-à-vis other products." He adds:

> The essence of strategic product planning requires . . . a commitment about what your product or service is and how you want it perceived. You can't have it be all things to all people. It can be the best or the cheapest, traditional or innovative, entertaining or educational. To try to be everything at once is to be nothing.[3]

To position an organization in the fund-raising market, then, a careful definition of an organization's products must be made. Often the organization's internal description of its services has to be recast in broader, more basic terms to appeal to potential contributors. For example, the American Film Institute's campaign to preserve old film negatives from physical deterioration is presented to potential donors as a program to preserve an essential element of America's cultural heritage.

Prime fund-raising prospects are found where there is a coincidence of interest between the goals of an organization's program and those of a potential donor. Solicitations will be designed to highlight such a match of interests. The overall universe of potential supporters must be broken down, according to this paralleling of interests.

"No organization can satisfy all the needs of the 'general public'," Lazer and Culley point out in their text *Marketing Management.* By way of illustration, they add, "The March of Dimes learned through marketing research that it should concentrate its fund-raising efforts on large donors and opinion leaders rather than appealing to the undifferentiated population."[4]

In a well-conceived marketing effort, the underlying motives which prompt funding sources to give, as well as their announced criteria for gifts, will also be carefully researched. The form and content of appeals will then be tailored to the interests and nature of specific funding targets. In every case, the form and manner in which the appeal is communicated to the donor will be as crucial as the content of the message.

For instance, if alumni loyalty to a school is seen as the primary motivator of giving, an educational institution will organize a peer system of raising funds from the bulk of its alumni; viz, an alumnus of each class (i.e., class agent) will be appointed to conduct a mail solicitation of funds from his or her classmates. This effort will be backed up by phone calls by the agent and other graduate volunteer alumni or occa-

---

[3] *Direct Marketing, Strategy, Planning, Execution* (p. 215) by Edward L. Nash, 1982. Excerpts reprinted by permission of McGraw-Hill Book Company.

[4] Lazer and Culley, *Marketing Management* (Boston: Houghton Mifflin, 1983, pp. 835, 840).

sionally by current students. Cultivation of very wealthy alumni for major gifts will be handled by personal visits by university officers, primarily the president.

For nonprofit institutions without a hard core of loyal supporters, targeted segments of the public may be solicited by volunteer door-to-door canvassers; this usually requires publicity for success. Appeals may also be cast in the form of invitations to expensive theater benefits or dinners honoring a well-known figure, both of which require a good target list of upscale potential ticket buyers to attain their goals.

If the best potential fund providers are foundations or government agencies, usually a skillfully written grant application is required. But carefully planned personal contact with officials will also be important in helping the nonprofit organization understand the funding source's interests as well as its criteria and process for making awards. Besides, being known to funding officials never hurts.

A marketing approach to fund-raising will also be premised on a realistic assessment of the potential of the organization to raise money. Past efforts of the organization, results achieved by comparable organizations, and soundings of prospects will inform the judgment as to how successful a campaign is going to be. Fund-raising goals will not be defined solely by the cost of the programs the organization wishes to conduct. As discussed in the chapter on budgeting, programmatic aspirations must be tempered by a realistic assessment of the market potential for raising support.

The entire fund-raising effort should be centrally coordinated to avoid duplication of effort by various parts of the institution and the inadvertent application for funds from the same source by more than one department. An attempt should also be made to balance and diversify the sources of support so an organization is not beholden to one or even a handful of powerful benefactors. Wherever possible, vulnerability to the inevitable restlessness of government and foundation funders should be minimized by the solicitation of private support. Indeed, a prudent nonprofit institution that obtains foundation or government support will anticipate from the outset that such aid will be phased out some day and plan, as best it can, for alternative sources of funds. (In other words, hope for the best, but plan for the worst.)

At the same time, a marketing approach to fund-raising is a two-way system: it involves planning and formulating the institution's appeal for funds to potential donors, but it is also an important source of information as to how well the institution's product is being received in the marketplace and for changes that may be taking place in that marketplace. A marketing network thus serves as an intelligence system.

Peters and Waterman point out in their study of successful American businesses, *In Search of Excellence*:

> Excellent companies are better listeners. They get a benefit from market closeness that for us was truly unexpected, that is, until you think about it. Most of their real innovation comes from the market.[5]

[5] Peters and Waterman, p. 193.

In sum, marketing is a deliberate and conceptual approach to raising funds; it is a disciplined managerial process involving analysis, planning, and execution. It is an *assertive* process; it sees a nonprofit organization as *earning* the support it receives by conferring important benefits upon funding sources rather than simply appealing to the good will of benefactors.

Approaching Funding Sources

The four major sources of funding are government, corporations, foundations, and individuals. Each of these sources may be regarded as a separate donor market with its own special characteristics and requirements.

GOVERNMENT

In our modern economy it is a way of life for private organizations, whether for-profit or not-for-profit, to seek contracts from government. Exempt organizations are providers of social goods, and by far, government is the largest purchaser of such goods. The government is thus a natural partner for many nonprofit institutions in their efforts to carry out their social missions.

Indeed, for some nonprofit activities or projects, there is no alternative except to seek government support. The scale or nature of a particular project, for example, may dictate government funding as the only available resource. For example, take the case of a research project like Princeton University's Plasma Physics Laboratory where the payoff, if any, in harnessing hydrogen fusion to provide energy won't come until the year 2000. The annual cost of this research runs into millions of dollars. Industry won't pick up the tab. The only realistic source is the federal government.

For many nonprofits there is no choice but to seek some level of government support. Such organizations need to appreciate the limitations and risks inherent in government funding and minimize these dangers whenever possible by diversifying their sources of revenue.

Government Funding: Special Costs and Risks

The basis of government support is ultimately political; that is inherent in the nature of government. But political priorities can shift quickly, and thus a nonprofit enterprise heavily dependent on government funds can suddenly find itself out in the cold.

In an early 1960s study of the impact of government funding on a major private university, it was asserted that one need have "no concern about the overall level of government aid for higher education." But this failed to anticipate the support President Reagan would marshal for the curtailment of government budgets in the 1980s. Under President Reagan, aid to education has leveled off in the face of a continuing increase in educational costs. Continued availability of any form of government support is *inherently* uncertain as political priorities change over time.

Moreover, government officials often become restless in committing funds to the same organization year after year. They don't want their funds all tied up in the same enterprise; they want to move on to doing new things. If they cannot quietly persuade their superiors to allow them to cut off support to an existing grantee in favor of adding new organizations, they sometimes will seek to undermine the reputation of the longstanding recipient. Negative comments about such a recipient may be leaked to the press or to legislators looking to embarrass the funding agency's head. I am familiar with several actual situations in which government staff, unable to get their superiors to cease funding a popular organization, fed disparaging material about the organization, in one case to a critic of the agency in the legislature and in another to "investigative" reporters. Months of effort and substantial expense were incurred by the organizations to clear the air and restore their good reputations.

A major drawback in seeking government funding is the frequent need to obtain funds from a variety of governmental agencies with conflicting program priorities and requirements, in order to raise enough money to support a single program. A classic illustration of this is the way public broadcasting is funded by the federal government. The Corporation for Public Broadcasting, the government institution charged with both channeling funds to public television stations and helping them to develop programs, has nowhere near the amount of funds required to finance programming for the system. One year, CPB's entire budget for developing new programs was $8 million. The stations (even with their own efforts to tap public support), in combination with the resources of CPB, can rarely afford to pay for the programs the system requires. For example, the bulk of the $11 million required to produce 65 shows for a Children's Television Workshop series on science and technology was provided by the Workshop from its own funds, the National Science Foundation, the Office of Education, and the United Technologies Corporation. Less than $1 million was provided by the Corporation for Public Broadcasting.

In contrast, the commercial television networks in this country provide "one-stop shopping" for program producers; if a network wants a program, it can and will pay the costs of its development. (Commercial television budgets are traditionally far larger than those in public broadcasting.) The result is that producers for public television must not only sell a show to the stations, but then comb the woods to provide some combination of governmental agencies and private corporations willing to help fund the program. This kind of search is not only frustrating and expensive to conduct, but even where successful, often involves jockeying back and forth between the conflicting goals of the various funders, shaping and twisting a concept to please diverse interests. The wonder of the public broadcasting system is that somehow so many quality programs are produced in spite of it.

The difficulties and costs of raising public money for television are by no means unique; rather, the cited problems plague a wide range of social efforts dependent on government support, as an excerpt on the following pages of this text from Elizabeth Sturz's book, *Widening Circles,* illustrates so pointedly.

Success in obtaining government money also poses its problems. There are some subtle, and some not-so-subtle, dangers in living on government funding. Government funding poses the risk of:

- distortion of the institution's true interests to conform to governmental objectives.
- creation of "have" (government-funded) and "have not" (no outside support) departments in the same organization.
- the establishment of a special class of personnel whose only connection to the institution is their work on a government contract. For instance, for many years the Plasma Physics Lab at Princeton, with more than 200 employees, had only two university departmental faculty members associated with the project. The vast bulk of lab employees became a special class of employees who sought different salary arrangements (together with the best benefits offered to the regular university staff) than those of university employees in general, creating all kinds of problems and tensions.
- detailed, far-ranging government audits that threaten the heart of an institution's freedom and that are expensive to defend even if the organization can eventually refute all claims. For example, a 1973 audit by the Department of Health, Education, and Welfare, a funding source for Children's Television Workshop's "Sesame Street" series, recommended the government review of CTW executive compensation policies even though no one earning more than $30,000 was charged to the government grant. The 1973 audit also recommended greater reuse of prior show segments to reduce costs, which thrust the government into the heart of programming judgments. In the same audit, HEW staff also recommended the CTW put out to competitive bid the segments of the "Sesame Street" series performed by the famous Muppet characters Big Bird, Ernie, and Burt. To government auditors, these marvelous and unique puppets were as replaceable as nuts and bolts.
- the imposition of requirements that are unrelated to the substance of the funded project, but which further the funding sources' collateral aims. For instance, the Department of Education required CTW to caption "Sesame Street" for the deaf at a cost to CTW of $150,000.
- voluminous bureaucratic reporting requirements and reviews which absorb so much of a nonprofit organization's time and energy as to distract it from its main tasks. Elizabeth Sturz is executive director of Argus House, a community organization in the South Bronx, New York, which deals with troubled and troublesome youth. In her book *Widening Circles,* she provides a compelling case history of just how distracting and debilitating it can be for an organization to comply with governmental red tape. She writes:

> Ours is a holistic approach. We believe it is more fruitful to address the needs of the whole adolescent rather than give treatment for separate problems such as drug addiction, alcoholism, emotional disturbances, social maladjustment, unemployment. But the government, and many foundations, make grants in discrete problem areas. In order to construct something like a coherent program, responding to the needs of

our enrollees, we have put together funding from a number of public and private sources. At times this creation resembles a Frankenstein monster, out of control and with the crude stitches barely holding together at the seams. We have grants to operate a drug-free day treatment program, a child-care program, various employment programs, several training programs, and key bits and pieces financed by private foundations or corporations. In addition, the New York City Board of Education outstations fifteen teachers on our premises under an arrangement known as a cluster or institutional school. All of the government-funded programs and the Board of Education school have their separate eligibility requirements. Numerous documents must be collected, not because they make our interactions with the adolescents more effective but simply in order to prove eligibility in terms of the statutes, rules and regulations. The hours spent at these tasks may seem reasonable, on the surface, as a way of accounting for the tax-payers' money, but in actuality the process is counter-productive and wasteful, as it cuts deeply into the time we could spend in effective work with the kids. We produced better results in the years before 1978, when the paper collar was put around our necks and tightened to the point of strangulation. We do not object to being held accountable, but we believe that a method can be devised to assure that funds are not wasted and that programs do what they say they are going to do without eating into the productive hours and paralyzing effectiveness.[6]

The frustration of dealing with a stream of red tape is often compounded by the efforts of so many bureaucracies to cloak their staffs in anonymity, precluding recipients from identifying *individuals* who are responsible for their actions. Again, let me quote from Elizabeth Sturz:

Of course, there are always, within any bureaucracy, individuals who will put your papers on the top of the pile and push them along expeditiously and will do anything in their power to help. They are decent, conscientious persons, and they deserve much praise. I have found generally that commissioners and people at the top are intelligent and understanding.

One of the problems we face nowadays is not that bureaucracies don't change, but that they change too quickly and too often. Officials seem to have a different title, phone number and office every time you talk to them. They can scarcely remember you, and they often don't know who has taken over the management of your contract or what the guidelines currently are. After several meetings and much negotiation, terms are agreed upon, then just as the plan is to become final it is scrapped. The old guidelines have been discarded; the former negotiators are no longer on the scene: and the whole laborious business has to be started again from scratch.[7]

The moral here is not that government funding inevitably poses unacceptable risks. Rather, the point is that the government funding terrain is no place for the unwary

[6] *Widening Circles* by Elizabeth Sturz (pp. 20–21). Copyright © 1983 by Harper & Row, Publishers, Inc. Selected excerpts reprinted by permission.

[7] Sturz, p. 300.

and unsophisticated to hazard. Nonprofit management must therefore assess the extent to which the operation of an institution is vulnerable to the reduction or cutoff of the flow of government funds. In particular it should examine in advance whether a potential reduction or cutoff would affect:

- core programs.
- long-term personnel commitments.
- indirect costs that have been allocated to government projects, costs that can't be eliminated despite loss of funding.

If it is at all possible, such program commitments and costs should be funded, at least in part, with nongovernmental money to contain the extent of damage to an institution if its government funding is curtailed.

Building an Organization to Seek Government Funds

An entity which must regularly approach government for significant support needs a professional staff with experience in dealing with public agencies. This staff should: process applications for funds; coordinate the search for funding by different departments; maintain contacts with officials of key funding agencies, and with the legislators who play decisive roles in controlling such agencies' funding or overseeing their operations; ensure compliance with government regulations; and stay abreast of shifting governmental priorities and interests. Where necessary, it must also learn how to pierce the veil of anonymity of a bureaucracy and find the points of leverage to make the agency more responsive. A nonprofit organization must be as professional in seeking government funding as the treasury department of a large corporation is in raising capital from Wall Street.

In particular, such staff must also master the nature of the government appropriation process. An understanding of the process—and the key players in it—is required in order to support the efforts of a friendly executive department in securing funding from the legislature with which to fund an organization's program and to plan for when funds are going to be available. The risks of delay in getting funds from the government has to be taken into account in the cash flow planning of an organization.

Nonprofit institutions playing the government funding game must be prepared, on occasion, to mount a political campaign to protect their interests (the politics of self-defense). In order to be able to mount such a campaign, over a period of time an organization has to develop a political base it can call upon. It has to cultivate relationships with the legislature and within the executive branch, as well as with public constituencies, to be able to bring them into play when necessary. It's too late if a nonprofit organization is caught in a fire storm and then has to go out and look for support. In the 1970s, there was a move in the U.S. House of Representatives to eliminate or curtail the charitable deduction. In the end, the movement was defeated not by neatly argued position papers (though these were prepared) or by lobbying members on the Hill (though this was done), but by developing grass roots support for the deduction in every congressman's home district. The organizers of this effort received their highest accolade when one congressman told them, "You guys are as tough as the unions!"

NONGOVERNMENTAL SOURCES OF REVENUE SUPPORT: AN OVERVIEW

Before delving into how to approach nongovernmental funders, it may be useful to develop a profile of both the principal sources of nongovernmental support of exempt organizations and the levels of support various classes of such organizations have received. Our profile is drawn from two sources: A 1981 Chemical Bank study entitled *Giving and Getting,* updated in 1984, and the *1975 Report of the Commission on Private Philanthropy and Public Needs* (the so-called Filer Commission).

As previously noted, there are four principal categories of supporters of not-for-profit enterprises: individuals, corporations, foundations, and bequests. The vast majority of support of exempt organizations in this country is provided by individuals (79 percent in 1974, according to the Filer Commission study).

The Commission also reported that "a disproportionate amount of philanthropic giving comes from the highest income levels" and cited a 1973 survey showing that some 21 percent of individual giving came from the less than 1 percent of households earning above $50,000 a year.[8] The same survey indicated low and middle income families—the 87 percent of households with incomes below $20,000—provided 54 percent of all individual philanthropy.

Taking 1979 as the latest year for which I found comprehensive data, the contributions break down in dollar terms as follows:

Table 1.   TOTAL CONTRIBUTIONS (in billions of dollars)[9]

Total	Individuals	Corporations	Bequests	Foundations
$43.31	$36.54	$2.3	$2.23	$2.24

Over the period 1955–1979, the share of giving by individuals remained in the 78–86 percent range, with the share provided by corporations fluctuating during the same period—generally in tandem with variations in corporate profits—while the share provided by bequests and foundations declined over this time frame (see Table 2). (Actually, since bequests represent giving by individuals through their estate plans, the amount of giving by bequests could be added to the total for individual gifts.)

[8] *Filer Commission Report,* pp. 55, 56.

[9] Tables 1, 2, and 3 were drawn from *Giving and Getting* (New York: Chemical Bank, 1981, p. 181. Updated 1984, pp. 9–11). The original figures were taken from *Giving USA: 1980 Annual Report* of the American Association of Fund-Raising Counsel, Inc. (AAFRC), New York.

Table 2.   **TOTAL CONTRIBUTIONS BY CONTRIBUTOR CATEGORIES**
(percent of total)

	Individuals	Corporations	Bequests plus Foundations	Bequests	Foundations
1955	85.7%	6.2%	8.1%	3.6%	4.5%
1960	81.3	5.1	13.7	6.1	7.6
1965	78.0	5.9	16.2	7.7	8.5
1970	76.7	3.8	19.5	10.3	9.2
1975	81.7	4.0	14.3	7.5	6.8
1979	84.4	5.3	10.3	5.1	5.2

The 1 percent of U.S. households that earned more than $50,000 in 1974 tended to give most of its money (93 percent) to nonreligious exempt organizations. The 87 percent of the country's households that earned less than $20,000 in 1974 gave more of their money (66 percent) to religious organizations.[10]

Among the recipients of private giving in this country, religious institutions tended to be the major beneficiaries over the years from 1955 to 1979 (see Table 3). However, their shares of total giving tended to decline in the more recent part of the period, with an increase in gifts to arts and humanities.

Table 3.   **TOTAL CONTRIBUTIONS BY RECIPIENT CATEGORIES**
(in billions of dollars)

Total Contributions	Religious		Arts & Humanities		Educational Institutions		Health Org. & Hospitals		Social Welfare Organizations		Civil, Public & Other	
	$	% of Total	$	% of Total	$	% of Total	$	% of Total	$	% of Total	$	% of Total
1955 $6.66	3.33	50.0	.199	3.0	.733	11.0	.596	9.0	1.53	23.0	.272	4.1
1979 $43.31	20.14	46.5	2.70	6.2	5.99	13.8	5.95	13.7	4.35	10.0	4.14	9.6

The above figures show that for the 24 years from 1955 to 1979, charitable contributions increased from $6.66 billion to $43.31 billion, or at a significantly greater rate than inflation during the period.[11] This means there was a *real* increase in giving over the period. Remember, however, that the 1960s and early 1970s were periods of rapid growth in the American economy, and there is a question whether charitable giving grew as fast as the economy as a whole over this time frame. Toward the end of the period, as inflation intensified in the 1970s, giving did not keep pace with the rising level of prices in this country. The Filer Commission concluded on the basis of its study that the purchasing power of giving did not keep pace with the growth of

[10] *Filer Commission Report*, p. 59.
[11] *Giving and Getting*, 1984, pp. 9, 19.

the economy through the expansive years of the 1960s and 1970s, and that in recent years it has fallen off absolutely when discounted for inflation.[12]

Between 1979 and 1982 total giving increased from $43.31 billion to $60.39 billion, or some 39 percent. The bulk of the increase came in 1981 and 1982, and over half of it came from increases in giving by individuals.[13] During the same period, inflation, as measured by the consumer price index, rose only about 24 percent. The start of the decline in inflation in mid-1981 and the bull stock market, which began in the summer of 1982, as well as the increasing imagination and aggressiveness of nonprofit organizations in raising funds, undoubtedly helped account for the significant increase in *real* giving between 1979 and 1982.

Foundation Grants

There are some 24,000 foundations in this country, but the bulk of foundation resources and activity is concentrated in approximately 19 percent of the nation's total foundations. The tenth edition of *The Foundation Directory,* published by The Foundation Center in 1985, lists 4,402 foundations accounting in 1983 for $63.1 billion in assets, or 97 percent of all the assets of active grant-making foundations in the United States. These foundations made a total of $4.1 billion in grants in 1983, or 85 percent of all the grants paid out in that year. According to *The Foundation Directory, 10th Edition,* approximately 82 percent of the foundations (numbering over 19,000) account for only 3 percent of total foundation assets and 15 percent of total foundation giving.

Foundations vary widely not only in size, but also in character of staff and style of operation. A good number of foundations are family foundations set up by a wealthy individual to support activities of special appeal to the donor and are typically administered by family members or legal counsel. At the other extreme are the professional foundations that support a wide range of activities according to priorities set by their boards of trustees, and which are administered by full-time professional staffs.

Foundations are also sometimes organized by corporations to give away the up to 5 percent of a company's adjusted net income which they are allowed to deduct against corporate taxes. Some of these corporate foundations are casually administered on a part-time basis by a member of the corporate staff with other duties, or in some cases by a full-time staff specially hired for the purpose. In addition to the foundations that make grants to others, there are operating foundations, which use their resources to conduct their own research or to provide a direct service. Obviously, these types of foundations are of little interest to an organization seeking funds for its own programs.

Many people assume blithely that foundations are interested in any good work they hear about. In fact, almost all foundations of any size now have very well-defined program objectives; certainly this is the case for professionally staffed organizations.

---

[12] *Filer Commission Report,* pp. 70–75.
[13] *Giving and Getting,* 1984, p. 5.

As a rule, foundations do not like to provide general institutional support but prefer to back specific new programs that would not be undertaken but for the foundation's help, and they must mesh with the institution's defined program objectives. Most foundations are hesitant to make grants for endowment or for buildings. They prefer to fund an operational program.

Foundations like to make grants that they are convinced will have an impact, not only on the recipient, but on others as well. They also tend to favor "leveraging" their funds, by which they mean attracting others to contribute to the financing of the program in which they invest.

The degree of precision with which foundations express their objectives, as you might expect, varies widely from institution to institution. For instance, three foundations may all be similarly concerned with helping higher education, but one will announce its goals as "aiding higher education," another as "helping colleges and universities deal with their management and financial problems," and the third as "improving instructional methodology and content, especially projects which cross traditional lines between disciplines." Without specifically inquiring of each foundation, it would be impossible to tell from a simple reading of these statements whether they would all support similar specific programs or have very different aims in mind.

To illuminate how a foundation's program goals can shape its grant-making, let me review how one foundation developed its program. Lloyd Morrisett, head of the Markle Foundation (about $60 million in assets), explained to me in an interview in the summer of 1983 the rationale he presented to his trustees in 1969 that led to the redirection of Markle's program from support of medical school professionals to communications. In our conversation Lloyd recalled that he recommended that the foundation center its efforts on communications because:

1. The communications industry was an area of great importance, but it had been largely ignored by philanthropic institutions. The Ford Foundation was active in supporting public broadcasting, but the entire terrain of commercial broadcasting was largely unattended and ignored by foundations.

2. Even a small foundation like Markle could have an impact since the target audience, the senior officials in the fields of publishing and broadcast communications, was quite small in number, perhaps no more than 10,000. The number of people and the number of institutions one had to influence was thus relatively small, say, in comparison to public schools in this country. Lloyd was convinced that the principal reason for the failure of a foundation project is "under-capitalization financially or intellectually." Thus, finding a small enough universe that Markle could fund adequately with its budget was critical to him.

3. Government regulation of broadcasting as well as of copyrights, and the court's interest in First Amendment issues, would inevitably raise significant public policy issues. Such issues are a place where it is relatively feasible for a foundation to fund efforts which will be useful. Moreover, the scope of such issues in broadcasting is more readily definable than in such broad fields as education.

4. Lloyd's own experience before coming to Markle indicated broadcasting was a good field in which to leverage funds. As a vice-president at the Carnegie Foundation, he initiated the idea of creating the Children's Television Workshop, producer of the famed "Sesame Street" television series, and he spearheaded the successful effort to put together a consortium of foundations and the federal Office of Education to provide $8 million to launch the workshop in 1969.

5. The people-skills needed for grant-making in communications involve an analytic orientation, an understanding of economic, social, and legal issues, and an appreciation of the impact of public policy on an industry. These skills are general enough so that many people could acquire them relatively quickly, especially in comparison to a specialized area such as, say, pediatric endocrinology.

6. The timing was right. There has to be a receptivity in the larger public, as well as in important institutions, to the foundation's aims. The amount of resources even the largest foundation can marshal won't have an impact unless the climate is hospitable. As an example, he cited the start of the Children's Television Workshop to produce "Sesame Street" in 1969 as a case of "perfect timing." The public was focused on preschool education, and friends of such a program were in the right places in government and foundations.

Many foundations, once they have identified an area of general interest, such as communications, will develop a set of more specific objectives. For instance, they may try to foster more effective "children's educational programming" and "informational" programming within the field of communications. Under Morrisett, however, Markle has resisted this approach. In Lloyd's view, "If an area is important, I'm not sure I would place many limits on decisions to grant support in the field . . . beyond the limits of imagination and available resources."

Many foundations today have an as clearly articulated rationale for the choice of program interests as Markle. Accordingly, the basic focus in seeking a foundation grant has to be on matching an organization's program goals with those of a specific foundation.

There are a good many sources of information about foundation activities; a good starting point is The Foundation Center, a nonprofit organization with research centers in New York, Washington, D.C., San Francisco, and Cleveland. The Center issues a series of publications including *The Foundation Directory,* which provides capsule descriptions of the program interests of some 4,400 foundations, and *Foundation Fundamentals: A Guide for Grantseekers.* (For a list of other publications on grantsmanship, see note four at page 447 of Kotler's *Marketing for Nonprofit Organizations.*)

Since even the most narrowly focused descriptions of foundation interests are likely to be somewhat elastic, a fund-seeking organization should go beyond published descriptions and study what type of grant awards the foundation has in fact made. The foundation's annual report is a good source for this information, and The Foundation Center's *Foundation Grants Index* may be helpful.

Even with this research, informal contact with the foundations an organization thinks offer potential will save time in the long run.

A good application takes effort to prepare; if filed blindly, it may sit for weeks at a foundation that has no interest. A phone call, even in a case where no one in the organization knows an official at the foundation, can produce helpful hints as to whether a particular activity is likely to be of interest. A brief letter may also serve to avoid the preparation of a full-blown application which is of no interest to a foundation.

If a preliminary inquiry is encouraging, try to arrange a visit to talk with a foundation official before filing a formal application. Find out what the foundation's internal process is for awarding grants and what criteria it applies in making awards. Learn the timing of its funding cycle and try to ascertain what kinds of things really interest the staff person who will review the grant proposal.

For example, would it help to invite the person to visit your organization? Is there something compelling you could show a foundation representative which would give life and power to what would otherwise be dry words on paper? Is the staff person only interested in the content of an organization's program, or is the overall quality of its management, especially financial administration, also crucial? Can you distinguish your program in some fashion from your competitors? What kind of demonstration would the official be interested in to show that a grant will have impact beyond the boundaries of your organization? Is leveraging funds important to this particular foundation?

Finally, nonprofit organizations, if they can afford to, should cultivate potentially supportive foundations on a regular basis, not just when they want to put in a grant proposal. Larger institutions, such as major private universities, typically will assign a development staff officer (an account executive) to make regular calls on a list of target foundations, partly to keep up contacts and partly to learn of new directions or interests developing at the foundation. The account executive sometimes arranges for a senior officer of the university or a distinguished faculty member to accompany him or her to a talk about some aspect of the university, not necessarily one for which funding will be sought.

For instance, one of the most interesting discussions I heard about college admissions policy was an after-dinner debate at Princeton between William Bowen, president of the university, and MacGeorge Bundy, former Harvard dean and then head of the Ford Foundation. Bowen and Bundy differed sharply on the ability of the Ivy League colleges to select with any accuracy the actual "best" students from their pool of highly qualified applicants. The issue had nothing to do with any potential business between the university and the foundation, but was the kind of exchange the two principals enjoyed, and it served to further cultivate their relationship.

The point is that success at grantsmanship has less to do with the altruism of an organization's aims than the skill with which it identifies a foundation with matching interests and then cultivates this interest.

Corporate Support

Many corporations provide support for charitable activities, as the federal tax code permits such businesses to deduct up to 5 percent of their adjusted gross income for gifts to charities. Some corporations, as noted earlier, organize their charitable activities in the form of a foundation; some operate quite informally. But some programs of nonprofit organizations may also be funded out of a corporation's regular operating budget, if it furthers a specific business purpose of the company. For instance, the underwriting of a public television series may be charged to the corporation's public relations or advertising budget, while counseling services for chemically dependent employees or job training may be funded by the personnel budget. In considering the potential for corporate support, therefore, nonprofit institutions should begin by analyzing how their program can serve the self-interests of specific business entities.

Initially, in attempting to narrow the universe of corporations to a prospect list that can be explored in depth, the following criteria may be useful:

Geographic proximity: Corporations tend to favor supporting nonprofit organizations located in the same area, especially where it can be shown that the service provides some benefits to the corporation's employees (e.g., a local health care facility or cultural activity).

Specific benefit to the corporation: Corporations will favor supporting a necessary service provided by the nonprofit enterprise directly to a company, such as counseling the corporation's chemically dependent employees. Other services may be attractive to companies because they have a general need for them, although the benefit to the company may be only indirect in the case of any particular nonprofit organization. An example is engineering schools seeking support from companies which hire large numbers of engineers.

Personal relationships with key officials: Knowing someone personally in the right corporate department or, at least, someone senior enough to steer a nonprofit institution to the right person in the corporate structure, is an obvious advantage. Board members of a nonprofit organization, as well as professional staff, should always review their corporate contacts as part of a fund-raising search.

An image fit: A corporation's own advertising and public relations efforts may suggest themes or objectives for which the nonprofit institution's program can provide support. An example is provided below in the discussion of how Children's Television Workshop gained the support of United Technologies Corporation for a new children's television series.

Existing area of interest: Corporations may have previously supported similar programs. For example, Mobil, Exxon, and Atlantic Richfield corporations are known for their interest in underwriting public television series, so a nonprofit entity with a public TV project might consider them as possible prospects. Other companies will be known for their active support of the performing arts, museums, hospitals, and so forth.

These criteria, however, are just a starting point in approaching a corporation for funding. In preparing to approach specific companies, keep in mind that corporate support for nonprofits is prompted by a pragmatic interest in enhancing some aspect of the corporation's goals. Hence, in seeking corporate funds, a nonprofit organization should be able to explain how supporting its program will in turn further a particular corporate objective.

For example, take United Technologies' $2 million grant in 1979 to the Children's Television Workshop to help fund "3-2-1 Contact," a public television series on science technology for children between the ages of eight and twelve. At the time, United Technologies was a conglomerate spending substantial sums on trying to build a corporate identity as a leader in the technology field. Its public relations department had just added two executives who had been at Mobil Corporation and who had worked on that oil giant's active underwriting of public television series. The public relations staff was contacted informally to see if UT might have an interest in being the sole corporate sponsor of the show. An affirmative indication led first to a presentation to that staff and eventually to Harry Gray, UT's chief executive officer, and his key aides. In pitching UT, CTW was aware that in public television an underwriter of a show only receives a brief oral and visual mention of its name at the end of the show after the production credits are shown. This isn't much exposure, especially when compared to commercials for the much larger audiences attracted by commercial television. How then did CTW induce UT to contribute $2 million to "3-2-1 Contact"?

In all its presentations to UT, the Workshop stressed that underwriting "3-2-1 Contact" could give UT substantial public relations benefits, provided that it vigorously promoted its association with the show via newspaper and other forms of mass media advertising. Of course, this meant UT would have to spend a good deal of additional money advertising its underwriting of the show. But such advertising would bring wide attention to UT's underwriting regardless of how many viewers actually watched the series on public television and noticed the brief underwriting credit at the end of each show. United Technologies bought CTW's concept.

Just before "3-2-1 Contact" went on the air, United Technologies placed ads in selected major U.S. newspapers and national magazines with the headline, "Will there ever be another show as worthwhile as 'Sesame Street'?" That gave United Technologies the double benefit of underwriting a show for children on science and technology and an association with "Sesame Street," the most widely known children's television show in history.

Tie-in promotions with vendors of commercial products or services are another means of tapping corporations to support nonprofit causes. A tie-in promotion involves a commercial vendor linking its product to a charitable cause. For instance, Frito Lay potato chips contributes funds to cancer research based on the runs scored by the New York Yankees baseball team. Frito Lay advertises its contributions on radio broadcasts of the Yankees games, publicizing itself as well as the charity.

The tie-in promotion approach reflects an increasing focus by a corporation on the connections between its charitable efforts and its own business interests. *The Wall Street Journal,* under a lead story headlined "Companies Change The Ways They Make Charitable Donations," chronicled the spectacular tie-in promotion done by American Express in connection with the campaign to refurbish the Statue of Liberty. The *Journal* reported:

> With deep gratitude, the Statue of Liberty-Ellis Island Foundation recently accepted two special traveler's checks totaling more than $1.7 million from American Express Co.
>
> The gift, along with contributions from others, meant the grande dame of New York Harbor could be restored to past glory, Americans could gaze upon it with renewed pride and the donor could be hailed a corporate patriot.
>
> Moreover, by doing good, American Express managed to do well. It generated the gift money by promising in a national ad campaign in last year's fourth quarter to donate a penny to that statue for each use of its charge card and a dollar for most new cards issued in the U.S. The result: Card usage increased 28% during the quarter over the same period in 1982; before the campaign was devised, the company had forecast a card-usage increase of 18% for last year's fourth quarter. New card holders rose more than 45% during the campaign, and the company's card business had its best fourth quarter ever.
>
> "The wave of the future isn't checkbook philanthropy, " says Jerry C. Welsch, an American Express marketing executive. "It's a marriage of corporate marketing and social responsibility."[14]

According to the *Journal,* American Express has worked tie-ins with charities in 31 other markets around the country. The company calls this effort "cause-related marketing."

Carter Hawley Hale Stores is another example cited by the *Journal* of companies that have begun to relate their charitable efforts more closely to their business interests. The *Journal* reported:

> At Carter Hawley Hale Stores, Inc., enlightened self-interest has steered the Los Angeles retailer to contribute for the most part only to the visual and performing arts and only in major cities. Until recently, Carter Hawley had a potpourri of charitable interests; its decision to narrow its approach was based on bringing its name, in connection with its charities, to the attention of the people who really count in its business—the decidedly upscale.
>
> "There's been a real determination to bring the contributions program in concert with corporate goals," says Jeanette McElwee, Carter Hawley's corporate contributions

---

[14] Wendy L. Wall, "Helping Hands, Companies Change the Ways They Make Charitable Donations," in *The Wall Street Journal,* June 21, 1984, p. 1. Excerpts reprinted by permission of *The Wall Street Journal,* © Dow Jones & Company, Inc., 1984. All rights reserved.

manager. "You have to look at the second layer: Is this good for Broadway? Is it good for Neiman-Marcus?" (Both are Carter Hawley units.)[15]

Corporations, according to the same story in *The Wall Street Journal,* are extremely interested in finding alternatives to cash gifts. The *Journal* cited gifts of everything from staging management seminars to donating vacated office space. The *Journal* noted:

> In a Conference Board survey of 286 firms, such donations accounted for 29% of total giving in 1982. Even if the surge to that level can be laid in large part to recession-induced cash conservation, the proportion may well remain high even in better times. As with their manufacturing operations, companies have been "learning to orchestrate everything they've got," says Kathryn Troy, a Conference Board researcher.[16]

Individual Donations

Private individuals are the backbone of voluntary giving in this country. As noted earlier, over the last nearly twenty years, some 76–85 percent of the support for exempt organizations has come from individuals. In dollar terms, by far the largest share of such giving comes from wealthier individuals. Filer Commission studies show that 75 percent of the gifts to higher education in 1970–71 were large gifts (more than $5,000) and that nearly 27 percent of such gifts were in the form of property (securities, real estate assets, etc.).[17]

The tax benefits to a donor in giving a gift to charity are an important part of raising funds from individuals. Of particular significance are the special benefits to a donor in making a gift of substantially appreciated property. For example, assume that a donor owns a piece of real estate with an appraised value of $110,000 and an original purchase price of $10,000. The capital gains tax would equal 20 percent of $100,000, or $20,000, leaving an $80,000 profit if the land were sold by the donor. If, however, the donor gives the land to a 501(c)(3) organization, he or she will receive a tax deduction of $110,000, which will save the donor $55,000 in taxes if he or she is in the 50 percent bracket.[18] The resultant saving in taxes is $25,000 less than the after-tax profit in the case of a sale. If there is no ready market for the property the donor can get an immediate tax deduction by giving the land to an exempt organization, whereas it may be years before he or she can find a buyer for the property. In such a case, the tax deduction for a gift may be very attractive.

However, certifying the value of a gift for the purpose of establishing the amount of the donor's tax deduction is a practice all nonprofit organizations should avoid.

---

[15] Wall, in *The Wall Street Journal,* June 21, 1984, p. 1.

[16] Wall, in *The Wall Street Journal,* June 21, 1984, p. 1.

[17] *Filer Commission Report,* Vol. 2, p. 486.

[18] The deduction on long-term appreciated securities is now limited to 30 percent of a donor's adjusted gross income, but an excess deduction may be carried forward for five years.

The danger is too great that the organization will be perceived as colluding with the donor to inflate a gift's value. Establishing the appropriate amount to deduct for a charitable gift should be left entirely up to the donor. The exempt organization may properly provide a donor with a receipt for a gift and evidence of its tax-exempt status, but no more.

Most nonprofit entities readily accept gifts of appreciated marketable securities. Such securities are easy to handle and to sell. But fewer tax-exempt entities seek out other forms of property, such as real estate or art, which require specialized skill to manage and to sell in order to convert the asset into liquid funds. Thus, a nonprofit institution that develops know-how in the management and sale of works of art, undeveloped land, or income-producing buildings may have an edge in attracting new forms of giving.

Tax benefits by no means constitute the entire reason for individual giving. A range of different motives underlies individual giving to exempt organizations, even among supporters of the same institution. For instance, in the case of schools, colleges, and universities, donor motivation will range from traditional school loyalty, to ego enhancement via putting one's name on a new building, to gratitude for an education which the donor believes enabled him or her to prosper or enjoy life more fully. Kotler, in his *Marketing for Nonprofit Organizations*, asks:

> Is there such a thing as giving without "getting"? Some people give and say that they expect nothing back. But actually they have "expectations." They expect the organization to use the money efficiently; they expect the fundraiser to show gratitude; and so on. Even the anonymous giver, while wanting no acknowledgment, may privately enjoy the self-esteem of being "big enough" to give money without requiring recognition.[19]

He goes on to list the complex of motives that may underlie giving in an interesting table excerpted in full here:

1. Need for self-esteem. Person attempts to build his self-esteem through self-image, playing "God," or feeling good from giving. Opposite of this would be shame or guilt.

2. Need for recognition from others. Person attempts to build his social status or enhance his prestige in the eyes of others. There is a strong need to belong.

3. Fear of contracting disease. The need centers around an insecurity in people that they will contract the disease or that a member of their family will. They hope in some sense for immortality.

4. The habit giver. This person gives out of habit for no real reason other than a desire not to be embarrassed by not contributing to the cause. These people are very indif-

---

[19] Kotler, *Marketing for Nonprofit Organizations*, p. 427.

ferent to contributions, but feel that they must give to someone because everyone else does.

5. Nuisance giver. This person only gives to get rid of the caller. He feels contributing to a cause to be of no real significance, but would rather donate a few dollars than be troubled by others.

6. Required to give. These people are required to give at work; they are under pressure from superiors to donate part of their checks to a fund. They therefore demand efficiency, credibility from the organization that they contribute to.

7. Captive givers. These people feel real sorrow for someone they know who might have contracted the disease. They are other-centered in that they earnestly would like to aid the victim in some way. Givers in this category may contribute at the death of a friend, rather than sending flowers, etc.

8. People-to-people givers. These people have a real feeling of the "commonness of man," a solidarity with other people. This group of people has internalized the idea of helping others because they want to.

9. Concern for humanity. This segment of givers are concerned about others for religious reasons and because they are "God's children." They feel a moral obligation to contribute to a charity. They have accepted the love-for-humanity idea because it is a requirement of their faith.[20]

The motives of potential givers provide important clues about how to appeal to them. For example, an institute that treats chemically dependent children may hold a theater benefit, not only to offer the families and friends of children who have been helped a chance to express their gratitude, but also to appeal to the even wider audience of parents who *fear* their children might become dependent and want "to do something" to help reduce their risk.

Schools carefully cultivate and develop an alumnus' sense of loyalty through colorful mailings of information about the school and classmates, as well as by staging special events encouraging alumni to return to the school. Actual fund-raising solicitations are staged separately but seek to capitalize on the attachments reinforced by such communications and events.

Kotler provides further illustration, in his *Marketing for Nonprofit Organizations,* of how understanding the motivation for giving provides clues to shaping an effective fund-raising strategy. He notes:

> . . . appeal levels . . . vary greatly . . . within medical charities people give most readily to the American Red Cross ($381.5 million), American Cancer Society ($139.7 million), Easter Seals ($99 million), American Heart Association ($87 million), March of Dimes ($68.5 million), and Mental Health Association ($20.9 million) (figures as of 1978). Some of the difference in the amount raised is due to the fact that these organizations have different life spans and different degrees of effectiveness at fundraising. A larger

[20] Kotler, *Marketing for Nonprofit Organizations,* p. 427.

part of the difference in giving levels is due to the opinion people hold about specific diseases, particularly about the disease's *severity, prevalence,* and *remediability.* Thus, heart disease and cancer are severe diseases—they kill—whereas arthritis and birth defects are considered less serious since they do not kill. Cancer has a higher prevalence than muscular dystrophy and therefore attracts more support. Finally, people believe that cures or preventions are possible for heart disease and less so for birth defects and this leads to more giving. If the March of Dimes wants to attract more funds for its cause— birth defects—it must try to increase the perceived severity, prevalence, and remediability of birth defects.[21]

Many organizations have discovered that it is more effective to appeal for support for programs that have produced results or that promise to provide specific benefits, rather than to solicit help on the basis of the organization's general needs. That is why most colleges and universities, for instance, draw up tables of need that list an array of new projects that cost various amounts to implement, as a means of exciting potential donors with different giving potentials.[22]

In general, people respond better to messages detailing programs that will enable an institution to progress than to pleas about its financial predicament. Indeed, the credibility of organizations for efficient administration and good, well-run programs is an important plus. For instance, Princeton commonly stresses in its fund appeals its successful record of financial management and, in particular, its excellent record of endowment management. The point is to assure donors, especially of capital gifts, that their funds will be used efficiently and effectively.

The Wall Street Journal recently reported that among corporations there is growing insistence that nonprofit agencies be soundly managed and have strong prospects for survival before the companies make donations. "Corporations don't want to put money behind an organization that's going to go under in a year," the *Journal* quoted an executive of the Chicago Donors Forum, a cooperative association of grant-makers.[23]

Once in a while, donors will respond to an emergency appeal to bail out a troubled but worthwhile organization. But an organization can go to the well too often with such appeals. As a consultant to a financially troubled cultural organization warned, "The public [tires] of supporting an organization which constantly promises better management and more fiscal responsibility, but year after year falls deeper into debt."

Lively, well-conceived, and emotional appeals also stand a better chance of success than dry, fact-laden solicitations. Stirring people's hearts is always an effective fund-raising strategy.

---

[21] Kotler, *Marketing for Nonprofit Organizations,* p. 426.

[22] At the same time, raising funds only for specific projects can leave the institution without sufficient unrestricted funds to spend on general needs. One remedy is to structure a gift specific enough to appeal to a donor's special interest, but which still generates unrestricted funds for the recipient institution—for example, an endowed professorship in a donor's name. The donor's funds are restricted to support the professorship, but they will free up the university's general funds to support other university needs.

[23] Wall, in *The Wall Street Journal,* June 21, 1984, p. 1.

There is also no harm in injecting some fun for the audience into a fund-raiser: it's a tactic as old as the church picnic and as modern as a star-studded telethon.

Building perceived momentum toward an announced goal can be important in appeals to a broad grouping of donors. Schools, colleges, and universities, for example, will seek to raise customary levels of alumni support by announcing the start of a major capital campaign with a specific goal to be reached within a specified time period. Typically, the launching of the campaign will be supported by an announcement of a significant number of major pledges toward the campaign goal.[24] The pledges, of course, have been negotiated (usually with wealthy trustees and selected donors) beforehand. Other charities such as the March of Dimes, prior to a television appeal for funds to the general public, will stage a series of separate fund-raising events and announce the results of those prior efforts at strategic points in the telethon.

The time and effort invested relative to the amount that can be raised potentially also needs to be factored into any fund-raising strategy. Segmentation according to the donor's giving potential is thus important. If a fund-raiser spends 30 hours on a prospect, it is obviously far better if that donor is in a position to give $100,000 than $3,000. But broadening the base of giving is also important. Thus, if the same 30 hours can produce a campaign which yields $100 from each of 10,000 alumni, the broader-based effort is a far more productive one.

The organization's resources also have to be factored into the choice of fund-raising strategies. A theater benefit may be an excellent fund-raising vehicle for a nonprofit with a relatively sizable and affluent group of supporters. A series of fund-raising events aimed at the general public may work for an organization like the March of Dimes, with its high public visibility and a corps of volunteer workers to promote the events. Direct mail solicitation may serve colleges and universities with large, active alumni bodies. But a relatively new and small organization, perhaps seeking private funds for the first time, may find its most cost-effective strategy lies in one-on-one soliciting of private donors known personally by its board members.

For organizations without an existing constituency ready to provide financial support, one has to be built. For this need, the role of the board is critical. There must be one or two persons among board members with the talent for encouraging people of substantial means to give. This prime mover does not have to be extraordinarily wealthy, though he or she must be in a financial position to make substantial contributions. This mover must also have the time to invest in a campaign and the flair for getting others to give, as well as a network of associations to tap into. For instance,

---

[24] After World War II, schools, colleges, and universities found that ordinary levels of support could be increased by organizing a capital gifts campaign and building up staff and promotional efforts as part of such a campaign. Once the time period for the campaign ended, however, the additional staff was released and the extra promotional effort curtailed, turning the fund-raising effort back to a minimal level. Now schools typically find that it pays to maintain a sustained effort to raise funds all of the time and, from time to time, to increase the level of effort and its visibility under the umbrella of an announced campaign.

in the case of a small, fledgling social service agency, a board chairman was successful in raising money through a network of people who were traditional supporters of charities in the city served by the agency. Over the years, he had developed acquaintances with members of this circle of donors through his own modest giving activities. Now he called in his chits, asking this circle to support "his charity."

Astute fund raisers also understand that a fund provider—whether a private citizen, foundation officer, or government official—requires continuing attention after the funds have been raised. The cultivation cannot end with receipt of the check. If you slight individual donors or funding source officials in this way, you run the risk of incurring a rejection the next time you seek funds from them. A good fund-raising organization will devise ways to continue to pay attention to financial supporters and to give them the opportunity to give advice without letting them inappropriately interfere with the operations of the donee institution. Visiting committees and alumni gatherings of colleges and universities provide one model for "involving" financial supporters without getting them in management's hair.

In sum, in soliciting funds, nonprofit organizations must employ modern marketing techniques in the same way business does, and experienced, skilled people must be hired for the task. Professionalism vs. amateurism in fund-raising makes all the difference. But in all the efforts to be sophisticated about fund-raising, don't overlook the fact that there are substantial numbers of people who want to make modest gifts because they believe in an institution's work. Millions of individual Americans give support to good causes simply because they believe they ought to.

3

Making A Profit for Your Nonprofit Organization

HOW TO COPE WITH RAPIDLY INCREASING COSTS is driving many nonprofit organizations to consider a range of options for building up the flow of their revenues. More and more, such organizations are discovering that dependence on the benevolence of others will no longer suffice.

An aggressive and professional fund-raising effort makes sense for organizations in a position to undertake one. But not all nonprofit institutions have a constituency that can provide significant financial support. Moreover, more than a few nonprofit institutions have mounted imaginative and aggressive fund drives only to find they still were not able to offset their rapidly escalating expenses. The repeated inflations and recessions of the 1970s and 1980s have been a difficult climate in which to raise increased sums from contributors.

THE NEED FOR NEW REVENUE SOURCES

Increasingly, not-for-profit entities must consider generating new sources of revenues from their own activities. Such income may be derived either from commercial enterprises or by developing new customers for the organization's traditional services. In either case, the distinctive feature is that revenue is *earned* by the organization rather than received as a gift or grant. Many nonprofit entities do not consider this option, thinking it impossible or inappropriate and for some it is not a feasible strategy. But a good number have also been successful at developing new sources of earned income.[1]

[1] See pages 56–58 for examples.

The primary focus of this chapter is on the ways and means of earning income from commercial activities because this continues today to be a relatively novel and controversial strategy in the nonprofit world. But marketing traditional services to new clients is a no less important way of earning new revenues.

STARTING POINT: PART OF THE VALUE SCHEME

How does a nonprofit organization, long dependent on the charity of others, begin to find ways to make money on its own? The starting point is the organization's system of values and its attitudes toward itself and its customers.

Think for a moment about the term "not-for-profit." It is an inherently negative way of describing an organization. The term sets up an invidious comparison with business. People tend to associate profit-making with success and its opposite as implying "loss," and thus something short of successful. In the not-for-profit world this misplaced analogy has too often engendered a dependent mentality and defeatism about the prospects of achieving financial viability and independence.

Put another way, an organization that incorporates financial independence into its central value scheme will seek systematically and aggressively to identify and develop opportunities for revenue diversification. An organization that falls prey to the psychology of dependence will miss opportunities to improve its own financial fate.

Generating income is not inherently alien to nonprofit organizations. Artistic organizations give performances before the public; universities, museums, and other institutions invest endowment funds in the securities markets; and public broadcasting stations solicit corporate underwriting for programs. But, typically, such income generation is seen as a by-product of the organization's efforts rather than as the result of a deliberate focus on how the organization can market its services.

Developing Marketing Orientation

To find new revenues today, nonprofit enterprises must consciously adopt a "marketing orientation" in the same fashion as a successful profit-making enterprise.[2] Kotler, in his text on nonprofit marketing, characterizes a marketing orientation for nonprofit institutions as "customer-centeredness," meaning the focus of the entire organization is not on developing products or making sales but on satisfying "customers' changing needs and wants."[3] The point is that nonprofit organizations need to be in touch with what the marketplace wants, not just their own ideas of what the public ought to want.

---

[2] Philip Kotler and Sidney J. Levy, "Broadening the Concept of Marketing," in *Cases and Readings for Marketing for Nonprofit Organizations*, Philip Kotler, O. C. Ferrell, and Charles Lamb, eds. (Englewood Cliffs, NJ: Prentice-Hall, 1983, pp. 3–4). Selected excerpts reprinted by permission from the *Journal of Marketing*, January 1969, published by the American Marketing Association.

[3] Kotler, *Marketing for Nonprofit Organizations*, p. 22. Peters and Waterman (p. 14) characterize a marketing orientation in private companies as being "close to the customer" with a focus on providing "unparalleled quality, service, and reliability."

Kotler argues that the organizations that move toward a marketing orientation take on characteristics vital to their survival . . . becoming "more responsive, adaptive and entrepreneurial."[4]

A survey of planning in American corporations by Yankelovich, Skelly, and White, Inc., for Coopers and Lybrand observes:

> Marketing strategy is the most significant planning challenge in the 1980's, regardless of industry type or size of company. Central to the planning and social trends are the beliefs among participants that most of their businesses will not enjoy unlimited growth in the future, and that economic success will depend primarily on which competitor can capture, hold, and increase its share in existing and/or closely related markets. Most importantly, they believe that to be successful, their companies must develop a more pragmatic view of their abilities, and focus on developing, improving, and implementing competitive marketing strategies and specific marketing tactics.[5]

The nonprofit organization that consciously seeks to expand its revenues develops, as a business does, a realistic feel for its competitive environment. It recognizes that nonprofit entities compete against each other, not only for paying customers and a share of financial resources, but also for public attention and support. Peters and Waterman, writing in *In Search of Excellence* about profit-making corporations, describe "customer orientation" as a "way of 'tailoring'—a way of finding a particular niche where you are better at something than anybody else."[6]

A nonprofit enterprise needs a sharp sense of what is distinctive or special about the services it offers, what we call its "comparative advantage."

Capitalizing on Comparative Advantage

The concept of "comparative advantage" can be explained as concentrating an organization's activities in those fields in which it has expertise not equally possessed by its competitors. More simply, Peters and Waterman in *In Search of Excellence* express the idea as "sticking to your knitting." The authors assert, "Our principal finding is clear and simple. Organizations that do branch out (whether by acquisition or internal diversification) but stick very close to their knitting outperform the others. The most successful of all are those diversified around a single skill. . . ." The authors add that there is overwhelming evidence that successful companies "have strategies of entering only those businesses that build on, draw strength from and enlarge some central strength or competence."[7]

---

[4] Kotler, *Marketing for Nonprofit Organizations*, pp. 24–27.

[5] Yankelovich, Skelly, and White, Inc., *Business Planning in the Eighties: The New Competitiveness of American Corporations*, (New York: Coopers and Lybrand, 1983).

[6] Peters and Waterman, p. 182.

[7] Peters and Waterman, pp. 293, 294.

A nonprofit organization needs to plan how best to capitalize on its special advantages. Such an analysis can identify opportunities to generate new sources of revenue through the organizations's own activities.

Opportunities to Earn Income

Numbers of nonprofit enterprises have successfully earned significant amounts of income through business endeavors. Children's Television Workshop, for example, was founded in 1969 with a combination of federal and foundation support. From the outset, the Workshop sought to reduce its dependence on such sources of funding by developing revenues from commercial activities. With the help of a major grant from the Ford Foundation in 1972 and the merchandising power of the "Sesame Street" television series, especially the unique Muppet characters, the Workshop had earned sufficient business revenue to be financially healthy by the 1980s. Indeed, by the mid-1980s the Workshop had built up a fund of some $12 million to finance development of future projects.

Few organizations can expect to have a "Sesame Street" television series with which to build a merchandising business, but they may have opportunities to earn income that they are overlooking.

The Denver Children's Museum offers an example of how initiative and ingenuity in developing business-based revenues can lift an organization toward financial independence. In 1976 the museum nearly went under. The three grants which made up its sparse $300,000 budget expired and no new ones were forthcoming. Desperate, the museum set out to earn money. By 1983, the museum's annual budget was $65,000—95 percent of which was derived from earned income.

In addition to case studies on the Denver museum and others, Crimmins and Keil published in *Enterprise in the Nonprofit Sector* a survey of "income-producing activities that are beyond the normal mission" of nonprofit institutions. They found for the period 1978–81:

- Sixty-five percent of the organizations in their sample generated some of their revenues from these activities and almost one-fourth earned at least 10 percent of their revenues from such sources.
- All organizations with annual budgets over $10 million have some amount of such income.
- A significantly greater number of organizations expanded their revenues from such sources during the period than experienced a contraction in such revenues.
- Those organizations in which such income became a larger share of total income saw their total budgets expand far more rapidly than organizations in which such income declined as a share of total revenues.[8]

[8] James C. Crimmins and Mary Keil, *Enterprise in the Nonprofit Sector* (Partners for Livable Places and The Rockefeller Brothers Fund, 1983, pp. 35–39, 123–133).

New Markets for Traditional Services

New income may be derived by finding new consumers for an organization's traditional services. For example, in higher education the static or soon-to-decline undergraduate enrollments (as the country produces fewer 18-year-olds) may be offset by the appetite of older adults for education. Community mental health organizations can offer corporate employee assistance programs that utilize their staff health counselors, and public television enterprises might extend their work to the audiences that will use the new communications technologies (e.g., cable, computers, and the emerging forms of interactive television transmission).

Commercial Sales

Nontraditional sources of income also may be derived from the marketing of products or services related to the organization's principal activities. For example, New York City's Metropolitan Museum of Art nets substantial revenues from its restaurants, and from its sale of art reproductions, greeting cards, and other publications in its shops and bookstores.

Full Utilization of Assets

Imaginative employment of under-utilized assets also may be a source of increased revenue. For example, Stanford University, and later Princeton University, saw that their vast campus land holdings were far greater than they could ever use for educational purposes. Both initiated a large-scale office park development on some of their excess acreage, appealing to companies who wanted to be located in proximity to a university's unique resources. Today, these universities earn very handsome sums from what would otherwise be idle, non-income-producing land. In the same vein, a good number of universities whose campus facilities would normally be idle in the summer now produce income in that season through summer semesters and the hosting of conferences and other special groups, including sports camps for youngsters.

New York City's Museum of Modern Art has demonstrated that an institution may have "underutilized land" even though it appears to take up 100 percent of the land on which it is located. In this case, the Museum sold the air rights above its quarter-acre building site to commercial developers for $17 million.[9]

The Wall Street Journal recently reported another example of exploiting previously underutilized assets:

> In 1981, the Young Women's Christian Association of Washington, D.C., studied the feasibility of raising $1 million to construct a new headquarters building. The conclusion:

---

[9] "Real Estate Transaction," in *The Buck Starts Here: Enterprise on the Arts*, A Conference for Nonprofit Organizations on the Legal Aspects of Making Money, Volunteer Lawyers for the Arts, 1984, p. 65.

it couldn't possibly win needed corporate support for the fund-raising effort because the capital's few major corporations were inundated with applications, and the YMCA had never received any corporate support.

But they hired a consultant, as nonprofit organizations are wont to do these days, and put together a business plan: It would sell its old building, use the proceeds to build extra stories on its proposed new building and rent out office space on those floors to generate income.

Corporations were impressed with the hardheaded approach and the attention to cash flow, according to Susan Scribner, the campaign's fund-raising coordinator, and they came through with $150,000, enough to put the drive over the top and get the building built. Now Miss Scribner is herself a consultant, showing other nonprofit agencies how to apply such techniques.[10]

OBJECTION: COMMERCIALISM

Despite the existence of opportunities, efforts by a nonprofit organization to generate revenues from its own activities or programs may run into objections that they are inappropriate. In the public mind, nonprofit institutions are devoted to worthy causes that lose money regularly. Their very existence is perceived as dependent on charity rather than vigorous self-reliance. Earning income is seen by some as incompatible with a charitable posture.

To some extent, this tin cup image is encouraged by the nonprofit sector itself. Many nonprofit organizations hold to the view that to be businesslike—to seek ways to generate funds internally, to diversify sources of income, to stick to a financial plan— is to succumb to a "commercialism" incompatible with the pursuit of high artistic, scholarly, or social goals. Contrary to such fears, however, nonprofit institutions have been able to carry on commercial activities in ways that are not incompatible with their basic mission or image. Institutions have successfully imposed high standards of quality, as well as conditions designed to protect their image with consumers, without impeding the financial success of commercial efforts. In the chapter "Changing the Nonprofit Mind-Set Toward Commercial Income," these issues are discussed in detail.

TAX CONSIDERATIONS

Engaging in business activities need not jeopardize the exempt status of public charity organizations, although private foundations may not own more than 20 percent of a business. As we discuss in the chapter on tax planning, the tax law does not bar nonprofit enterprises (other than private foundations) from actively engaging in business activities and even earning a profit, provided the profit is used to support the organization's exempt purposes and does not inure to the benefit of private individuals.

[10] Wall, in *The Wall Street Journal*, June 21, 1984, p. 1.

In general, as discussed on pp. 162–164, as long as the generation of income is a means of promoting the organization's social aims rather than an end in itself, it is an appropriate activity for a nonprofit institution.

However, the fact that an organization (other than a private foundation) may freely engage in business activities without jeopardizing its exempt status does not mean the income from such endeavors will necessarily escape taxation. As discussed in the section below, as well as in the chapter on tax planning, certain kinds of income earned by nonprofit organizations may be subject to taxation.

Legal Forms of Profit-Making Activities

The structure of the profit-making component of a nonprofit organization can take varied forms: a working group, division, or a separately incorporated subsidiary, which can be either nonprofit or profit-making in form. Of course, by definition, the separately incorporated profit-making subsidiary will pay corporate income tax on any net profit it earns.

In the case of a group or division organized within the not-for-profit corporation or a nonprofit subsidiary, the excess of the component's revenues over its expenses—i.e., its profits—may or may not constitute taxable income. As pointed out on pp. 168–169, if the revenues are generated by an activity that is *related* to the organization's exempt purpose, they will be exempt (e.g., Children's Television Workshop, producer of "Sesame Street" and other educational television series for children, also publishes an educational magazine for children). If the income is generated in a manner that is *unrelated* to the organization's purposes (e.g., if a university owns a shoe factory), it will be subject to federal income taxes with certain classes of exceptions—generally passive income in the form of dividends, interest, rents, and royalties. This holds true whether the component is organized as a working group within the nonprofit division or a nonprofit subsidiary.

The determination whether to classify a profitable activity as unrelated (and therefore subject it to federal income taxation) or related (and therefore exempt) should *not* be made solely on the basis of tax legalities. Such determinations rarely involve black-and-white situations. The financial gain from claiming tax exemption needs to be compared with certain intangible benefits of profit-making status. Establishing an activity as profit-making may be very important in setting the tone for the enterprise. Moreover, a nonprofit enterprise that engages in a highly visible commercial endeavor but claims that the income is exempt from taxation may generate criticism or attract the attention of the IRS.

These risks are much greater if the enterprise is competing with tax-paying business firms. There have been numerous instances in which such firms complained that they are facing unfair competition and triggered investigations by the IRS or provoked the concern of legislators. Simply put, an exempt organization must consider carefully the real potential for public criticism if it generates significant income from active participation in profit-making enterprises, yet pays no tax at all on such income.[11]

OPERATIONAL CONSIDERATIONS IN ORGANIZING PROFIT-MAKING ACTIVITIES

Marketing traditional services to new customers should not, as a rule, present formidable problems for a nonprofit; but the operation of a business enterprise by a nonprofit institution is a complex managerial challenge. In the first place, it is difficult to attract and appropriately compensate people with the skill and mind-set to run business enterprises for a nonprofit institution. People are attracted by an organization's purpose and values. People who care most about making money in their work tend to be drawn to profit-making organizations. Moreover, people who can generate profits want to be rewarded for their success. This means paying them additional compensation over their base salary, if they meet their financial goals. The tax law does permit incentive compensation if it is reasonable and normal for the position. (See chapter: "Tax Planning: Forethought Rather Than Afterthought.") But such incentive-based compensation is not easy for management to offer in nonprofit organizations typically accustomed to paying only fixed salaries and often modest ones at that.

Beyond the problem of staffing, there is a subtle but clear risk of confusion of purpose. The cultural values of a nonprofit and profit-making enterprise are quite different. Typically, profit maximization is the overriding goal of a business venture. The single-minded clarity of this objective is an important force in guiding such operations, while the value structure of nonprofit enterprise is more diffuse. At the center is the nonprofit organization's mission; it is the chief value that attracts both the personnel to work for it and the external support for the institution.[12] It also shapes the enterprise's priorities. But financial survival is also important. Thus, a not-for-profit entity is an organization with fundamental duality of purpose—social mission and financial well-being (which is, of course, a far more limited objective than the profit maximization goal that drives profit-making enterprises).[13]

[11] See "When Should the Profits of Nonprofits be Taxed," *Business Week*, December 5, 1983.

[12] Lloyd Morrisett, president of the Markle Foundation, writes in "Corporate Planning for Foundations" (in *Strategic Planning in Private Non-Profit Organizations*, p. 29): "The overall goal for the Markle Foundation is to achieve results and contribute to the solutions of problems in its area of concern. . . . The professional who is drawn to nonprofit work may well have economic reward as one of his important goals but of necessity he also has achievement and contribution to the solution of problems as important goals." See also Waks, in *Strategic Planning in Private Non-Profit Organizations*, pp. 5, 9–12.

[13] Norman Waks, chief management scientist in the not-for-profit research organization the MITRE Corporation, declares in *Strategic Planning in Private Non-Profit Organizations* (p. 3), quoting from an SRI publication: "Non-Profit means simply that no individual realizes profit or personal financial gain from SRI operations." In other words, it puts the emphasis more on what the enterprise does or does not do with any money it makes than on whether and what rate it makes it. He goes on to say (p. 7), "Profit-making not-for-profits . . . are organizations which have a positive spread between their dollar expenses

This duality of objectives makes it difficult for a nonprofit institution to manage a commercial business well. Simply put, there isn't likely to be the clarity of *business* purpose essential to an effective profit-making operation.

For example, assume that an activity, closely related to an organization's main purposes and offering the potential of producing income, fails to turn a profit. Should it be discontinued, or does its social value justify its continuation?

The mere possibility that such an activity may be continued, despite running at a loss, can undermine the necessary focus on creating profits. If profit-making is not central to the organization, then even those working on a profit-making venture may excuse themselves from the pressures of trying to produce a profit. If earning a profit is not the supreme value, then you can be more relaxed about meeting budgets and timetables that are necessary to produce a profit, but which impinge on the effort to turn out the highest possible quality product. In a nonprofit environment, perfectionism may indeed substitute for a bottom-line orientation.[14]

Accordingly, where both nonprofit and profit-making activities coexist within the same enterprise, there is a strong risk of confusion of objectives and operating style between the two components. This is not to say that nonprofit institutions cannot insulate profit-making activities from those nonprofit values and operating styles considered inimical to the success of a profit-making venture, but special care has to be taken in organizational design to achieve such insulation.

The Princeton Forrestal Center of Princeton University provides a model of a successful profit-making enterprise undertaken by a nonprofit organization; the reasons for its success within a nonprofit environment now seem fairly apparent. The Center was launched in 1973 with twin objectives. They were:

- to convert idle university owned land into income-producing property with a rate of return at least comparable to that of the successful return earned by the university's endowment.

- to upgrade the quality of development rapidly taking place in the vicinity of the campus.

Ten years later it is clear that the center has achieved both these objectives. In fact, the project significantly bettered its financial goal, and a series of factors may be isolated that account for the success of the center's development.

First, the concept of developing university-owned land commercially was initiated only after exhaustive consideration of various alternatives in a series of wide-ranging

---

and their dollar income. Thus, they may be considered to be profit-making organizations . . . however, while the so-called profit they make is not unimportant to them, because of the independence and management flexibility it gives them, they do not consider pursuing such 'profit,' much less trying to maximize it, as even *one* of the major goals of their operations."

[14] See Waks, in *Strategic Planning in Private Non-Profit Organizations*, p. 12.

discussions with the administration, key faculty members, local community leaders, and the board of trustees.

Second, university officials with pertinent skills teamed with outside real estate professionals to organize and lead these inquiries. The team did its homework, and its presentations were thoroughly professional.

Third, during the formative stage of the development, a senior university officer close to the president was actively involved in overseeing the development and ensuring it had the necessary support within the university and local community. The project was staffed with outside professionals experienced in real estate development, but they were not burdened with the task of winning the ongoing support of the university. That role was played by the senior officer, who was specifically designated by the president to handle the assignment.

The senior officer was involved in the day-to-day details of the project's management but continued to play his regular institutional role within the life of the university. He served, if you will, as knowledgeable "champion" of the development, dealing and brokering with the politics, nonprofit predilections, and anxieties of the university community. After a fashion, he played a role similar to that described by Peters and Waterman in *In Search of Excellence* of the executive champion of corporate entrepreneurs.

Fourth, the president fully comprehended the financial and institutional risks involved in the development. He understood particularly the pressures such risks created for him (e.g., external or internal complaints about the concept of the venture or its manner of execution).

Fifth, the day-to-day development work was carried out by the cadre of professionals from the commercial real estate world. They provided not only the needed skills but also established the profit-oriented environment for the project's management.

Sixth, the university's officials and its outside professional team limited their development efforts to planning the site, obtaining government approvals of the plan, and then finding and leasing land to companies wishing to build offices or to develop the hotel/conference facilities or housing units planned for the site. By restricting its development role, Princeton avoided the complexities and risks of building and leasing finished space—and thus limited its business efforts to areas in which the university team had clear competence and experience, notwithstanding that its outside management group had experience in construction.

Seventh, at the outset, a contract was established with the outside professionals that keyed the bulk of their compensation to the financial success of the development, and which provided them with the opportunity to earn a profit on their efforts comparable to what they could earn in a similar development launched by a profit-making enterprise.

Eighth, it was established from the outset that the policy decisions about the development, including whether to initiate it, were to be made by the board of trustees and, within the board, by a committee made up entirely of trustees with relevant business backgrounds. The committee quickly established that the development was to be treated as a business: they understood the risks involved in the development, did not flinch from backing the venture with university funds during the start-up phase, and at critical moments provided active personal assistance to the project team.

Ninth, the project team was housed away from the university campus and in its day-to-day activities it rarely mingled with the university community outside of meetings specifically related to the project.

Tenth, the center's financial goal was quite explicit: to provide a better return on the assets utilized in the development than the university's endowment. While the center was also charged with attaining a high level of quality, which would influence the caliber of development in the region, there was no ambiguity about the priority of its profit-making goals.

The Princeton Forrestal Center is not a unique structure in the nonprofit world. For instance, Harvard University's endowment funds and real estate assets are managed by a university-owned corporation of full-time professionals located in Boston, rather than at the university campus in Cambridge; this unit works under compensation arrangements comparable to similar professionals in the profit-making world. The group reports to the treasurer of the university who is a fellow of the Harvard Corporation. The treasurer is a part-time official drawn from the professional investment world.

The basic point here is that the creation of a successful profit-making component within a not-for-profit environment—the building of a culture-within-a-culture, so to speak—is a difficult business. The chances of successfully doing so will be enhanced if:

- the for-profit component is, from the outset, clearly labeled as such, and its different objectives and need for a different operating style are recognized from the start.

- the profit-making component employs its own set of professionals from the profit-making world.

- separate compensation policies are adopted for the component that provide appropriate incentives for profit-minded professionals.

- the relationship between the component and the institution is managed by a senior executive of the nonprofit who is charged specifically with championing the project and insulating it from inappropriate interference by the institution's staff.

- ultimate responsibility for the project is vested unequivocally in a group of the institution's board of trustees, who themselves are experienced participants in the profit-making world.

- the component is physically separated from the institution.

In short, the greater the separation in terms of form, staffing, oversight, and location, the greater are the chances that the profit-making component will be able to function with the necessary clarity of purpose and operating style appropriate to its objectives.

FINANCING SELF-GENERATED REVENUES

When it comes to financing a new business activity, there is a variety of financing options for nonprofit organizations. The real art is to understand exactly what role financing can play in furthering that business. Each financing option can make a different contribution to a business beyond simply providing money. A nonprofit organization needs to establish what it wants from a financial source beyond money before it can really determine where to go in search of financing.

Financing Options

A nonprofit organization may raise financing:

- from funds generated by existing revenue-producing activities. Unfortunately, few nonprofit enterprises have such resources available to fund a new endeavor.

- from venture capital or other conventional public and private financing sources available to fund qualified new businesses. Such financing may take the form of either equity or debt, or some combination, depending on the business' needs and financial condition. Either the business itself is strong enough to attract funding in its own right, or the nonprofit organization may put its credit on the line to secure capital. The terms of financing would be the same as those granted to a profit-making organization of similar resources launching a similar venture.

- by licensing a commercial profit-making company to develop the business in exchange for a royalty based on either sales, net profits, or some in-between standard.[15] Under a licensing arrangement, the commercial firm typically provides all the capital and the active management of the business. The nonprofit organization confines its role primarily to exercising quality control over the licensed product. Where the nonprofit organization receives a royalty based on sales revenues rather than on a share of profits, the income will be exempt from federal income taxation. (See chapter "Tax Planning: Forethought Rather Than Afterthought.") To be in a position to negotiate such a royalty arrangement, the nonprofit organization must have a name or other property elements (e.g., popular television characters) which can enhance the sale of a product.

- by forming a joint venture with a commercial company to develop the business. The joint venture can take the form of a partnership, stock corporation, or a contract between two entities to develop a business jointly without forming a new legal entity to operate it. The relative amount of capital and know-how contributed by the nonprofit organization and the commercial company will vary from case to case. If the

[15] Most alert nonprofit institutions avoid any royalty based other than on gross revenues in order to avoid getting involved in the morass of another company's accounting practices.

organization's name or other intangible assets are of enough value to the business, the organization may be able to negotiate for a significant ownership share without having to invest its own funds in the venture.

Each of these options offers a different control–risk trade-off. For instance, the nonprofit institution will have the greatest control over a venture financed entirely with its own funds, but it will bear also the complete financial and management risk. The least risk exposure is offered by the licensing route, but this route provides the nonprofit organization with the least degree of control over the business.

At the same time, each of the options offers a different range of support for a new undertaking. To determine the kind of support that will be most valuable, an analysis should be made of (1) the skills and resources the nonprofit organization brings and does not bring to the proposed venture; (2) the availability within the proposed commercial financing source of the particular skills and experience necessary to execute the proposed business; and (3) the goals the nonprofit organization is seeking to achieve from the venture.

Such analysis will help to identify the characteristics of both the financing and of the financing source that make the most sense for the intended business. If you don't go through such a process, the risk is seriously increased of seeking the wrong type of money from the wrong source.

For instance, a nonprofit organization may have an opportunity to generate revenues from a commercial venture, and the organization's name, trademark, or affiliation with the business may be important to the exploitation of the opportunity. But the organization may not wish to expose itself to the financial or managerial risks of undertaking a business venture. It may also have few skills to bring to the development of the business. In such cases, the appropriate strategy is probably for the organization to license another firm to exploit the particular commercial opportunity in exchange for a royalty based on the revenues generated. Note, too, that the tax law treats passive royalty income as tax-free to the organization. Active involvement in a business thus has to offer a handsome return to provide more net after-tax income than tax-free royalties.

Licensing

For example, Children's Television Workshop decided years ago to license a series of established commercial firms to produce toys, games, clothing, and other items under the "Sesame Street" trademark. CTW wanted to earn nonbroadcast revenues from the uniquely valuable trademark. But the Workshop, especially in its first years, did not have the capital or desire to invest in manufacturing and distribution businesses, nor did it wish to generate taxable income. Moreover, it was concerned that active involvement in an intensely competitive nonbroadcast business would divert management attention and focus from its primary mission of producing educational television shows for children. Accordingly, licensing others to produce and market "Sesame Street" toys, books, and clothing made the most overall sense for CTW, even though the Workshop's control over the production of products bearing its name was limited. When a product is licensed, the nonprofit licensor will retain rights to approve the quality of the product (CTW also had rights to approve advertising and marketing plans), but a right to approve quality does not provide the same power over the shape of the ultimate product as an active role in its creation.

Joint Ventures

Of course, licensing may not always be feasible or desirable. A nonprofit organization may find that the product or service it wants to market commercially is so new it will require a genuine act of invention to create the product, or that its reputation will be so linked to the product or service that it cannot delegate responsibility for its production to others. It is one thing to license the use of a nonprofit institution's name or properties in connection with an established product; it is another kind of risk to do so where the product first must be created. In such cases, the institution is likely to decide it must play an active role in the development of the product or service. This can lead to the institution either undertaking the venture on its own, with a combination of its own capital for equity and conventional lending sources for debt financing, or to entering a joint venture with an established commercial firm. The joint venture can allow the nonprofit institution to play a strong role in product development. At the same time, it can bring to bear expertise of a commercial partner that complements its own talents, as well as make available the commercial firm's equity capital and credit resources.

For instance, using its own funds over the period of a year, CTW conceived of an educational play park attraction for children (ultimately known as *Sesame Place*), in which children play actively on a unique set of play elements, science exhibits, and computers. The park was projected to cost some $10 million. The park is a different form of attraction from the ride-oriented, passive entertainment of traditional theme parks, and CTW wanted to be an active participant in the creation of this new concept. At the same time, the Workshop recognized that experience in park construction and operating and marketing amusement parks would be crucial to success. The Workshop was also in a position to invest only a small part of the total equity capital required to build a series of parks, and lacked the credit to obtain the necessary debt-financing for multiple parks (as well as the willingness to take on such a large financial obligation).

The Workshop decided to reject offers of funding from venture capital groups and turned instead to the theme park division of Anheuser Busch to form a combined venture to own, build, and operate jointly proposed parks. The Workshop looked to Anheuser Busch, not only to provide the bulk of the equity capital for the parks and the credit for the necessary borrowing, but just as importantly the personnel required to construct, operate, and market the project in conjunction with CTW's creative team. Anheuser Busch thus played a role in the development of the parks that no purely financial institution would be willing or equipped to undertake.

However, despite the array of complementary talents provided by the joint venture—and the strong appeal of the attraction to young children—it has never attained the hoped for financial results. Construction cost overruns in the case of the initial park and a poor location choice in the case of the second facility, are among the reasons for the shortfall in financial return. None of these failings can be attributed to the form of the enterprise; they were errors in execution, in which I was a full participant.

Production Advances

In contrast, when CTW planned its entry into the production of educational computer software, it decided that such an effort was a direct extension of its principal business of providing educational television programs for children. Computer software was seen by CTW as two-way, or interactive, television programming. The Workshop's board of trustees determined that it could not share the ownership or operating control of an activity so close to the heart of the Workshop's main mission; so it rejected overtures from both venture capital groups and from operating companies (e.g., traditional print publishers) for a partnership to produce such software.

Instead, the Workshop determined to provide the necessary start-up capital for the business from its own resources. However, to cut down its capital exposure, CTW sought contracts with companies interested in marketing and distributing the Workshop software, under which the distributors financed a major portion of the costs of producing the CTW software (including the inventory risk involved in manufacturing the disc or cartridge for the software) and the costs of marketing the output. In exchange for this production and marketing financing, the distribution companies kept a substantial portion of the revenues flowing from the sale of the software. In effect, CTW sold to these companies an "equity" in the products of the Workshop's software company. The financing approach allowed CTW to retain complete ownership and creative control of its software company but reduced its financial risk—by giving up some portion of the return on sales and control of marketing.

Such an arrangement was, of course, not unique to CTW, since many other software producers operate in the same way. Again, the financing arrangement did not guarantee success; when the computer software market did not develop as CTW (and many others) originally hoped, the Workshop incurred financial losses despite its financing approach.

The Business Skills of Financing Sources

As part of the process of determining what contributions are needed from a financial source, a realistic assessment ought to be made of the limits on a nonprofit organization's ability to implement a business. Organizations—both profit-making as well as nonprofit—tend to overestimate the transferability of their competence from one field to another, and thus often forego the opportunity to find a partner that can supply the skills and assets they may lack.

In contrast, Princeton University recognized from the outset its limitations in developing the 1,600-acre mixed-use real estate development on holdings adjacent to its main campus. The university determined it had an expertise in planning and developing the uses of land, processes in which it was regularly engaged with respect to its campus and adjacent holdings, but not in designing, building, or financing commercial structures, which it had never done. Hence, the university decided to sell or lease land to developers and private companies to build their own office, research, and housing facilities, and to limit its role to land planning and development, and to design and quality review. This strategy not only confined the university's role to its area of expertise, but also reduced the capital it had to advance and limited its financial exposure.

Shared Values

As part of the process of defining what contributions a financial source can make to a venture, it is useful to set out, with as much specificity as possible, a list of the characteristics desired in a financial partner—for instance, bringing to the venture expertise in managing construction, operations, marketing, and so forth. But the list should also entail the qualitative characteristics wanted in a partner—such as an appreciation for the values and culture of the nonprofit institution, a shared commitment to producing a quality product (even at the expense of foregoing some short-run profitability), and recognition of the importance of the public's perception of the quality and integrity of an organization.

In short, it is necessary to see if there is a common set of values shared by the partners. If there isn't, they will eventually become antagonists, however much both may want to realize a profit from the venture. For example, CTW spent nearly two years fruitlessly trying to negotiate a computer software distribution arrangement with one of the country's leading integrated hardware and software companies. In the end the deal could not be made because the commercial company's primary focus was on quick exploitation and short-run profits, rather than on product quality and long-range return.

In the end, however, whichever financial approach or internal organizational setup it adopts to develop a business, the nonprofit organization will have to acclimate itself to the culture of the commercial world. This is never easy for organizations driven primarily by the desire to advance social goals rather than by the profit motive. But the point is, to achieve its diverse aims, a modern not-for-profit must be a hybrid: a classical, charitable organization in purpose and a successful business in raising revenues. Where these two values coexist in proper balance, you can expect to find a vibrant not-for-profit organization.

4

Changing the Nonprofit Mind-Set Toward Commercial Income

RECENTLY, TWO OFFICIALS from an international nonprofit organization sought my advice on how they could persuade their board that it was appropriate and necessary for the organization to expand the sources of its commercially derived revenues. The two executives wanted to pick my brain on how we had "succeeded" at Princeton University and at Children's Television Workshop in inducing those organizations to turn to commercial opportunities to help pay their bills.

Within their own organization, the executives reported there was opposition to increased commercial efforts, out of fear that government funding would be cut back as a consequence. There was also strong concern that the organization's volunteers, who played a major role in fund-raising, would react negatively to increased commercial endeavors.

The two visiting executives from the international organization told me that they had prepared a proposal for their board to set up a separate profit-making arm dedicated to expanding the organization's commercial activities. They were interested in how Princeton had been persuaded to use professionals from the profit-making world to develop the Princeton Forrestal Center real estate project (as described in "Making a Profit for Your Nonprofit Organization"), and what factors had led Children's Television Workshop to set up its computer software production group as a profit-making subsidiary.

I asked if they had identified specific business ventures to be pursued by the profit-making entity. They replied that they had referenced only a few vague suggestions of new business activities, and that the focus of their proposal had been on organizational issues. I told them to expect to encounter considerable difficulty in persuading their colleagues and board to set up a separate profit-making group to exploit unspecified commercial ventures. Instead, I advised them to begin to develop specific, attractive commercial ventures, and to get approval for participation in those ventures, on a case-by-case basis.

I added, "In my experience, in order to persuade initially reluctant colleagues and board members to plunge into the commercial arena, you need to present an appealing specific venture which is both compatible with the organization's image and promises to generate significant income without undue risk."

I told them of my own efforts at Children's Television Workshop, after I had been with the organization for more than six years as the executive vice-president, to set up a separate profit-making subsidiary dedicated to developing new business ventures. The Workshop at the time had an active and quite successful program of licensing its name in connection with the sale of "Sesame Street" products for preschool children. It had also been engaged in the active operation of several business ventures. But the Workshop needed even more income to keep pace with rising expenses.

The plan had been to spin off a couple of executives, myself included, to devote full time to finding new business ventures. The separate entity was to be supervised by a small group of trustees chosen from the full CTW board. In addition, certain capital funds were to be allocated to the new entity, to be appropriated for specific ventures with the approval of the entity's board. The proposal included the identification of four specific business opportunities. But the ventures were at such an early stage of development that business plans for pursuing them were not presented. Indeed, the whole thrust of the proposal was to focus on the initiation and creation of new business opportunities rather than to seek the blessing for a specific set of opportunities. In the end, the proposal failed to win support.

The board and other senior executives finally agreed to set up a separate profit-making subsidiary to pursue one of the ventures—the production of educational, entertaining computer software. But support was obtained only after the idea was fully developed and a complete business plan for it presented for review. In other words, the creation of a separate profit-making structure came about because of the commitment to a particular venture rather than to the idea of pursuing profit-making opportunities in general.

Even then, the board might have declined to pursue the software venture if there had not been continual education over a long time frame about the need to develop additional commercial opportunities in order to expand the Workshop's revenue base.

Even this educational process might not have succeeded if it had remained strictly a theoretical proposition. But in the early 1980s, for the first time in some five years, the Workshop's expenses exceeded its revenues, and thus the warnings that had been given to the board over the years became a reality. Indeed, at the very board meeting where the board was presented with the options for cutting costs, including substantial staff layoffs to deal with the first budget deficit in years, it was also presented with an outline of the new business opportunities that were open to the Workshop. In short, the budget crisis was seized upon to focus the board's attention on the possibility of increasing the Workshop's explorations of new business ventures. Crisis thus became the catalyst for eventual change.

The two executives conversed briefly with each other as to whether there were warning signals within their own organization that their proposal to set up a separate profit-making arm was in trouble. They saw some of the same reluctance developing toward spinning off a separate profit-making enterprise with a broad charter to find attractive commercial ventures. They then pressed me to try to formulate some generalizations about how to persuade nonprofit management, board members, and organizational supporters to undertake a specific commercial activity that promised significant financial return. I replied that persuading a nonprofit organization to step into the business area can be a very difficult task.

For starters, any campaign to persuade a not-for-profit institution to seek revenues from a commercial source, and to do so on a businesslike basis, may run into an unexpressed but strongly felt organizational ambivalence about the appropriateness of entering into the commercial arena. Frequently, nonprofit organizations are staffed with people who, for a whole variety of deeply felt personal reasons, have chosen to work in the not-for-profit world rather than the commercial world. In many ways, they are personally uncomfortable with the environment and culture of commercial endeavors. It is not unusual for such professionals to be quite self-conscious about establishing that they are different from the people who populate the commercial world. Accordingly, the proposed entry into commercial activities may cut against the grain of deeply held feelings.

Typically, the people who run not-for-profit organizations are also unfamiliar with how businesses are run. Usually, such nonprofit professionals have concentrated their careers on social issues and have little training or experience in business. This makes them, appropriately enough, wary of becoming involved in such endeavors. Moreover, in seeking to move a nonprofit entity toward a commercial enterprise, you are dealing with what is still a generally controversial notion—that not-for-profit organizations can be successful at undertaking commercially oriented activities.

Beyond these environmental barriers to commercial activities, there are some genuinely tough policy and operating issues regarding how you mesh nonprofit activities and commercial endeavors within the same overall organization. These substantive issues are complex and not always susceptible to a clean-cut resolution.

What are the fundamental substantive objections to a nonprofit enterprise undertaking a commercial venture? They are a set of policy concerns relating to the "appropriateness" of such ventures and of issues relating to the "competency" of nonprofit organizations to undertake profit-making activities.

Most of the expressed reservations boil down to a fear that the values inherent in pursuing commercial success are at variance with the values underlying a nonprofit social mission. Profit, rather than product or service quality, is seen as the single-minded objective of the commercial sector. Therefore, in the minds of some, pursuit of commercial gain inevitably means sacrificing quality. This line of reasoning is pressed vociferously in the institutions that are especially image-conscious, such as colleges and universities. On the contrary, a good number of businesses are built on the delivery of very high-quality products or services. The high end of the market is their niche. Thus, superior quality can be as important to commercial success as it is to the mission of a nonprofit enterprise.

Often masked in the debate over quality is an underlying reluctance of nonprofit personnel to accept, as constraints on their actions, financial limits designed to preserve a "profit" element. People whose driving motivation is linked to the content of their work, rather than its profitability, may find it difficult to balance profitability and artistry. This is true, not only of nonprofit staff, but also of artisans in many fields. In their minds, art simply should not have to yield to finances. But the trade-off between returning a profit and some higher level of product quality is a judgment that both nonprofit institutions and profit-making businesses can make.

A related reservation is that the pursuit of commercial gain will be carried on in a way that is insensitive to important social and ethical considerations. In particular, very real concerns can be expressed about the use of a nonprofit organization's name to endorse a commercial product. On one hand, such endorsements can present good opportunities to earn income where the organization's name carries weight with the consumer. On the other hand, the integrity of the organization can be jeopardized if people perceive that it is lending its name to products that do not measure up to the standard the public associates with the institution, or that it is allowing its name to be inappropriately exploited. Case-by-case determinations are, by and large, the most practical approach to resolving such issues.

For instance, Children's Television Workshop's entry into the licensing of children's commercial products was initially opposed by some because of concern about product quality and fears that "hard sell' television advertising techniques might be used to pitch young children. But the Workshop found an answer: insist on stiff quality review by its own staff and prohibit television advertising of licensed products in hours when young children are watching.

As the CTW experience illustrates, a nonprofit institution's concern for its values can often be made an explicit part of the commercial program, and not necessarily at the cost of profitability. In fact, protecting the organization's image can be important to the success of a commercial venture. For instance, television advertising of the Workshop's products to preschool and young children might have alienated parents who, after all, are the real market for such products.

Or take the case of Princeton University's development of the Princeton Forrestal Center, the 1600-acre commercial real estate venture on land adjacent to its campus. As part of its development plan, Princeton dedicated significantly more land to the preservation of open space and environmental protection than was required under the then-applicable zoning ordinances for the area. The university adopted stricter standards because of its environmental concerns, but these tougher specifications also enhanced the value of the land dedicated to development. Thus, social commitment and pursuit of profit were by no means incompatible.

Another typical reservation is that profit-making endeavors will lead to a focus on making money rather than on the program of the organization. The corollary to this argument is that commercial activities will bring into the organization a breed of employee who will not share his or her fellow employees' dedication to its mission.

In fact, employees bent on making profits (and reaping the personal rewards from such success) may initially have less understanding of a nonprofit institution's program interests than those hired to administer the program. But that may be more a matter of exposure and education than irreversible bias. In any case, the experience of CTW and other nonprofit organizations is that it is possible to find business executives who share the organization's social objectives.

Another frequently raised concern is whether commercial success will undercut the willingness of government funding sources and private donors to support a nonprofit enterprise. The argument is advanced that the flow of income from business ventures will make government and charitable support seem unnecessary. The risk of this happening does exist, but there are two countervailing arguments.

First, substituting business income for inherently volatile and uncertain government aid is desirable. (See chapter "Expanding the Revenue Base: Traditional Sources.") Second, the fact that a nonprofit organization is earning some part of its revenues from commercial endeavors may well encourage private donors, and even government agencies, to think more highly of the organization. At Princeton, much was made to potential alumni donors of the university's skillful management of its endowment and its successful development of the Princeton Forrestal Center real estate project. At Children's Television Workshop, interested members of Congress were kept apprised by CTW of its efforts to build up its business revenues.

Policy issues aside, there is a series of well-taken concerns regarding the competency of nonprofit organizations to participate in commercial endeavors. Typically, the most formidable practical barrier to a nonprofit institution's entry into the commercial arena is its own inexperience in business ventures. Few nonprofit personnel tend to be trained or experienced in business endeavors, and so have only a limited sense of how to evaluate commercial opportunities or how to begin to exploit them. To overcome this, nonprofit organizations that are neophytes in commercial matters had best turn to the business members of the board and their contacts for advice and assistance. Professional consultants can also be helpful in examining an organization's potential to generate income from commercial sources.

Once determined to participate in a commercial venture, it is possible for nonprofit institutions to hire persons experienced in the business, and a good number have done so successfully. But it is not a simple task. Often business personnel fear that working in the nonprofit world will stigmatize them if they later seek employment again in private business. (Fair or not, a good many in the business community see the nonprofit arena as a "soft" world lacking the drive and discipline of the profit-making sector.) At the same time, nonprofit organizations tend to be reluctant to provide the type of compensation, especially incentive compensation, that attracts able business talent.

Of course, seeking to meet the financial expectations of profit-making business executives is not without potential complications for a nonprofit organization. If the compensation offered profit-making personnel engaged in commercial undertakings is higher than that of nonprofit program staff, there is the potential of internal conflict, especially if the program personnel feel it is their efforts which are being exploited commercially. Nevertheless, nonprofit institutions can and have provided compensation arrangements which are competitive with comparable undertakings in the profit-making world without tearing their organizations apart. (See chapters "Tax Planning: Forethought Rather Than Afterthought," "Developing Human Resources," and "Making a Profit for Your Nonprofit Organization.")

The potential resentment of higher salaries for commercial personnel can be minimized if the organization carefully prices the compensation offered for comparable positions by business enterprises and also engages in a process of evaluating, from the standpoint of internal equity, the salaries attached to different positions in the organization. (See chapter "Developing Human Resources.") In addition, the organization can tie these higher rewards for commercial staff, in some part at least, to the success of the business venture on which they are working. At the same time, as a practical matter, resentment of the compensation paid to profit-making personnel will be lessened if it is made clear to the traditional staff that success of the commercial venture is helping pay their salaries.

I recall one day at Princeton being stopped by a faculty member as I walked across the campus during the summer. The professor objected strenuously to renting the university's otherwise empty facilities during the summer to "outsiders." I replied, "Well, we don't have to, but the income we will earn this year will support about a dozen junior faculty members." The professor expressed surprise that the rental program meant so much to the university and wished me luck with it.

Finally, there is the danger a nonprofit will fail to make clear the ground rules under which it operates a profit-making enterprise, with the consequent lack of clarity as to whether the venture's goal is profit-making or advancing the organization's social mission. But clarity of objectives can be achieved, especially if the commercial venture is sufficiently separated from the nonprofit organization in terms of policies, personnel, and even location. This point is discussed at some length in the chapter "Making a Profit for Your Nonprofit Organization."

In sum, to enter the commercial arena, nonprofit management must attract and appropriately motivate competent business professionals, balance and clarify its competing social and profit-making interests, and ensure that all employees, whatever their tasks, are sensitive to the organization's crucial values. These are functions able non-profit institutions can perform and thereby enable them to tap business opportunities that exist.

5

Endowment Management in the 1980s

FUNDS INVESTED TO PRODUCE INCOME to support an organization's current activities are commonly referred to as an "endowment." Endowments tend to be the province of the wealthier nonprofits, since the smaller, more fragile organizations constituting the bulk of our tax-exempt charitable enterprises are pressed to use every dollar to meet current expenses; they don't have the luxury of husbanding some capital to invest, using only the income from such investments to support current operations. For institutions with endowments, the skill with which they are managed can make a critical difference in the magnitude of resources available to the organization. For this reason, this chapter is considered an integral part of this volume.

In addition, the appropriate division of labor in managing such funds between trustees and professional staff illuminates the larger issue of the respective roles that trustees and professional managers can best play in running a nonprofit. Finally, the trade-off between greater current spending or conservation of the endowment for the future touches an issue affecting even those nonprofits without endowments that are constantly pressed to balance present vs. future needs.

INTRODUCTION

In 1976, Burton Malkiel, then a professor of economics at Princeton and now dean of the Yale School of Organization and Management, and I published a booklet entitled *Managing Risk in an Uncertain Era: An Analysis for Endowed Institutions*. The volume was the product of work we had done over two years as we sought to convince Princeton's trustees to abandon their system whereby a trustee investment committee picked individual securities for the university's endowment. Dean Malkiel and I favored trustees to concentrate on strategic and policy issues and to delegate the selection of individual stocks and bonds to full-time professional managers who were not members of the board. In 1977, a year after I had left the campus, Princeton finally decided to adopt the recommended change in procedure.

In the introduction to the volume, Malkiel and I spoke of the difficulty of managing investments at a time when the economy was suffering from a series of shocks (oil prices, staggering inflation, etc.), and monetary and fiscal policy seemed incapable of dampening objectionably high inflation rates without producing a harsh decline in the level of economic activity. Today, the task of managing institutional funds may be just as formidable as when we wrote our treatise.

The Malkiel-Firstenberg thesis was this:

> The performance of the economy, of course, in large measure governs the performance of investment funds. But allowing for this point, policy and strategic choices, rather than the selection of individual securities, are the major determinants of portfolio performance.[1]

Let me begin now with a discussion of this thesis and then turn to specific alternatives for the day-to-day management of an endowment portfolio.

Trustee Role

Trustees must exercise oversight over all phases of portfolio operations. They can, however, choose to make all decisions concerning the portfolio themselves or delegate some decision-making authority to professional advisors. In order to structure the management of the portfolio, trustees must therefore determine which decisions they will make themselves and which decisions, if any, they will delegate to others.

Establishment of policy and strategy constitutes the core of the trustee's fiduciary responsibility in overseeing an endowment. As a trustee of a major university has observed, "How you decide to commit funds to various types of investment media is likely to prove more important than how you decide to select particular investments."

The surveys Dean Malkiel and I did of the experiences of universities with major endowments indicate that the institutions which did not achieve their investment goals were, in general, the ones at which trustees had failed to exercise adequate control over strategic decisions. Too little direction was given with respect to the composition of the portfolio or to the risk levels the trustees were willing to accept. Moreover, we found a temptation to engage in rearrangement of advisory services even when the most urgent need was to reexamine the basic investment philosophy of the university. Such cases smack a little of firing the baseball field manager when it is really the front office which has not done its job right.

[1] Paul Firstenberg and Burton Malkiel, *Managing Risk in an Uncertain Era: An Analysis for Endowed Institutions* (Princeton: Princeton University, 1976, p. 7).

We concluded from our survey that there is no single organizational approach to managing investments that produces superior performance. Disappointing performance has come about under a variety of management systems: delegation to a single manager, to multiple managers, or to a captive or semicaptive firm. Thus, the failure of a nonprofit organization to attain its investment objectives generally can be traced either to a policy or strategic decision by its trustees that proved to be incorrect or, perhaps more commonly, to leaving such critical choices by default to the investment managers themselves.

There are at least four basic policy and strategic decisions trustees must make, including:

1. setting the risk level for the portfolio in light of the institution's financial needs.
2. determining the composition of the portfolio.
3. establishing the method by which securities are selected and controlling portfolio turnover.
4. establishing a spending rule: how much of annual return and what portion (income only, or realized and unrealized gains as well) should be distributed to meet current expenses and how much reinvested. At stake is the trade-off between current and future needs.

The starting point is adjustment of an institution's return objectives to the level of risk it can accept.

Setting the Risk Level

One of the best documented propositions in the field of investments is that, on the average, investors receive higher long-term rates of return for bearing greater risk. This principle has been documented in the case of the stock and bond markets. Although there is less formal evidence available, risk and return also appear to come into play with regard to investments in real estate and other investment media. It follows that the "risk level" set for the overall portfolio is of critical importance in determining the performance of the endowment.

What is meant by a portfolio's "risk level"?

In capital market theory, the concept of risk for investors is related to the chance of disappointment in achieving expected return. Hence, the definition of risk is the probable variability of future returns. A security or portfolio with returns not likely to depart much, if at all, from its average or expected return, is said to carry little or no risk. A security or portfolio whose returns are likely to fluctuate widely from year to year (and for which sharp losses are typical in some years) is said to be risky.

An investment portfolio promising a stable and dependable 9 percent each year is less risky than another that averages 9 percent but may return 36 percent in a bull (up) market and minus 18 percent in a year when the market falls.

Simply stated, "risk" is the fluctuation in returns from time period to time period. The term "risk level" thus refers to a comparison of the riskiness or variability in returns of one portfolio relative to another portfolio. It is simply a shorthand way of expressing the concept of relative variability of returns.[2] Often the "market" portfolio, as measured by one of the broad indexes such as the Standard and Poor's 500 Stock Index, serves as the standard of comparison. Indeed, the responsiveness of a portfolio's rate of return to market swings is perhaps the most widely used measure of risk. Under this definition, stocks in general are risky. Chart 1 shows the annual price performance of the Standard and Poor's 500 Stock Index over the thirty years from 1954 to 1983. The wide swings in stock prices over relatively short time periods illustrates the "riskiness" of stocks.

Historically, there has been a close relationship between the risk level of a reasonably well-diversified common stock portfolio and the rate of return the portfolio has produced. Diversified portfolios with returns that have been relatively more volatile than the market from year to year (i.e., riskier), have tended to produce over the long term a higher return than the market as a whole (as represented by a broad cross section of stocks). But such portfolios, while enjoying greater price appreciation during market upswings than funds of lower volatility, suffer more depreciation during market declines. On the other hand, portfolios made up of somewhat more stable stocks on the average will produce lower but less volatile returns than riskier funds.

The comparative return of bonds versus stocks further illustrates the relevance of a portfolio's risk level. On the average, rates of return for corporate bonds historically have been lower than stocks, but bond returns also have been somewhat less volatile than stock returns.

Accordingly, portfolios made of stocks "balanced" with bonds have tended to produce more stable but somewhat lower returns than those for the broad stock indices. The following summary (Table 4) of key indices of stock and bond prices illustrates how stocks have offered greater returns than bonds over most time spans.

Table 4.   ANNUALIZED TOTAL RETURN PERFORMANCE RESULTS PERIODS ENDING DECEMBER 31, 1982

	Three Years	Five Years	Ten Years	Twenty Years
S&P 500 Common Stock Index	15.3%	14.1%	6.7%	8.3%
DJIA (Stock Index)	14.4	11.2	5.7	7.0
IDA (Stock Index)	29.8	23.0	10.5	—
Salomon High Grade Bond Index	11.5	5.8	6.1	4.5
CPI Bond Index	8.3	9.5	8.7	6.0

SOURCE: The Vanguard Group

[2] However, this definition can sound anomalous in certain situations. If variance results from better-than-expected returns, it is hard to call that result "risk."

Chart 1.   RANGE OF ANNUAL RETURNS ON COMMON STOCKS 1954–1983

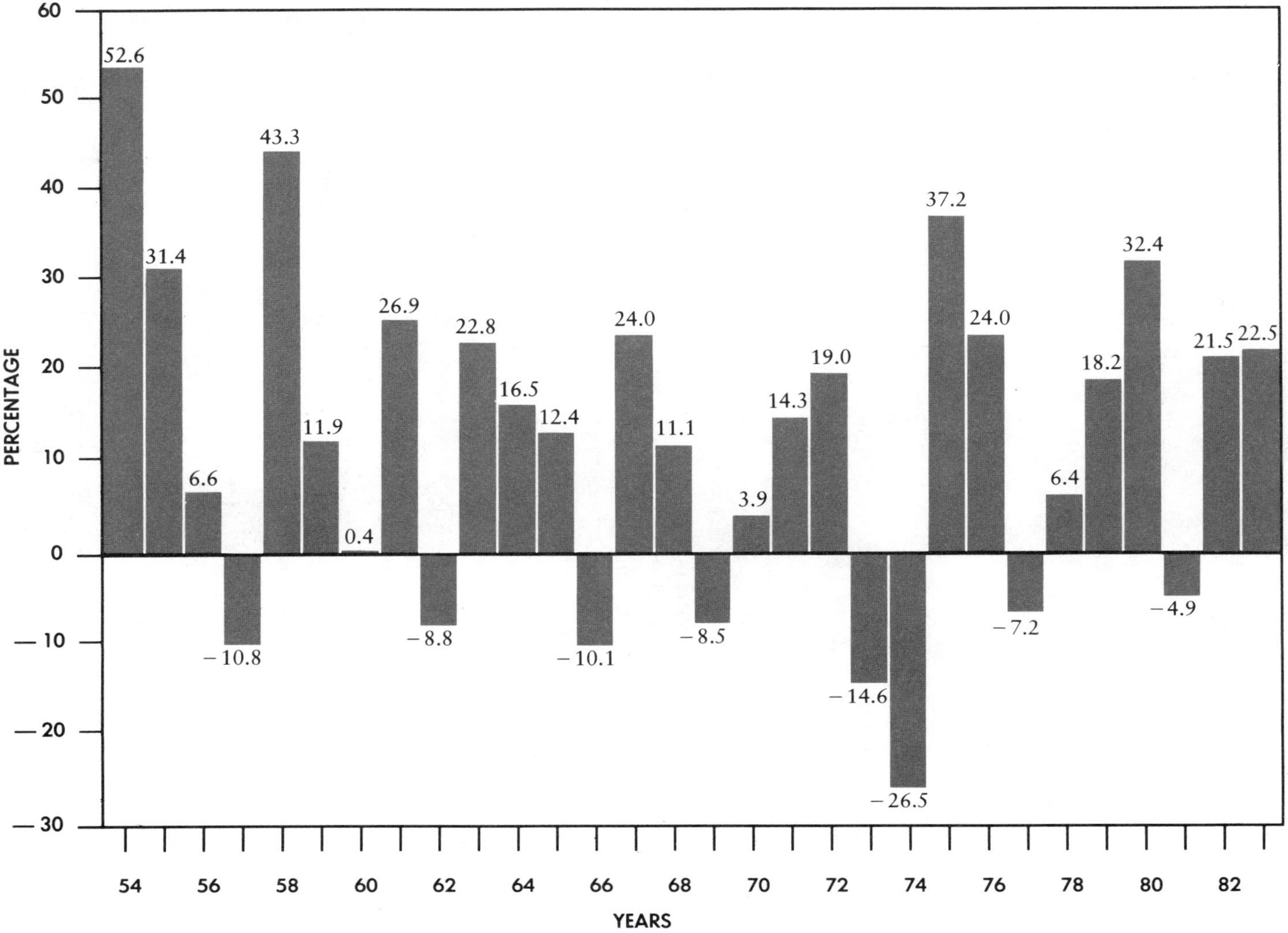

SOURCE: The Vanguard Group

A more complete set of stock and bond indices is included at the end of the chapter as Table 5 and Chart 7.

Decisions regarding the general categories of securities placed in the portfolio (e.g., aggressive, high-volatility "growth" stocks versus defensive, low-volatility stocks) thus are likely to prove more important than decisions regarding which particular stocks in a given category are added to the portfolio.

The higher return one can expect to receive for accepting high risks should not, however, lead a not-for-profit organization, or indeed any other investor, to strive to maximize return and ignore risk or volatility. Even for a nonprofit entity that spends currently only the dividends and interest earned on its endowment, excessive variance (fluctuations) in the value of the portfolio can create difficulties in budgeting the amount of spendable funds available to the organization, particularly if the portfolio does not generate a sufficient amount of dividend and interest payments during down markets. If such receipts decline too far below the level of the nonprofit institution's need for current funds, its trustees may be forced to decide whether to sell securities in a down market, even if such a step is unsound from the point of view of maximizing long-term endowment growth, or to cut the amount of spendable income available to the institution.

The dilemma exists especially for institutions that have adopted a total-return concept of spendable income. The operation of any such plan implies perversely dipping into capital (endowment) during low points in the market and adding to capital during good times. If the portion of the total return earned annually by the endowment and expended currently by a nonprofit organization remains constant while the market value of the endowment is declining, the result is that the value of the endowment fund is being reduced when stock prices are falling. Obversely, if spending remains stable when the market value of the endowment is rising, this means adding to the value of the endowment when stock prices are rising. In effect, this contradicts the ancient maxim, "Buy cheap, sell dear." It follows arithmetically that the more volatile a portfolio is, the more permanent damage there will be to the long-term growth in value of the endowment fund.

A reasonable degree of predictability in the amount of funds annually available from the endowment is important from the point of view of financial planning. Programs and activities cannot be turned off and on according to the vicissitudes of the capital markets. Indeed, predictability may be sufficiently important in stabilizing an organization's financial planning to warrant adopting a policy that provides a more consistent but lower total return than one that provides a greater return over the long term, but is vulnerable to sharp fluctuations. At the same time, a risk position that is too conservative, and a resulting return that is too low, could force an organization to make painful budget cuts. Trustees must select the appropriate return objective for the portfolio in light of both the level of risk considered acceptable and the institution's needs.

The question of the appropriate level of risk to be taken by university endowments was a matter of controversy involving the Ford Foundation in the late 1960s. MacGeorge Bundy, head of the foundation, became increasingly impatient with university presidents who came to the foundation seeking relief from their financial woes without having first put the management of their own endowments in order. This prompted the foundation to organize and publish the *Barker Report,* which was widely read as calling for a more aggressive investment posture by endowment managers, implying that "risk" could be ignored.[3]

In fact, the *Barker Report* was directed at the large numbers of colleges and universities which had very substantial portions of their endowments invested in bonds in the 1960s, producing fixed but very low yields. Surprisingly, not that many universities in the 1960s had committed themselves to an equity-oriented investment strategy. The *Barker Report,* quite correctly, was critical of universities that failed to strike an intelligent balance between stocks and bonds.

The year 1969, of course, turned out to be a sharp bear market and thus exacerbated the feeling that the *Barker Report* had ignored "risk." In the preface of the second edition, published in July 1972, Mr. Barker calls for more emphasis in endowment management on how a fund will react to severe market fluctuations.[4]

Determining Portfolio Composition

Once a targeted return objective and risk level are set for the portfolio as a whole, the trustees must determine the mix of investment assets that is most likely to achieve the overall performance goals established for the endowment. Deployment of portfolio assets among different types of investments—in short, diversification—is a way to reduce risk without sacrificing significant return.

Diversification of a portfolio means the fortunes of the various securities in the portfolio are not all dependent to the same degree on the same economic variables. If the price movements of the various investments selected for the portfolio do not move in completely parallel directions (e.g., when one goes up, the others always go up), there will be some reduction in the overall risk level of the portfolio.

Diversification cannot reduce all risk because stocks usually tend to move up and down together in response to economic trends. Even a well-diversified portfolio is risky—that is, its returns will fluctuate over time. The returns from such a portfolio will continue to fluctuate in response to general market trends. Still, diversification is

---

[3] The *Barker Report* is the popular name given to the report, published by the Ford Foundation in the summer of 1969, entitled *Managing Educational Endowments;* it was prepared by an 11-man advisory committee chaired by Robert R. Barker, a partner in William A. Burden and Co.

[4] For a description of recent efforts by colleges and universities to increase their endowment return by participating in higher-risk investments, see "College Funds Taking Steps to Raise Yields," (*The Wall Street Journal,* August 10, 1983, p. 10). The article refers among other things to the Common Fund, a fund that allows smaller colleges to pool their funds, i.e., a mutual fund for endowments.

useful because it can eliminate some risks: namely, the variability in a stock's price (and therefore in its returns) that results from factors peculiar to that particular company (e.g., a sudden labor strike or a major oil find).

The whole point of a diversification strategy is that to the extent stocks do not always move in tandem, variations in the returns from any one security will tend to be washed away or smoothed out by compensating variation in the returns from other securities.

The importance of diversifying investments was underscored in an editorial by Peter Bernstein in the spring 1983 edition of *The Journal of Portfolio Management*. Mr. Bernstein, an experienced commentator and counselor on investments, compared the results that had been obtained by the median performing pension fund over the last twenty years (from 1960 to 1980) with a hypothetical worldwide, diversified portfolio, investments including not only U.S. and foreign stocks and bonds, but also U.S. and foreign real estate, and various metals. Despite whatever imperfections might exist in the collection of this data, Mr. Bernstein's analysis shows that a well-diversified portfolio, encompassing all media of investments, not just stocks and bonds, substantially outperformed the median U.S. pension fund during the 1960s and 1970s. In particular, Mr. Bernstein noted that the failure to include international equities and U.S. and foreign real estate in a portfolio would have seriously and adversely affected the portfolio returns. Mr. Bernstein concluded:

> All of this points to the deepest meaning of diversification and its essential contribution to portfolio construction. The evidence here goes beyond the traditional view—amply proven by these data—that diversification reduces variability and thereby enhances compound returns over time. This experience demonstrates that managers cannot afford *not* to be exposed to every possible opportunity, no matter how dim (or even imprudent) any particular opportunity may look at the moment of decision. None of us knows what the big play of the future is going to be—if we did, it would not be a big play. Diversification is the only rational deployment for our ignorance.[5]

Stocks as the Core of the Portfolio

Common stocks continue to be the best bet for the core of a well-diversified portfolio. Stocks have historically provided, over time, the highest rate of return of the major categories of financial assets, including real estate, gold, bonds, and U.S. Treasury Bills. This point is illustrated by Chart 2. Stock returns, *over time,* have also tended to be well in excess of the inflation rate as measured by the annual rate of increase in consumer prices.

[5] Peter Bernstein, *The Journal of Portfolio Management,* Spring, 1983.

Chart 2. ANNUAL RATES OF RETURN 1947–1983

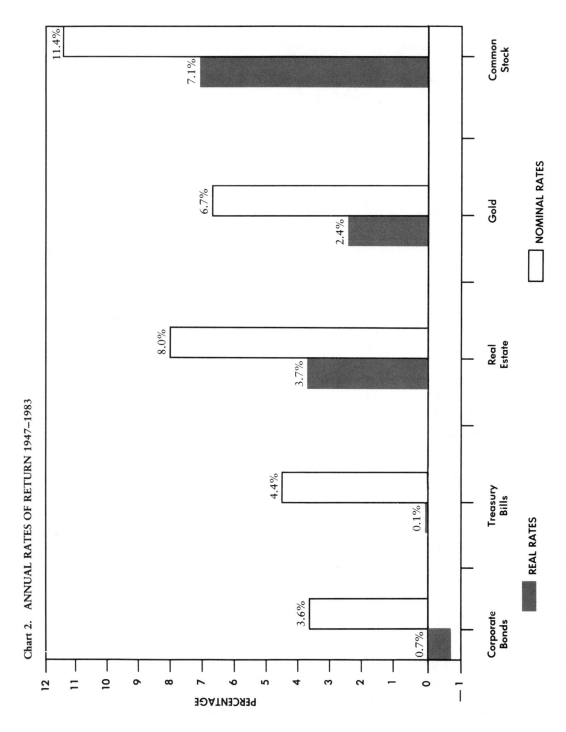

SOURCE: The Vanguard Group

In addition, the price/earnings ratio of common stocks in general looked reasonable in relation to past ratios. The P/E ratio reflects the relationship of stock prices to a company's earnings.

The aggregate price/earnings ratio for the stocks in the Standard and Poor's 500 Index from 1927 to 1983 ranged from a high of 22.4 to a low of 6.5, averaging 14 over the period. In 1984, the Index's P/E ratio hovered at about 9—well below average.

This evidence, with historical studies documenting that stocks will over time produce higher returns than bonds, suggests that common stocks should continue to form the core of an endowment portfolio.

However, while stocks may provide the best returns compared to other investment media over long periods of time, in the short run the other forms of investment may prove more attractive. For instance, during recent periods of inflation real estate has offered, in general, better returns than common stocks. Moreover, stock returns are highly variable with very wide ranges in year-to-year gains and losses (e.g., 25 percent or more). There have also been periods of five years or longer when common stocks have actually produced negative rates of return.

In addition, bonds may now better compensate investors for expected inflation than at any time since World War II. Indeed, as discussed below, they currently offer attractive real returns. Inclusion of bonds may thus offer the opportunity to lower overall portfolio risk without sacrificing the ability to earn an attractive real rate of return.

Accordingly, while portfolios will undoubtedly continue to place heavy reliance on common stocks, diversification among different investment media will increasingly become crucial to achieving successful investment returns.

Methods of Selecting Securities

Stocks (The Efficient Market Thesis). The question of how you select the stocks to be included in an endowment portfolio is likely to produce heated debate among investment professionals.

Studies indicate there is no evidence that most professional firms can produce above-average returns on a sustained basis from managing stock portfolios of equivalent risk, primarily because in an organized central marketplace such as the stock market, prices at any point in time usually will reflect both the problems and opportunities inherent in any given stock. With hundreds of security analysts thoroughly studying most, if not all stocks, the publicly available information that affects security prices is digested quickly and reflected in the prices at which securities are traded. This assumes, of course, that a large number of investors understand the information that is available and make rational decisions.

A market where all developments are reflected quickly in security prices is characterized as an "efficient market." One conclusion is that in such an environment, few professional money managers can hope to be consistently wiser in analyzing stock values than their competitors, at least without the benefit of inside information.

In fact, the S and P 500 Stock Index has a record over the past several years that is superior to most institutional accounts being actively managed by banks, insurance companies, and other investment professionals.

Chart 3 shows that while there were variations in relative performance on a year-by-year basis, for the full fifteen-year period the unmanaged Index outpaced 68 percent of all managed accounts. The S and P Index rose by 204 percent in this period, the assets managed by professional advisers by 165 percent.

Of course, there *are* investment advisers that do better, but the point is that investment managers that consistently surpass the market indices are *extremely* rare. To make matters worse, there is no overwhelming evidence that those few who have produced a superior record in the past will repeat this success in the future.

John C. Bogle, chairman and chief executive officer of the Vanguard Group of Investment Companies, upon reviewing the foregoing data, observed:

> The lessons to be learned from these "facts of life" are at least twofold: first, give due consideration to the role of a less active investment strategy—more conservative objectives, up to and including indexing—in the management of your assets, perhaps as the core of your investment program. And, secondly, if you use active investment managers in the hopes of enhancing your investment returns, pick them carefully and with good reasons, use them to diversify your portfolio mix, evaluate them carefully, and do not change them too quickly.[6]

Even investment professionals who insist that it is feasible to organize the analytical capability to make a superior selection of individual securities do not deny that it is exceedingly difficult to identify overvalued and undervalued stocks. Accordingly, you can conclude that the primary reward to be expected in making stock investments is compensation for assuming a higher level of risk than other investors are willing to accept.

The efficient market hypothesis has important potential implications for the manner in which a stock portfolio is constructed. If you accept the idea of an efficient market for stocks, instead of seeking to pick individual securities that will outperform the market, you would seek to own a widely diversified group of stocks whose overall market value moves in close parallel with the market in general (measured by some proxy such as Standard and Poor's 500 Common Stock Index).[7] You would adjust the risk level of the overall portfolio according to your goals and objectives. Such a strategy

[6] John C. Bogle, "Chance, the Garden, and Investing," (Remarks to the Philadelphia Chapter of the Financial Executives Institute, April 5, 1984).

[7] See Burton Malkiel, *Risk and Return, A New Look* (National Bureau of Economic Research, Inc., NBER Reprint No. 291) on the limitations of the S and P 500 (or any other index) as a proxy for the market. Any proxy is an imperfect proxy at best.

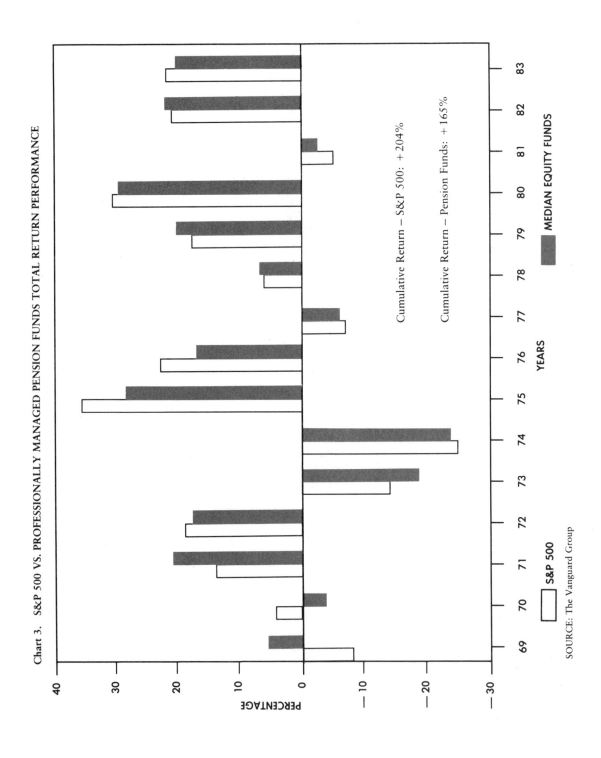

Chart 3. S&P 500 VS. PROFESSIONALLY MANAGED PENSION FUNDS TOTAL RETURN PERFORMANCE

Cumulative Return – S&P 500: + 204%

Cumulative Return – Pension Funds: + 165%

MEDIAN EQUITY FUNDS

S&P 500

SOURCE: The Vanguard Group

PERCENTAGE

YEARS

would directly contradict the perceived experience of most professional money managers and is contrary to the method by which institutional investors have selected stocks over the years.

At present, when most institutional investors buy or sell an individual security, they make a judgment as to whether the potential return that the security might earn is sufficient to justify the risk or uncertainty that such a return will be realized. This judgment is made in large part on the basis of information available about the financial condition of the company, the strength of the demand for its goods or services, the quality of its management, how well its main lines of business are likely to fare, projections of its future earnings, and the extent to which its stock price reflects all these various factors.

However, if you accept the concept of an efficient market and modern portfolio theory, then this kind of analysis is not pertinent. Under the efficient market approach, the critical factor to examine in making assessments of risk is the sensitivity of securities included in the overall portfolio to general market fluctuations. This means analyzing the degree of the volatility of stock returns relative to the market in general and then making sure that the portfolio is sufficiently diversified to eliminate risk that is peculiar to individual securities.

In determining the kind of process to be employed in selecting individual stocks for a nonprofit organization's portfolio, trustees should weigh the merits of the conflicting views about the efficiency of the market. They can opt to accept or reject the concept.[8] However, in establishing overall policy for the portfolio, the importance of calculating the trade-off between risk and return is not dependent on acceptance of the efficient market theory as opposed to analysis of underlying stock values.

Even those professionals who believe that skilled selection of individual securities can affect return agree that there is a trade-off between the degree of risk and the rate of return enjoyed over the long term. Moreover, many professional portfolio managers, even as they assert they can outperform the market through superior selection, now employ risk measurement techniques as tools to evaluate the extent to which market factors or selection skill contribute to portfolio returns.[8a] (For the latest discussion of risk measurements, see Malkiel, *Risk and Return: A New Look*.).

If the evidence shows that a manager cannot consistently discriminate between overvalued and undervalued securities, then the portfolio can be diversified to make it

---

[8] They will find plenty of ammunition for either outcome among both practitioners and academicians. For the evolving debate over modern portfolio theory see the July, 1985 issue of *Institutional Investor* magazine and Burton Malkiel, *A Random Walk Down Wall Street*, (New York: W.W. Norton & Co., 4th ed., 1985, pp. 169–170, 185–236).

[8a] See Burton Malkiel and Paul Firstenberg, *Managing Risk in An Uncertain Era: An Analysis for Endowed Institutions* for a discussion of risk measurement techniques. See also James H. Lorie and Mary T. Hamilton, *The Stock Market*, (© Richard D. Irwin, Inc., 1973, Homewood, Illinois) pp. 178–247, 265–266.

correlate more closely with the general market, thereby eliminating the specific risk of trying to pick the "right" companies. If the evidence indicates that a manager is demonstrably good at picking the "right" stocks, then trustees may want to encourage the manager to try to outperform the market. Thus, without accepting all of the implications of the efficient market thesis, the employment of risk measurement techniques can assist the trustees in evaluating investment performance.

Fixed-Income Investments (Bonds).   Most nonprofit organizations invest some portion of their endowments in fixed-income securities. During the years following World War II, the trend was to reduce the investment in long-term bonds. However, the impact of the recent inflations on the capital markets has now impelled most institutional investors to reassess the stock-bond mix.

Risk and Reward from Investment in Fixed-Income Securities.   Bonds generally have provided lower rates of return but more safety than common stocks. However, bonds are by no means immune to variations in value. The prices of long-term bonds fluctuate with interest rates. In any one year, long-term bonds can lose 10–15 percent of their value, and over several years of secularly falling bond prices, drops of 25–30 percent are possible. In 1981–82 bond prices were more volatile than usual, as interest rates fluctuated more rapidly and more widely. To some investors bond price volatility was beginning to resemble that of stocks. Bond price volatility was in fact greater than stock price volatility during some periods in the later 1970s and early 1980s. Nevertheless, over the long pull, fluctuations in bond rates of return, including interest and capital changes, have tended to be considerably smaller than corresponding fluctuations in equities.

Table 5 and Chart 7 present figures on long-run rates of return for long-term bonds (pp. 113–114).

Bond returns, like stock returns, are also related to risk. In the case of bonds, risk is determined by quality. Rates of return vary among bonds of different quality or risk level. Bonds are rated as to quality by various rating services. Ratings range from AAA to CCC for corporate securities, although "investment grade" securities—those considered acceptable for institutional investors to buy—are generally regarded as carrying a rating of BAA or better. In general, higher returns can be obtained by accepting lower quality bonds—bonds for which the assurance of payment is considered less certain than more highly rated bonds.

Lower quality bonds, over time, have provided higher yields and total returns than higher quality bonds, although the spreads have varied, with interest rates fluctuating much further on obligations of lower quality. When rates rise, the yields on bonds of lower quality tend to rise further. This accentuates the risk level in holding obligations of lower quality.

During the period 1980 through 1983 long-term industrial bonds with a credit rating of BAA provided a variable spread of from 100 to 300 basis points (i.e., 3 percent) higher yield than 30-year treasury issues (the peak spread was in 1982, before the market rally). For most of the period, the added return was probably worth the greater apparent credit risk associated with BAA industrials. Careful credit analysis of the lower-rated bonds shows the risks of a default on such bonds was not as great as the market anticipated, and thus one could gain a greater return from such securities than treasury bonds offered, without taking on much added risk. This is an "inefficiency" in the bond rating system.

Similar "inefficiencies" may exist in the case of individual bond ratings. Within the same quality ratings there will be opportunities to identify individual issues which offer higher returns than similarly rated bonds. For instance, the bond default of a legally independent power system in the state of Washington tarnished issues of the state government though in fact the state's credit was not behind the power facility. As a result, Washington State bonds carried a higher yield than their actual creditworthiness seemed to warrant.

Bonds and Inflation. In the 1970s many investors would have nothing to do with bonds because they had proved to offer no protection against inflation over the previous several decades.

It is well to remember, however, that from the beginning of World War II through 1951, bond yields were pegged at artificially low levels by the United States Treasury and the Federal Reserve System. (Bond yields at the end of World War II were only 2.5 percent on government issues and no more than 3 percent on corporate bonds of high quality.) Only during the 1950s was the market freed from controls and allowed to adjust to levels that reflect the free interplay of the forces of supply and demand as well as inflation.

One reason nominal interest rates are relatively high at the present time is that investors now recognize the danger of continued inflation, and high interest rates in part compensate for the expected loss in the purchasing power of the dollar.

For investors the telltale rate is not the nominal yield on the bond but the yield relative to the rate of inflation, or the real interest rate of the bond. The top half of Chart 4 shows the historical pattern of yields on high grade bonds and the inflation rate from 1960 to 1982. As expected, they exhibit a high degree of positive correlation. The bottom half of the chart shows the *real* interest rate—the actual bond yield minus the inflation rate.

Throughout the 1960s, the real interest rate remained remarkably steady, with roughly a 3 percent differential between long-term interest rates and the inflation rate. The 1970s witnessed much greater volatility in the inflation rate and consequently in bond yields. Real interest rates became negative both in 1974 and in 1979 as the inflation rate accelerated unexpectedly, and bond yields took time to catch up.

But an unexpected development has unfolded in the 1980s. While the inflation rate has dropped dramatically—from a high of a 17 percent annual rate in the first quarter of 1980 to the current annual rate of, say 4 percent to 5 percent—long-term interest rates have failed to decline commensurately. In fact, while bonds rallied impressively in 1982 from their all-time highs of 17 percent (AA Utilities), they have since given up most of their gains.

As a result, in 1983 and 1984, the yield on long-term bonds provided a margin of as much as 8 percent over current rates of inflation. This is quite a spread considering the real return on long-term bonds had been thought to be in the range of 3 percent. Of course, it is possible that the actual long-run rate of inflation may prove to be greater than it is at present and thus the real interest rate gap may well narrow over time to approximate the historical norm. A good number of economists and investment professionals believe it will, though none wants to say just when this change in direction is likely to come about.

Still, bond yields now better compensate investors for expected inflation than at any time in recent experience. Indeed, with real interest rates at unprecedented levels, bonds today represent a relatively safe, high-yielding diversification tool—a second important component of long-term oriented portfolios.

Bond Management Styles. In recent years, the practice of buying bonds and holding them until maturity has been discredited in some circles, and the idea of active or intensive bond portfolio management has come of age. Professionals engaged in actively managing bonds believe that through a combination of techniques (primarily by discerning interest rate trends and anticipating supply–demand pressures between market sectors) they can outperform a portfolio of fixed-income securities which are passively held (i.e., until maturity) or a bond market index by 1–3 percent annually in added return.

To the extent that some investors may have made excess returns from active bond portfolio management, they have done so primarily because they correctly anticipated the long bear market in bonds. You have to wonder, however, about the wisdom of relying on a strategy of consistently predicting turns in interest rates. Predicting interest rate movements might prove as illusive as predicting turns in the stock market. Moreover, if the manager misses in his or her timing strategy, the bond portfolio will be penalized with the very heavy transaction costs (i.e., expenses associated with frequent sales and/or purchases) connected with high turnover rates.

To sum up, in the case of bonds, just as for equities, there is a clear relationship between risk and return. Higher risk implies higher returns. Therefore, to seek additional return will entail taking greater risk by investing in bonds of lower quality.

Risk, however, can be mitigated by diversification. If you hold triple-A rated bonds, a single issue will not expose you to much risk. With lower quality bonds you want to be widely diversified. If you hold enough issues, isolated losses can be absorbed.

Risk spreads do vary from time to time, suggesting that accepting more risk is not always equally attractive. But bond trading to anticipate such changes or interest rate trends is expensive, and few traders will be consistently correct. Controlling portfolio turnover is therefore important.

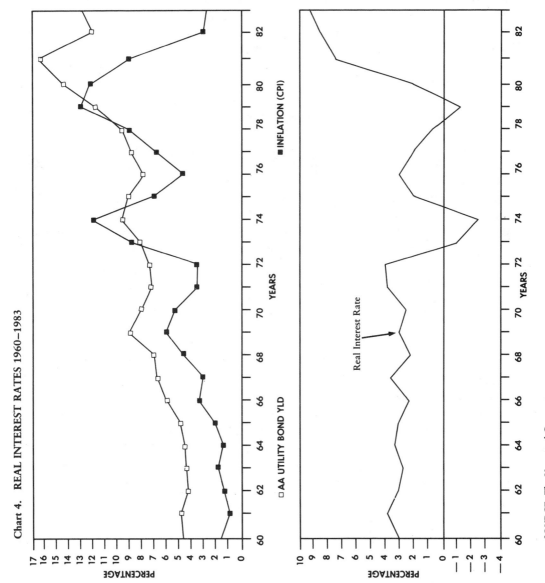

Chart 4. REAL INTEREST RATES 1960–1983

SOURCE: The Vanguard Group

Nonmarketable Investments.   From time to time, nonprofit endowments have invested in some form of asset or security that cannot be readily purchased or sold in an organized market. Among such types of investments are the financing of new or relatively new companies prior to a public offering of their securities—so-called venture capital—and real estate investments.

Venture capital involves investing in new or young companies prior to their entering the public securities markets. The acquisition of high returns from venture capital is dependent essentially on being able to bring the developing company in which one has invested to the public market, and to reap a significantly higher price from the public sale of its securities than you have paid for it.

Handsome profits have been made by some investors. But make no mistake: backing new, young companies is a very risky business. Success generally depends on investing in a portfolio of companies, which produces a few very big "winners" that more than offset the large number of run-of-the-mill returns, or even some losses. Considerable specialized skill is required to identify good opportunities and to nurture them to fruition. Therefore, for most institutions, the most practical method of participating in venture capital is to acquire a limited partnership interest in a professionally managed fund (the limited partnership confines the investor's liability to the amount of capital invested). In recent years, well-managed venture capital funds have provided returns in excess of 20 percent per annum.

There is a seeming plethora of such funds for an investor to choose from; indeed, there are so many funds in existence now that it's possible to speculate if there may not be too much money chasing too few good deals in which funds can invest. Moreover, to the extent that ultimate success depends on the state of the public securities markets, the diversification possible in making such investments may be reduced.

In contrast, real estate offers significant diversification possibilities from stocks and bonds; for this reason it is examined here in some detail.

Equity Investment in Real Estate.   Without a doubt, the largest field of nonmarketable investments is real estate. (As noted above, the term "nonmarketable" refers to the absence of an organized market such as exists for stocks and bonds, rather than the inability to sell an asset.) A study by the Ford Foundation describes real estate as one of the nation's largest capital markets.[9] Our focus here is on the characteristics of equity investment in real estate.

Equity investment in real estate offers the possibility of earning both current cash flows (or yield) as well as the potential for capital appreciation. In contrast, real estate mortgages with long-term fixed interest rates and amortization schedules are more akin to fixed-income bonds. Today, long-term mortgage loans secured by real estate offer

---

[9] See also Roger G. Ibbotson and Laurence B. Siegel, "The World Wealth Portfolio" *(The Journal of Portfolio Management,* Spring 1983).

somewhat more yield, for the same risk, than publicly marketed fixed-income bonds though the latter are more readily marketable.

The Imperfect Nature of the Market. Investment in real estate businesses means participation in a much more imperfect (or inefficient) market than the market for common stocks and bonds. Real estate investment can encompass not merely the purchase of land but participation in a multitude of varying and distinct businesses (viz., residences, shopping centers, office buildings, hotels, industrial parks, etc.) situated in different geographical locations with discrete market conditions.[10] Real estate transactions, being widely dispersed, are heavily influenced by the local supply–demand situation for the particular type of property. Even within cities, market conditions can differ. For example, one suburb could have a strong demand for apartments while another suburb of the same city could be overbuilt.

The chances of a project's success are largely dependent on location, the capabilities of the developer and property manager, the quality of the design and its amenities, local environmental requirements, community receptivity, timing, and so forth. To discern and evaluate these factors requires specialized expertise and experience, but even with such skills there is ample chance that judgments will prove to be erroneous. In contrast to the relatively efficient market for stocks and bonds, the ability and information to appraise any particular real estate venture is not possessed with virtual simultaneity by a mass of analysts.

Moreover, in the case of common stocks, it is equally easy to buy IBM if one is located in San Francisco, Denver, or New York City. In real estate, the evaluation has to be done on the scene. Many industry experts believe, however, that real estate is becoming much more of a national industry with a growing list of national and international players who can quickly develop a valuation for any perceived opportunity at any location. In this view, real estate is becoming a more efficient market than it once was.

In addition, a real estate transaction is far more complicated to execute than the purchase of stock, with an array of legal, financial, marketing, and other experts required to consummate a deal. All of these factors eliminate most individuals and many institutions from the real estate market. Thus, there may be a limited number of investors, in contrast to the number of participants in the securities markets, who can organize the array of skills necessary to identify particular projects in particular localities whose returns will exceed those of many other real estate properties.

Illiquidity. The lack of liquidity in real estate, at least relative to publicly traded stocks and bonds, is the other side of the coin to the advantages that certain investors may be able to derive from the imperfect nature of the real estate market. "Illiquidity" means that as a rule broad markets of buyers do not stand ready to purchase real estate (or to refinance it), at least to the same degree as the stock and bond markets.

---

[10] It is often said there are three principles of sound real estate investing: location, location, and location.

Therefore, equity investments in such properties cannot be as readily liquidated as publicly traded common stocks and bonds. Illiquidity also entails "opportunity costs": new investment opportunities cannot be exploited as fast if investment funds are locked into assets that cannot be readily sold.

A corollary to illiquidity is the difficulty of valuing real estate investments in the absence of a bona fide offer by a third party; short of this, the investment must be carried on the books at either an appraised value or by estimating a capitalization rate for the income stream, viz., the price an arms-length buyer would pay for the future stream of income. This system can produce valuations which may or may not represent what a particular property would bring if it were sold. Of course, it can also be argued that in the case of large holdings of some stocks, the price at which shares are shown to be traded may be significantly higher than the price that can be realized on the value of such holdings.

Profit Potential. In general, available studies show real estate equity returns to be roughly comparable to the long-run returns from common stocks, higher than stock returns during periods when inflation is accelerating, seemingly lower during periods of disinflation. However, the correlation between real estate returns and rates of inflation is a subject which is still being studied. It may be that other variables, which occur coincident with increasing or decreasing rates of inflation, may have more of an impact on real estate returns than changes in the price level. Real estate returns also appear less variable from year to year and thereby more predictable than returns from common stocks.[11] At the same time, real estate returns do not appear to move in parallel with stock prices. This factor, coupled with real estate's appeal as an inflation hedge, make it an important diversification tool.

Real Estate as an Inflation Hedge. Real estate investments can provide an effective hedge against inflation by being structured to (1) enable the investor to pass on inflation in costs related to the investment, and (2) put the investor in a leveraged position with a fixed-interest-rate loan. Loan-to-value ratios of two-thirds, three-quarters, and even higher have been common, due mainly to rapid appreciation of value following the original equity investment and especially during a period of inflation. A high loan-to-value ratio implies that even a modest extra return on the value of a total property over the mortgage financing rate causes a substantial percentage return on the far smaller equity. Historically, those in a net-debtor position benefit most from inflation that is unanticipated by the lender, since loans are repaid with dollars of less value than those borrowed originally.

However, as interest rates more accurately reflect the likely rate of inflation, the advantages of a debtor position are reduced. Moreover, at the 1974–75 and 1981–82 levels of interest rates, leverage is not always considered attractive as it imposes a heavy debt service burden on the cash flow of projects.

---

[11] See Malkiel, *A Random Walk Down Wall Street,* 4th Ed., p. 282.

In addition to leveraging a project at fixed and reasonable interest rates, the ability to raise rents along with or faster than the general price level or increases in operating costs is critical to the utility of real estate as an inflation hedge.[11a] Retail leases with a fixed minimum, plus a percentage of total gross sales, provide one example of an automatic escalation provision. For all these reasons real estate has proved to be a first-rate inflation hedge.[12]

Possible Investment Strategies. An institution should have at least $25 million available for investing in real estate in order to achieve a properly balanced program, but it should avoid any commitment to move specific amounts of funds within a predetermined period of time. That puts ill-advised pressure on investment managers to invest money rather than to select superior investments. Moreover, any real estate investment program must be managed by highly specialized persons with particular expertise and experience.

How do you find a vehicle for making investments in real estate, particularly one that will insulate a nonprofit institution from the risk of being required to step into the management of properties in areas remote from its location if some ventures founder? There appear to be two basic options for obtaining the necessary expertise and management skills to make equity investments in real estate:

1. You may invest in commingled funds managed by an experienced institutional investor. Here you get the benefit of a much larger pool of resources (and thus the benefits of diversification) as well as the scale of expertise that is available normally to a large pool of capital. At the same time, you must relinquish control over the way commingled funds are invested, and thus you may not be able to achieve the selectivity people want in investing in real estate in today's market. For example, should you decide to limit investment to existing properties that are being sold under distress conditions, the fund in which you invest may or may not be committed to such a strategy. More important, the valuation of the properties in the pool, which determines the price at which an investor could buy into it are matters of judgment (i.e., appraisal) rather than reflection of pricing in an organized market.

2. You may select a firm to act as a general advisor to the trustees to make investments in accordance with the specific strategy determined by the trustees. The advisor could be given full discretion to make investments within the guidelines established by the

---

[11a] Properties constructed during an earlier time period may benefit handsomely from a subsequent inflation, enabling their owners to raise rental rates rapidly while operating costs increase less rapidly than the price level. Sales of such properties will also reflect inflated price levels.

[12] However, all real estate is not a sure inflation hedge. If space is leased on a long-term basis without escalation provisions to permit increases in operating costs to be passed on or for rentals to be adjusted upwards, real estate is unlikely to serve as an inflation hedge. (Most of such nonescalation leases have disappeared with inflation.) Residential units subject to rent controls also have proved to be unattractive investments. Moreover, even where there are no legal constraints on raising rents to keep pace with inflation, market conditions can be a problem. In a local market suffering from a surfeit of all types of space from offices to hotel rooms, it has proved impossible to negotiate for higher rents when renting out hotel rooms, offices, or shopping center sites.

trustees or could be limited to recommending investments to the trustees. For example, the firm, under policies established by the trustees, could invest in packages of existing properties, finance selected developers of new projects,[13] participate with other institutions in one of the above, or purchase interests in REITs (Real Estate Investment Trusts). Such trusts may, at times, provide investors with an opportunity to purchase real estate at prices below the market values of the properties held by the trusts. During 1975, for example, many equity REITs could be purchased at substantial discounts below the estimated market values of the trust assets. (Another period of hard times in real estate would create similar opportunities for an investor with the funds to buy properties from financially hard-pressed owners.)

The fees charged by the firms rendering general advice are harder to categorize than in the case of stock and bond managers since there are relatively few such firms, and each arrangement is negotiated on a case-by-case basis.

One important risk in employing an advisory firm is the possibility that the advisor, if servicing more than one client, may not be able to apportion opportunities among all the accounts. At the same time, by investing in individual projects through an advisor, the institution's portfolio might be exposed to becoming the sole overseer of a venture should it founder. However, a skilled advisor should be able to work out situations in which participation is possible with other institutions with similar investment objectives. This cooperation can mitigate risks.

To sum up, investing in real estate can provide better-than-average returns, especially during a period of inflation. But it is not to be undertaken lightly. There appears to be only a limited number of real estate investment vehicles in which a nonprofit institution can invest, i.e., ones in which the main benefits are not tax-related. Whether you choose one of these, or feel you have the specialized expertise and sufficient capital to invest directly, you must be prepared to stay with your investment for an extended period of time in order to reap the benefits.

Following are some more general considerations involved in the management of an endowment portfolio.

Controlling Turnover

Minimizing transaction costs through controlling portfolio turnover can be important in improving the return of the portfolio at the margin. Portfolio managers who have high rates of turnover are penalized by very high transaction costs. The brokerage costs for a turnaround considerably understate the true cost of trading. Investors must take into account that purchases are made typically at a dealer's asked price and sales at the bid price, in addition to the problem that buying and selling activity per se tends

---

[13] Financing developers of new projects is obviously riskier than purchasing existing properties, but if successful, it is also more likely to produce higher returns. In the case of a new development, care must be taken in selecting a developer and in choosing an expert with the competence to monitor the development. Nevertheless, the ownership of existing properties is not necessarily free of management problems.

to make the market move away from the transactor. Some professionals have estimated that true costs of turnover amount to as much as 7 or 8 percent for each in and out trade, especially in "thin" markets. The amount of turnover in the portfolio should continue to be an important focus of concern on the part of trustees.

Regular Investing

For portfolios that have recurring flows of funds to invest, the best strategy is to be regular and systematic in making investments in stocks. Determine what percentage of the cash flow to allocate to stocks and then stick to it. The mathematics of investing works when you invest regularly. It is called "dollar averaging," and it means simply that when an equal amount is invested at regular intervals, more shares of stock will be bought when the price is low than when it is high.

The protection such a program affords is remarkable. For example, if a person had invested $1,000 per year beginning at the end of 1929—hardly the perfect time to begin—the cumulative investment over the next 15 years would have been $15,000. As shown in Chart 5, at the end of 1944 the value of your investment (assuming you had used the Standard & Poor's 500 Stock Price Index) would have been $29,000 (including reinvested dividends). For a $100,000 annual endowment fund contribution ($1,500,000 total for the period), the final value would have been a hefty $2,900,000. From 1929 to 1944, the Index itself actually went down from 21 to 13, but, with income, generated a total return of just 1½ percent annually. But the return on a dollar averaging program of the type I have described was 9 percent per year—six times as large.

Avoiding Market Timing

In both your asset allocation and regular investing decisions, the evidence strongly suggests you avoid what is called "market timing." The idea that you can discern just when to get in or out of the stock market is simply not credible. The business of forecasting the behavior of our complex economy and capital stock markets has proved too tricky for anyone to be consistently successful at the timing game.

The horrendous record of private pension plans in varying the percentage of assets they allocate to equities illustrates the folly of attempting to time the market. Chart 6 shows the annual returns of the Standard and Poor's 500 Index and the percentage of pension plan acquisitions of financial assets flowing into equities each year. In every major stock market cycle, pension funds have taken the incorrect course in allocating assets to equities. For instance, in the market runup in 1971–72, pension plans dramatically increased the percentage of assets going to equities—from a "norm" of 70 percent of cash flow in 1968–70 to 120 percent in 1971–72, immediately preceding the great bear market of 1973–74, when stocks went down about 40 percent. Then,

Chart 5. "DOLLAR AVERAGING" IN THE STOCK MARKET 1929–1944

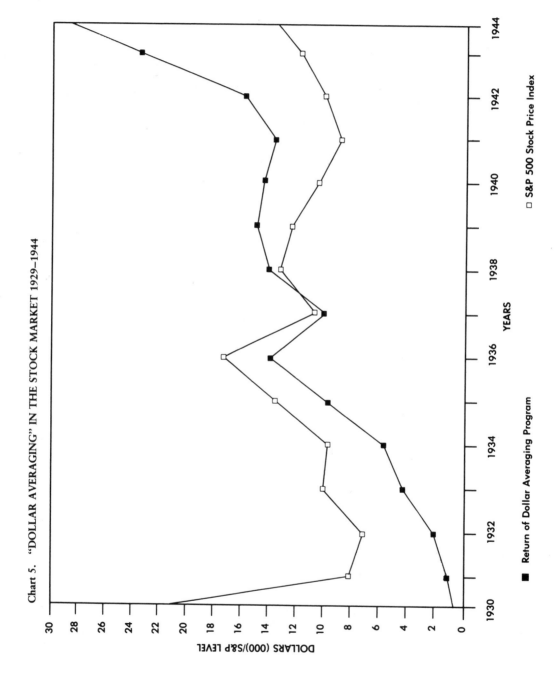

■ Return of Dollar Averaging Program   □ S&P 500 Stock Price Index

SOURCE: The Vanguard Group

Chart 6. PENSION FUND PURCHASES OF EQUITIES VS. EQUITY MARKET PERFORMANCE

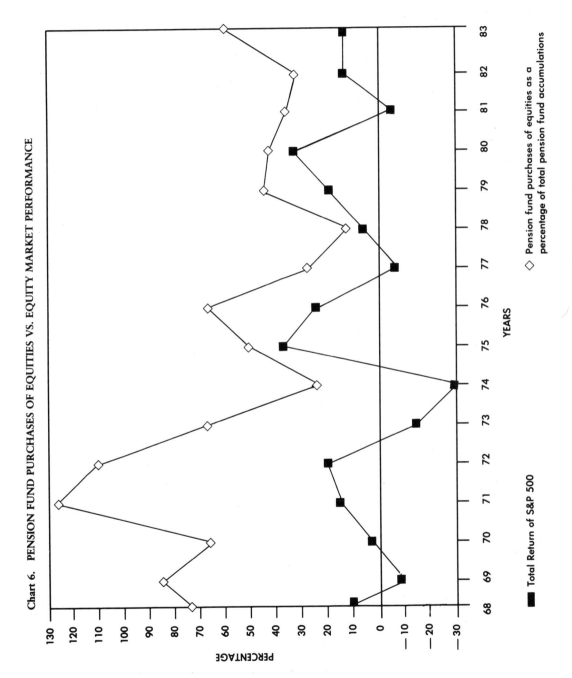

◇ Pension fund purchases of equities as a percentage of total pension fund accumulations

■ Total Return of S&P 500

SOURCE: The Vanguard Group

soured by their experience in that crashing market, they allocated just 22 percent of their 1974 asset purchases to equities, just at a time when stocks were cheap and they should have been increasing equity exposure to benefit from the "bounce back" of 1975–76. More recently, pension funds reduced their purchases of equities to just 30 percent of cash flow in 1981–82, apparently frightened by the modest decline in the market in 1981. Then they roared back into the market in 1983, largely *after* the market had exploded upward. The cost of these perverse asset allocations is incalculable; the benefits of a steady 60–70 percent equity allocation policy clearly would have been large.

Spending Policy

Portfolio returns are made up of current income (dividends, interest, rental payments) and capital gains (the appreciation in value of the underlying security or property). Spending policy determines how much of the total return from a portfolio (i.e., the total of current income plus capital gains) is to be made available to meet the current expenses of the institution and how much is to be reinvested in the portfolio to generate future returns. Hence, any policy on spending involves balancing a trade-off between current needs and those of the future.

There are two primary alternative approaches to a spending policy: (a) spend all interest and dividends actually earned in a given year and (b) devise a formula for spending a specified percentage of annual "total return," regardless of how much of such return is in the form of dividends and interest and how much is in the form of capital gains. Any form of spending policy should insulate the investment decisions of portfolio managers from the institution's spending decisions. Investment decisions should be made to maximize the total return to the institution, at an acceptable level of risk, rather than to affect the amount of funds available for current expenses.

An effort to generate current income on the part of portfolio managers can badly distort investment judgments. For example, to satisfy the need for current income rather than to provide the best total return at an acceptable level of risk, stocks paying high dividend yields are purchased because they offer more current income than stocks with low dividend yields. The latter, however, will usually provide a higher total return over time than high dividend yield stocks. Thus, over a period of years, there will be less total return available to the institution than if low yield stocks had been purchased.

As much as possible, spending policy should insulate investment decisions from current spending requirements. If the institution needs to spend more than the dividends on its stock portfolio, it should sell some of its stocks to realize a portion of the capital appreciation rather than invest in high-yielding securities, if the latter are not considered the best possible long-term investment.

In considering any spending formula, it has to be recognized explicitly that any increase in the amount of return spent in a current year reduces the endowment available to generate the larger amount of income needed in each succeeding year. The ability of an institution to maintain the purchasing power of the endowment into the future depends on reinvesting enough of the total return to enable the value of the endowment—and the income generated by the endowment—to grow at roughly the same rate as expenses increase. For example, if inflation is expected to be 6 percent a year, you must reinvest at least 6 percent of the principal value of the fund each year to keep pace with the rising price level.

The ability of the endowed institution to maintain its quality depends in large measure on its ability to maintain the purchasing power of its financial capital. Spending dollars to meet today's costs at a rate that erodes the real purchasing power of the endowment simply means the endowment funds will not grow at a rate which is adequate to meet the greater costs of future years.

A number of institutions have spent their endowments at rates that were overly optimistic with respect to investment returns and inflation rates, and which therefore could not be sustained. The result for many of these organizations is that income from endowment has been reduced at the very time as the institutions are facing increases in costs and declines in some other sources of income, thereby compounding their problem of retrenchment.

At the same time, few, if any, institutions can afford to reinvest every dollar of return. Most institutions must use some part of their endowment return to pay their bills in order to survive into the future. A trade-off between current needs and those of the future must be reached.

Spending currently only the interest and dividends earned is one possible form of spending policy. But an institution can't control the amount of dividends and interest it receives in a year. To base spending on such distributions puts the control over the compromise between current needs and future ones in the hands of those who declare dividends; such a policy uses a mechanistic approach that may not coincide with the balance which should be struck.

A total return formula is a more desirable approach. It allows the institution to decide consciously how much of the return from the portfolio—regardless of whether it is earned in the form of current income or capital gains—is to be spent for immediate expenses and how much is to be reinvested to keep pace with inflation, or to be reinvested to produce *real* future growth. A total return approach also allows the institution to establish a reasonably stable flow of spendable funds from the portfolio from year to year, regardless of the level of dividends or interest received.

One shortcoming in a pure "total return" approach is the risk that the amounts of spendable income will fluctuate widely from year to year. Since, under a total return formula, spendable income is determined as a percentage of endowment appreciation plus current yield, year-to-year variation in the return earned by the fund will vary the amount available for current spending. Forecasts of the returns a fund will earn in any year are necessarily uncertain. This lack of predictability can present a problem in budgeting institutional revenues. For this reason, there are proponents of adopting a fixed-percentage increase in the amount of available spendable income from year to year, based on assumptions about the expected total return the institution will earn over a period of time. Actual performance is then monitored to see if projections are met, and an adjustment of the spending formula is made if appropriate.

In an inflationary era it is not easy to generate enough total return from investments both to cover current spending needs and to maintain the real value of the endowment. For example, if inflation is 10 percent, a $10 million endowment fund must reinvest 10 percent, or $1 million, of annual total return just to keep the real value of the endowment corpus constant with inflation. Earning more than a 10 percent return to provide current spendable income is not an easy task, as is evident from the rates of returns for stocks and bonds shown in Table 5 and Chart 7. Thus, it is no mean feat to try to balance current needs against future ones. Typically, fewer voices take up the case for the future than cry out for current relief against inflation-driven expenses. That is why the trustees, who are charged with protecting its long-range interests, must finally determine an institution's spending policy.

Historically, in many states, only dividends, interest, and rents actually received by an endowment fund could legally be expended for current purposes. But the law has caught up with financial realities, and today the total-return approach to spending is legally appropriate in virtually all states in the administration of even a true endowment fund. (A true endowment fund is one in which a donor or outside agency has stipulated, as a condition of the gift of the funds, that the principal be maintained and that only the income earned be expended.) In most states, new statutes or judicial decisions make it clear that both realized capital gains and unrealized appreciation from an endowment may be expended currently under a soundly conceived total return spending formula.[14]

DAY-TO-DAY PORTFOLIO MANAGEMENT

The Alternatives for Investment Selection

When it comes to the choice of day-to-day portfolio managers, there are a number of options, including:

1. approval, in advance, of all transactions by an investment committee of the board of trustees (the committee may act entirely on its own or with the aid of an outside advisor).

2. delegation of investment discretion to one or more investment advisors under policy guidelines established by an investment committee.

[14] See William L. Carey and Craig B. Bright, "The Developing Law of Endowment Funds" (*The Law and the Lore Revisited*, Report to the Ford Foundation, 1974, pp. 1–19).

3. delegation of investment discretion to a staff specially organized by the institution for this purpose, along one of the following lines:
   a. formation of a separate corporation (a "captive firm") devoted entirely to handling the institution's investments;
   b. formation of a separate corporation that services the institution's account and others;
   c. hiring of a staff employed directly by the institution.

Option three is one that only institutions with rather sizable endowments can consider. For other institutions, the cost of such an approach would be too great, relative to the value of the assets under management.

The Alternative of Advance Trustee Approval of All Transactions

Those in favor of this system of portfolio management point out that it encourages active trustee involvement in the direction of the portfolio and thus promotes close oversight of the endowment by trustees. Also, the system may reduce investment advisory costs because responsibility for selection is vested with the trustees rather than an advisor.

The arguments advanced by various authorities against this approach and in favor of having trustees delegate the selection of investments, under appropriate guidelines and supervision, to professionals hired for this purpose, rest on four concerns:

1. The types of securities in which one invests and the general policy guidelines established are far more important than the individual securities selected. The trustees can better concentrate their main energies on such policy concerns if they do not also select individual securities. There is always the risk that preoccupation with day-to-day operations can distract trustees from critical policy choices.

2. Vesting the responsibility for selection of individual investments in a given trustee or group of trustees can, in the case of unsatisfactory performance, present the awkward situation of having to remove a trustee or trustees as portfolio manager. Obviously, it would be far easier, should results prove to be disappointing, to discharge hired employees than to move trustees aside.

3. The experience of a number of nonprofit institutions indicates, entirely apart from the risk of embarrassment that can result if a trustee fails to perform day-to-day operations in a satisfactory manner, that it is unwise to involve trustees in such operations. Merging the operational and policy-making roles of a trustee can deprive a nonprofit entity of the detachment from operations that is vital to the setting of sound policy.[15]

---

[15] As George Putnam, treasurer of the Harvard Corporation and in charge of the university's investments, observed in explaining Harvard's decision to establish a captive firm to manage the day-to-day operations of the Harvard portfolio: "Traditionally, the Treasurer has been the portfolio manager. What the Corporation wanted to do this time was to be sure that, in this world where portfolio management is very closely measured, the Treasurer was not the portfolio manager. He could then be entirely objective in looking at what kind of job was being done for the University's assets. And that's why I don't make my

4. Charges of conflict of interest might be asserted if a nonprofit organization's endowment were managed by a trustee who also had a responsibility for managing a private fund, as has been common practice in the past. If the two funds were to work together on a transaction, questions could be raised with respect to a conflict of interest on the part of the trustee or the organization.

Control over portfolio performance by trustees does not require advance approval or disapproval of every purchase or sale of stocks and bonds. Trustees can establish an "approved" or "eligible" list from which the advisors may select securities, or trustees can review transactions of the advisor on a post-transaction basis, requiring reversal if they believe a serious error has been made. Establishing an articulate investment philosophy for the advisor, and periodically reviewing the advisor's transactions, will achieve the kind of control trustees want and should have.

The Alternative of Delegating Investment Selection to an Established Advisory Firm

The delegation of discretion to make specific investment decisions to established professional advisory organizations is often urged as the best way to bring professional money management skills to bear on the selection of investments. The following considerations should be evaluated in determining whether to pursue this alternative.[16]

Importance of Management Expertise. There seems to be considerable agreement within the investment community that competition to find attractive stocks has become increasingly severe, and that the research capacity of brokerage firms is being cut back under the pressure of negotiated rates. From this, you might conclude that in the future an institution will require even more sophisticated stock selection techniques, in-house professional research capacity, and skill in negotiating trades, as well as an investment

---

office at Harvard Management Company or within the University. I'm the Chairman of the Board of Directors of the Harvard Management Company. But I'm independent of the money management; I don't make buy-sell decisions. So the Corporation has the Treasurer on their side when it comes to evaluating performance and [is] not in the position of defending his investment judgment." (*Harvard Gazette,* January 1975, p. 4)

[16] Another alternative is investing in the Common Fund. This fund was established to enable colleges and universities to pool their investment assets and is run by an independent board of trustees selected by the fund participants. Regular mutual funds may also provide an attractive means of obtaining outside professional management. Funds are available for almost every conceivable investment strategy and their asset values are published daily in the newspaper, facilitating periodic performance evaluation. Mutual funds may be particularly advantageous in the more specialized investment areas, such as foreign securities or small companies, where it may be hard for smaller institutions to find, on their own, the required expertise. Mutual funds generally charge the same expenses regardless of the size of an investment, unlike outside advisors whose fees as a percentage of assets are scaled down as the size of the assets under management increases. Hence, for smaller endowments mutual funds may be an economic way of obtaining professional investment management. As endowment size increases the use of mutual funds will usually lose its cost advantage relative to an independent advisory firm. Also, trustees must accept the investment policies of the funds, giving them less control than in the case of an advisory firm.

team that can work in close coordination and that has a wide spectrum of expertise. If this analysis is valid, then a nonprofit institution should seek an advisory organization having a critical mass of these skills.

On the other hand, you could conclude that the intensified competition to find stocks makes it harder than ever to consistently identify securities that are overvalued or undervalued by the market. If this is the case, then a nonprofit organization should seek a system of investment selection for publicly traded securities under which outside professional portfolio managers concentrate their time and energy on the selection of a portfolio that meets the risk and industry composition criteria established by the trustees and that also minimizes transaction costs. Capacity to research individual securities or to provide elaborate stock selection techniques would be of secondary importance.

Costs.   The fees of professional money management firms generally are presumed to be negotiable, particularly in the case of a portfolio in excess of $100 million. Fees generally are scaled according to the amount of funds under management, with the percentage rate decreasing as the size of the fund increases. Such fees may, depending on the advisor retained, include the cost of custodial services. You can expect to pay anywhere in the range of 0.16–0.30 percent of asset value to an established firm for management of a portfolio of stocks, bonds, and short-term funds, depending on the firm selected and the size of the fund assigned to the firm.

Management costs should be a factor in selecting advisors. This is especially so if you accept the accumulating evidence that you cannot identify with any genuine confidence a firm that will necessarily prove to be a superior performer over time in managing common stocks and bonds. Such an outlook argues for taking into account significant cost differentials in selecting an advisor, provided lower costs are not a substitute for basic competence.

Priority of Service and Conflicts of Interest.   Receiving first priority from an investment manager in terms of buying or selling securities can make a difference at the margin in the profits generated from endowment management. When a firm must choose whose shares will be bought or sold first, you would like to feel that the institution's stock would be part of the first block of shares bought or sold. The risk in having an outside manager is that unless a particular institution's portfolio represents a dominant portion of the firm's business, it may not receive priority of service. Of necessity, there is a potential conflict of interest situation whenever an advisor works for more than a single client.

Ease of Trustee Coordination and Supervision.   In the choice to delegate authority and still retain control over policy, there is an inherent risk of friction between trustees and managers. In the case of an established firm having many clients, views, and a style of its own, the possibility of deviation from set performance objectives is somewhat greater than with an endowment managed by a staff devoted only to servicing a single fund and directly responsible to the fund's trustees. On the other hand, if trustees do not give the advisory firm enough freedom, then the firm may say with some justification that it cannot be held accountable and that it was prevented from really "performing" in the way it did for other clients.

Avoiding Putting All One's Eggs into One Basket. Many nonprofit organizations believe that they should not rely on only one entity for the day-to-day management of the portfolio, regardless of whether the choice is made to delegate discretion to an existing outside firm or to establish the institution's own investment organization. Rather, it is argued that an institution should select several managers because a single advisor cannot provide a sufficiently broad perspective and point of view. Moreover, as any organization can suffer from loss of key personnel, internal discord, or a period of subpar performance, a nonprofit institution should try to minimize such risks by selecting a number of groups to handle different segments of the portfolio.

It is asserted that although you cannot perhaps select with confidence one advisor who consistently will obtain superior results, you can expect that if a group of, say, four is chosen, two will sufficiently outperform the market not only to offset the inferior performance of the other two firms, but also to put the portfolio as a whole ahead of the game.

These purported advantages need to be weighed against the drawbacks inherent in the multiple-manager approach. I am talking here about the selection of more than one manager to handle investment in the same medium (e.g., common stocks) and not the diversification of advisors to manage investments in different markets requiring distinctive expertise (e.g., common stocks and real estate). A combination of managers investing in the same area is no more likely to outperform the market than a single manager. On the other hand, these arrangements usually have encouraged managers to shoot for short-term performance resulting in increased portfolio turnover and unnecessary risk-taking.

Moreover, if the portfolio is split into too many pieces, the segments assigned to managers may not be large enough to ensure that a nonprofit entity will obtain priority of service from its investment advisors and may increase the costs of management (as fees normally increase in percentage terms as the size of the funds under management decreases).

Possibly, some of the benefits of diversification of managers can be achieved, and at the same time its pitfalls avoided, by dividing the management of the portfolio according to fields of investment. For example, a nonprofit institution might retain one manager for its common stock portfolio and a separate specialized manager to handle bonds, or assign the management of stocks and bonds to one organization and retain another manager for investment in specialized media, such as real estate.

Despite the arguments against employing multiple managers, most institutions in fact tend to engage in just such a practice. Indeed, although the foregoing objections to multiple managers were presented to Princeton University's board of trustees when

I was financial vice-president of the university, the advice was not heeded when the university reorganized its investment approach. Moreover, the university has had excellent success in its investments despite disregarding my advice on multiple managers.

Capability in the Execution and Negotiation of Transactions. The cost of buying and selling a security (going out of one security and into another) has, in the case of common stocks, been estimated to run as much as 7–8 percent per complete transaction. However, possibilities for reducing transaction costs have increased substantially in recent years with the growth of the "third" and "fourth" markets, the creation of automated quotation systems for over-the-counter trading in listed stocks, and the negotiation of commission rates. Consequently, skill in executing trades may become an increasingly important part of portfolio management. There is no reason to believe that the services of a skilled trader could not be made available, regardless of whether an external or captive firm is employed to select investments.

The Alternative of Delegating Investment Selection to a Staff Organized by an Institution

Institutions that employ their own investment staffs, or use some form of captive or semicaptive firm rather than employ outside managers, have done so primarily for three reasons. They are:

1. a conviction that they can select a staff of equal if not greater quality than that offered by established organizations and one that will concentrate all of its energy on servicing the institution.

2. a belief that the costs of operating one's own firm or staff will be somewhat less than the fees charged by established outside firms.

3. a desire to maximize trustee control over the policy governing the endowment and to ensure that the persons charged with day-to-day management of the portfolio will be responsive to the trustees' directions, and that there will not be an excessive focus on short-term performance.

If a nonprofit organization assembles its own investment staff and hires them as regular employees, it is forming an "in-house" management staff. If it organizes such a staff within a corporation that is legally independent but wholly controlled by the institution, it can be said to be forming a "captive" firm. The costs of either form of organization will be essentially the same. However, the seperate legal entity may serve to minimize potential friction within the nonprofit institution over the higher salaries generally paid to professional portfolio managers compared with its own staff, or to provide some insulation against the nonprofit staff injecting itself into investment matters, or undermining the investment group's focus on earning a profit (see chapter "Making a Profit for Your Nonprofit Organization"). Such nuances are important and may lead to the choice of one form over the other. But, as the in-house staff and captive firms perform the same functions, the term "captive organization" is used below to encompass either arrangement.

Formation of a Captive Organization.   To consider a captive organization model, an institution's endowment must be of considerable size or the costs of such a system will be out of proportion to the value of the assets being managed. The calculations below assume an endowment of some $500 million, but this is not necessarily the minimum size fund for which a specially organized staff would be feasible economically. For instance, many universities with endowments in the $250–300 million range have considered it advantageous to establish a captive portfolio management structure.

A captive organization, as conceived here, would operate under very clearly defined trustee guidelines for investment policy, particularly with respect to risk level and the composition of the portfolio. Although the organization would have discretion to select individual securities on its own authority, the object would be for the firm to operate in a manner fully responsive to the investment strategy mandated by the trustees.

Assuming a total endowment of $500 million (including short-term funds), the bulk of which is invested in common stocks and fixed-income securities, it would appear that operating a captive organization would cost in the range of $500,000–600,000 per year (before incentive compensation—cost of office furnishings and custodial fees).

Such costs assume a head of the organization, two common stock portfolio managers, and one fixed-income securities manager. A trader would place orders and engage in any ancillary operations such as stock lending and option writing. The fixed-income manager would control both long- and short-term securities.

No research on individual securities would be done in-house. It is anticipated that such research would be purchased from outside brokers with commission (or soft) dollars. If necessary, research could always be purchased for "hard" dollars (cash), although this would increase the cost of a captive firm. If trustees believe personnel need to be hired to evaluate investment firm research or develop independent analysis, this would add to the costs of a captive organization.

The structure of the proposed captive organization reflects the view both that trustees must make the strategic choices and that the stock and bond markets are efficient enough that expensive efforts to identify under- or over-valued securities are not justified. The arrangement envisioned could prove less expensive than the selection of an established outside advisory firm. A captive organization, as outlined above, would cost in the range of 0.1–0.12 percent on a $500 million portfolio, plus custodial fees. This is $200,000–300,000 less, before custodial fees, than the estimate of the lowest range of costs (0.16 percent) of an outside manager for a similarly sized portfolio. This differential could prove somewhat more or less than estimated, depending on the fee that could actually be negotiated with an outside advisor and on the actual amount of several costs of a captive organization that we have not been able to include in these calculations.

Advantages of a Captive Organization.   There are several advantages to the establishment of a captive organization.

Ability to Attract Top Investment People. A captive investment group can attract some of the very best investment analysts available, for several reasons. Working for a small organization, where the staff's full effort is expended on portfolio management and little time is spent on sales or administration, is extremely attractive for many money managers. Moreover, a working connection, even an indirect one with an important nonprofit institution such as a major foundation or a university, could be a powerful attraction to midcareer portfolio managers. Certainly, the experience of the universities that have chosen this route suggest this is the case.

Ease of Trustee Control. A captive organization servicing only its parent could be expected to develop a special rapport and intimacy with trustees, greatly facilitating trustee control of policy implementation. Of course, the obverse could prove a problem: namely, a captive organization may have difficulty in carving out a sufficient degree of independence from trustees in the selection of individual investments.

Exclusive Focus. The organization would be designed to service only the institution's account at least for some time. This concentration of focus is important if the firm is to provide the perceived advantages and to avoid the pressures inevitably accompanying the solicitation and servicing of new clients. (After the organization has been functioning effectively for some time, a carefully controlled expansion of clientele might be considered, to spread costs and to provide some diversity of activity for the staff.)

Disadvantages of a Captive Organization.   Creating a captive firm would impose a number of special burdens on trustees and involve certain not insignificant risks:

Start-up Costs. A substantial input of time and effort is likely to be involved in establishing an entirely new organization. A staff must be selected that is not accustomed to working together, and there may be other difficulties in getting a new organization established and working effectively. Apart from the time it takes to organize such a new venture, it may turn out that the chemistry of the personnel selected may not harmonize, and the organization may not function effectively for some time. Even if an institution is ultimately successful in putting together such an organization, it may thus have to bear a substantial "start-up cost" while the organization is getting off the ground.

Trustee Entanglement. Trustees would have to assume responsibility for the overseeing and administration of the organization (including such matters as compensation and personnel policies). These can be troublesome problems to deal with, particularly if it becomes necessary to reorganize a captive organization in an effort to improve its performance.

Inflexibility. In the event that the group's record does not prove satisfactory, it may be considerably more difficult to make a shift to a new team of advisors than if an unsatisfactory outside firm had been employed.

Research Costs Prohibitively Expensive. If you are convinced, as discussed above, that the selection of investments in the future will require extensive in-house analysis of individual securities, it is unlikely that a critical mass of research talent can be assembled within a captive firm without the costs of the firm becoming prohibitive. Of course, if you believe the primary focus of investment management should be on maintaining the risk level set by the trustees and evaluating opportunities for diversifying the composition of the portfolio to accomplish performance objectives, rather than on analysis of individual securities, then the lack of in-house research depth in a captive firm will be less of a concern.

Investment Philosophy is the Decisive Factor

There is no single organizational approach to managing investments that produces superior performance. In general, nonprofit institutions that have experienced the most disappointing results are the ones at which trustees failed to establish adequate policy and strategic guidelines for the investment of endowment funds. Indeed, one sometimes observes a temptation to engage in rearrangement of advisory services, when in fact the most urgent need is to reexamine the basic investment philosophy of the institution.

In the end, the choice between working with an outside advisory firm or a captive organization is going to prove less decisive than whether trustees develop a well-articulated investment philosophy for the management of the portfolio and monitor the investment advisor to ensure adherence to the guidelines they establish.

Table 5. MARKET INDEX PERFORMANCE COMPARISONS—TOTAL RETURN

	1974	1975	1976	1977	1978
Standard & Poor's 500	−26.3%	37.1%	23.8%	−7.2%	6.5%
Dow Jones Industrial Average	−23.5	44.8	22.7	−12.8	2.9
New York Stock Exchange	−26.9	37.4	26.2	−5.0	7.5
Indicator Digest Average	−33.6	47.1	41.9	6.7	5.0
American Stock Exchange	−30.7	42.2	34.4	19.1	20.2
NASDAQ	−32.8	35.2	28.8	10.0	14.6
Wilshire 5000	−28.4	38.5	26.6	−2.6	9.3
EAFE Index	−22.1	37.0	3.7	19.3	34.1
Salomon-High Grade Bond Index	−3.0	14.6	18.6	1.7	−0.1
Salomon-"A" Grade	—	—	—	—	0.6
Salomon-GNMA	—	—	—	—	—
Lehman IT Gov't./Corporate Bond	5.9	9.5	12.3	3.3	2.1
Lehman LT Gov't./Corporate (Baa)	−14.4	24.2	25.5	6.6	0.3
S & P-Preferred	−3.3	14.5	18.6	5.2	−4.3
Savings Account	5.25	5.25	5.25	5.25	5.25
3 Month T-Bills	7.9	5.8	5.1	5.2	7.1
Consumer Price Index	12.2	7.0	4.8	6.8	9.0

	1979	1980	1981	1982	1983
Standard & Poor's 500	18.4%	32.4%	−4.9%	21.5%	22.5%
Dow Jones Industrial Average	10.5	22.2	−3.7	27.1	26.0
New York Stock Exchange	21.7	32.2	−3.8	20.7	22.6
Indicator Digest Average	22.9	37.4	12.4	41.5	39.4
American Stock Exchange	67.6	44.8	−5.9	10.0	33.9
NASDAQ	30.8	37.1	−0.8	21.9	21.7
Wilshire 5000	25.6	33.7	−3.7	18.7	23.5
EAFE Index	6.1	24.4	−1.1	−0.7	24.8
Salomon-High Grade Bond Index	−4.2	−2.6	−1.0	43.7	4.7
Salomon-"A" Grade	−4.9	−1.6	0.2	43.6	7.9
Salomon-GNMA	0.2	0.4	1.5	40.1	10.0
Lehman IT Gov't./Corporate Bond	6.0	6.4	10.5	26.1	8.6
Lehman LT Gov't./Corporate (Baa)	−3.0	1.1	4.1	41.3	12.2
Bond Buyer Index	0.1	−14.8	−14.8	46.4	7.8
S & P-Preferred	−3.6	−5.5	3.0	30.1	9.0
Savings Account	5.5	5.5	5.5	5.5	5.5
3 Month T-Bills	10.0	11.4	14.7	8.0	9.0
Consumer Price Index	13.3	12.4	8.9	3.9	3.8

	Last 10 Years		Last 5 Years		Last 3 Years	
	Cum.	Annual.	Cum.	Annual.	Cum.	Annual.
Standard & Poor's 500	174.2%	10.6%	121.8%	17.3%	41.5%	12.3%
Dow Jones Industrial Average	154.0	9.8	108.2	15.8	54.2	15.5
New York Stock Exch.	210.5	12.0	129.0	18.0	42.4	12.5
Indicator Digest Average	481.5	19.3	274.5	30.2	121.8	30.4
American Stock Exchange	537.8	20.4	236.4	27.5	38.6	11.5
NASDAQ	289.3	14.6	163.9	21.4	47.2	13.8
Wilshire 5000	216.8	12.2	137.0	18.8	41.1	12.2
EAFE Index	186.4	11.1	61.8	10.1	22.6	7.0
Salomon-High Grade Bond Index	86.3	6.4	39.0	6.8	48.9	14.2
Salomon-"A" Grade	—	—	45.2	7.7	55.2	15.8
Salomon-GNMA	—	—	57.4	9.5	56.4	16.1
Lehman IT Gov't./Corporate Bond	134.5	8.9	70.7	11.3	51.3	14.8
Lehman LT Gov't./Corporate (Baa)	130.5	8.7	61.8	10.1	65.0	18.2
Bond Buyer Index	30.4	2.7	14.7	2.8	34.5	10.4
S & P-Preferred	75.9	5.8	27.3	5.9	35.0	13.5
Savings Account	68.8	5.4	30.7	5.5	17.4	5.5
3 Month T-Bills	123.7	8.4	65.4	10.6	35.0	10.5
Consumer Price Index	119.1	8.2	49.6	8.4	17.4	5.5

SOURCE: The Vanguard Group

Chart 7. MARKET INDEX PERFORMANCE–CUMULATIVE TOTAL RETURN (12/31/73 = 100)

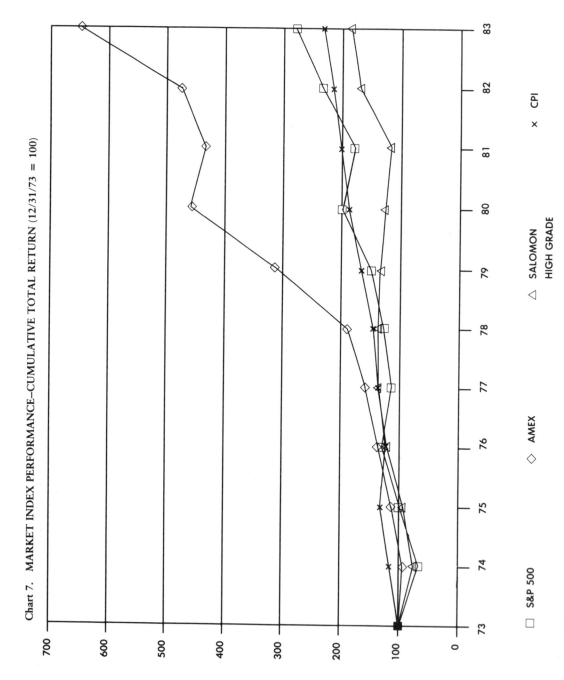

□ S&P 500   ◇ AMEX   △ SALOMON   × CPI
                                     HIGH GRADE

SOURCE: The Vanguard Group

III.

A Planned Approach
To Change

6

Strategic Planning: Playing To Your Comparative Advantage

THIS CHAPTER IS THE FIRST of four that deal with deliberative processes by which management can plan the course of an enterprise. Each chapter deals with a separate process: strategic planning, marketing, budgeting, and tax planning, but, as indicated in the introduction, any coherent effort to plan the direction and operating environment of an organization requires an integration of these actions.

PICKING YOUR SHOTS

The opportunities to try to improve the human condition seem limitless. Unless a nonprofit organization carefully picks it shots, it may fail despite the best will in the world. Good intentions have to be matched with the financial and human resources required to produce results. And the problem itself has to be amenable to correction. Unfortunately, not every ill can be overcome and not every wrong righted, even by the application of dedicated energy and skill.

MacGeorge Bundy, former president of the Ford Foundation, made a set of similar observations in an interview with me. In analyzing what factors account for a foundation's effectiveness, he cited, "The quality of its staff in identifying a problem and the means of attacking it." He added, "And there must be something in the environment that makes people ready to respond . . . a ripeness or readiness for change . . . someone must be interested besides the foundation . . . ."

Lloyd Morrisett, president of the Markle Foundation, sounded a similar theme when I interviewed him. This professional foundation executive, who also served as a vice president of the Carnegie Foundation, observed, "Most foundation projects fail because they are undercapitalized financially or intellectually. They suffer from not enough money or a long enough period of support. The idea may be good but the personnel available to carry it out aren't."

Morrisett continued, "And the problem has to benefit from the right timing. . . . The small resources any foundation can marshal won't work unless there is a hospitable climate for its programs."

The point is that a nonprofit institution has to select its objectives carefully. It has to identify a problem or issue for which it can organize the requisite resources and talents to effect change, and there has to be a public receptivity to its efforts. This process of picking your shots is the essence of strategic planning.

Strategic positioning is different from simply developing long-range financial projections. Developing estimates of an organization's future financial position can be a useful part of the process of developing a strategic plan for an organization. Such a financial planning exercise can help management to envision the impact of changing internal and external factors on the organization's aims and financial well-being. But it is not a strategic positioning of the enterprise.[1]

The emphasis in the planning process should be on the "strategic" aspects, meaning the focus is on the choices that will determine the nature and direction of the organization, and not a simple projection of current operations into the future.[2]

A well-conceived strategic planning effort will encompass a number of integrated steps:

- Determination of mission
- Evaluation of the behavior of rivals
- Evaluation of external environment
- Projections of multi-year expense and revenue trends
- Determination of specific goals (financial and programmatic).

Definition of Mission

At the heart of the strategic planning process is a clear definition of the specific mission the organization is seeking to accomplish. Simple and obvious as this sounds, a good many nonprofit institutions have not defined their missions, at least not with meaningful specificity. Unless this kind of analysis is undertaken, organizational resources cannot be allocated, or staff priorities set intelligently.[3]

---

[1] Kotler, in *Marketing for Nonprofit Organizations* (pp. 82–83), defines strategic planning as "the managerial process of developing and maintaining a strategic fit between the organization's goals and resources and its changing marketing opportunities."

[2] On strategic planning, see Benjamin B. Tregoe and John W. Zimmerman, *Top Management Strategy: What It Is and How To Make It Work* (New York: Simon and Schuster, 1983, pp. 11–17, 23–27).

[3] Raymond and Greyser note: "To get somewhere, an arts organization must define its purpose first—and very clearly. For the sake of survival, let alone prosperity, it must define itself realistically in terms of a distinctiveness versus the purpose of other groups in its field, a particular kind of art, a particular audience

Strategic positioning or planning for an organization must begin with a vision of what the organization should be—what its mission is. Virtually every day, an organization is confronted with critical choices: what population to service, what services to offer, how to allocate its resources. An enterprise needs a conceptual framework for making these choices. This is the role of a nonprofit organization's mission concept. A mission concept should serve to delineate what is the intended nature and direction of an organization—why it engages in certain activities and not others, and why it offers certain services and not others. As Kotler points out, "Each mission implies a particular type of customer and calls for a particular way of rendering value to a customer."[4]

Without such an organizing principle, nonprofit institutions drift into areas in which the enterprise is not strong. Loss of direction and unintended change in the character of the organization are possible, if not probable, outcomes. The concept of "mission" is the "driving force" which enables an organization to decide what should be the scope of its services, and what populations it should service.[5]

Precision in defining an organization's mission can make a significant difference in setting an organization's direction. For instance, the mission of Children's Television Workshop, producer of the "Sesame Street" television series for preschool children, may be defined as "employing television to educate young children" or as "employing the mass visual communications media to educate young children." Under the first definition, work with computers and video discs would not be seen as part of CTW's mission. Under the second definition, these new technologies would be included.

A well-crafted, sharply drawn mission statement serves as a central organizational compass. When drawn with enough precision, it enables management to sort out which activities it wishes to pursue and which it doesn't, and whom it wishes to serve and whom it doesn't. For the most part, the statement will address the same kind of questions a profit-making business needs to ask itself in its strategic planning exercise. (In the profit-making context, the questions are, "Why are you in the business you are in and not another? Why are you in the market you are in and not another?")

In defining a not-for-profit mission, attention should first be focused on identifying the particular *unmet societal need* the organization will seek to fill. This effort is an aspect of strategic planning unique to the not-for-profit world, and precision in defining the particular unmet needs should be coupled with an assessment of the *institution's special capability to affect that need.*

---

of community, and the like." Reprinted by permission of the *Harvard Business Review.* Excerpts from "The Business of Managing Arts Organizations" by Thomas J. C. Raymond and Stephen A. Greyser (July/ August 1978). Copyright © 1978 by the President and Fellows of Harvard College; all rights reserved.

[4] Kotler, *Marketing for Non-Profit Organizations*, p. 91. See also Tregoe and Zimmerman, and *Strategic Planning in Private Non-Profit Organizations* (MITRE).

[5] Tregoe and Zimmerman (p. 40) define "driving force" as "the primary determiner of the scope of future products and markets."

Simply put, you cannot define an organization's mission or aims in a vacuum. In defining an enterprise's mission, examine what the organization's edge is—its comparative advantage—in pursuing its proposed mission.

"Comparative advantage" means what an organization does better relative to its competitors, what it does uniquely well, what capitalizes on its natural strengths. It entails a realistic appraisal of an organization's strengths and weaknesses and how they compare to those of its competitors. Until an organization develops a clear viewpoint of what its strengths are in a highly competitive world, it cannot realistically define its mission.

To illustrate, assume an organization is concerned with mental health and experienced in training community mental health professionals. Over time, the organization becomes interested in affecting the problem of chemical dependency. It finds, however, that there are already organizations in its area providing good services to persons afflicted with such dependency. But the organization may have the capability to administer an aspect of the problem overlooked by other institutions and agencies: the training of medical professionals in the treatment of chemical dependency (most health professionals in fact now receive virtually no education in the subject). Such a focus will enable the organization to concentrate its energies in its area of expertise, the training of mental health care professionals.

The point of analyzing "comparative advantage" is to drive an organization to invest in its areas of strength and to cut back on areas in which it is competitively weaker. An enterprise wants to build on its principal areas of advantage. Over the long term, investing in a few areas of strength is the key to sustaining superiority.

Other criteria a not-for-profit organization may apply in defining its mission include:

- *cost–benefit effectiveness of meeting need (can society afford the cost of the perceived benefits?)*. The cost-effectiveness of the "Sesame Street" TV series is one of its appeals; for the roughly $10 million it costs to deliver the 130 new shows each year, the series attracts nine million regular viewers under the age of six as well as millions of other viewers. Children who regularly watch the show gain in skills. The size of the series' audience, relative to its production expense, means the cost of these benefits, on a per viewer basis, is quite small.

- *likelihood of drawing support for the programs in the mission (is there a market for the programs?)*. Dual test: Is there both a demand for the service and an effective constituency prepared to support, even fight for the program?

- *can the organization impact the problem?* Can the organization raise (or earn) enough funds to launch effective programs in support of its proposed mission? Can people with the requisite talents to mount such programs be recruited at a cost the organization can afford?

- *will the effort likely stimulate replications? Is it a model others will emulate?* One of the justifications for exempt organizations is to be at the cutting edge, to pilot new paths for others to follow.

- *importance to liveliness of the place/its reputation.* An organization that does not improve and doesn't modify or expand its program to keep abreast of the times, will gain a reputation as a staid entity, and will be perceived as dull and lifeless rather than as an imaginative and lively place to work. Ultimately, the perception of an institution's liveliness will affect the quality of people who come to work for it and the level of support it gains.

How to Choose a Mission Concept

The analytical framework we have outlined is useful in helping in the selection of a mission concept, but in the end, rational analysis doesn't lead by itself to any necessary conclusion. For instance, in the case of CTW, going through the analytical checklist above doesn't compel a choice between a narrow television-based or broadened communications-based concept of mission. Ultimately, the choice comes down to the personal system of values of those charged with determining the organization's mission. What do they believe is most important? What do they have the strongest convictions about? In the case of CTW, do they care so intensely about television that it is of overriding importance or is the center of their interest on mass communications media? This is a very personal decision.

Stripped of all analytic trappings, then, the determination of a mission is a statement of personal conviction . . . of personal commitment.

Tracking Rivals' Behavior

Competition is a fact of life for every nonprofit organization, though not all such organizations appreciate this. But in fact *all* exempt institutions compete at some level for either public financial support, or even where fully endowed, for the best talents, the best projects, and the most attention for their work. Very likely, an institution's own plan of action will be affected by the behavior of its rivals. Accordingly, the identity of an organization's effective competitors must first be delineated, and then the actions of such competitors monitored.

Tracking the competition has been long-practiced in higher education. Most colleges or universities keep closely abreast of the tuition, student aid, and faculty salary policies of the range of institutions with which they see themselves in competition. The first step, of course, is to identify the schools from which the most direct and intense competition is faced. (Few, if any institutions, have the resources to counter every potential competitor.) An alert college or university will survey the students who decline to attend once accepted, so that it can be learned what colleges or universities are seen by the marketplace (i.e., students) as competitive alternatives.

Once its principal rivals for students have been pinpointed, an institution will try to eliminate any gap that may exist in financial aid or student charges between itself and its competitors, if it feels such policies are adversely affecting its admissions. For instance, a school may begin to offer financial aid, regardless of need, to the students with the best academic records and have some success in attracting such students from its rivals. Observant competitors will very likely soon adopt a similar policy. Similarly, a college will be reluctant to raise its fees more rapidly than competitive schools with a high percentage of overlapping admissions. It will be reluctant to raise its faculty salaries much less than institutions who often make offers to members of its own professional ranks.

It can be a mistake, too, to limit the analysis of the competition a nonprofit organization faces. In some fields, the competition faced by a nonprofit may come from the commercial world. For instance, a public broadcasting station has a monopoly only on public television in its geographic broadcast area. It would be foolish to ignore the fierce and indeed often overwhelming competition it faces from commercial broadcast channels and, now, cable systems as well. Public television must and does take into account in its programming in such an environment, the broadcast schedules of its commercial competitors. For instance, the PBS stations would be foolhardy to put on a news documentary on a Sunday evening in a time slot competitive with the CBS network news feature series, "60 Minutes," one of television's most popular shows.

As you survey the competition, you want to look for ways in which you can gain an edge on rivals . . . for areas in which you can deploy your relatively greater strengths to play to your comparative advantage. A university, for example, may find that the colleges in its immediate area are really not its prime competitors for students, and that it can increase its appeal, relative to its real competitors, by offering joint programs with these neighboring institutions. Or a university may find that a major concern of students is getting into graduate professional schools. If it faces stiff competition for undergraduate students from institutions which do not have professional schools, it may advertise that its own professional schools look with favor on applications from the university's undergraduates. Or a small, community health services organization, in applying for a government grant in competition with larger organizations without a community affiliation, may tap the political power of its constituency to support its application.

The moral here is simple: you do not want to try to overpower the competition if there is any chance that you can outmaneuver it.

Evaluation of External Environment

In addition to analyzing present competition, an organization also ought to look down the road to see how it will fare in its competitive universe in the future. In particular, keep an eye out for changes in the external environment in which the organization operates. You cannot expect to predict all future changes, but at least you can be alert to the possibilities of economic, social, or technological change that could either adversely affect your organization or open new opportunities (e.g., in the case of educational institutions, the push for equality for women). You can also assess the possibility that other institutions will shift their directions and compete more intensely for your revenue sources and your market (e.g., arts channels on cable television seek out the public broadcasting audience).

Realistic Multi-Year Projections of Expense and Revenue Trends

Strategic planning also requires that you take your best shot at developing a multi-year forecast of expenses and revenues and the impact of economic trends on those projections. Failing to do so can have deadly consequences, as the experience of many universities over the last several decades illustrates.

Few universities had even heard of multi-year financial planning until the 1970s, when financial hard times pressed upon them. Prior to that period, they tended to operate and react according to the opportunities of the moment without examining longer-range trends. Reacting to demographic and government policies of the 1960s, many universities expanded willy-nilly, adding buildings and programs for which in-sufficient tuition revenue or government grants were available to finance within a few years. At the same time, they did not reinvest enough funds in their endowments to enable such funds to grow at the same pace as inflation-driven expenses. Moreover, in the 1960s universities overtenured faculty on the assumption that growth would be continuous. As a result, there was too-little room in the 1970s for new faculty when the economic slowdown struck.

In short, a good number of universities drifted over time into serious financial difficulty from which they found it acutely painful to extricate themselves. That the future of higher education would be different from the present was foreseen by some. But many universities had failed to look ahead, to make an effort to project future developments rather than to assume the present would continue into the future, and to assess the implications of potentially new conditions. Had they engaged in such long-range planning, many of these universities might have avoided mortgaging their futures.

A good number of nonprofit organizations find their current financial position so precarious that it is understandably hard for them to look beyond meeting next month's payroll to more long-range issues. But for others their plight stems—as in the case of universities—from the false expectation that past trends will continue into the future.

Of course, it is difficult to project future trends with precision. It is, however, possible to develop an informed sense of what the handwriting on the wall says. Look at William Bowen's study in the 1960s for the Carnegie Commission forecasting the impact of rising inflation on expenses in higher education.[6]

---

[6] See William G. Bowen, *The Economics of Major Private Universities* (Carnegie Commission on Higher Education, 1966).

You have to appraise the future availability of support sources realistically in the same way that a business would project the trend of revenues. For example, Children's Television Workshop decided as early as 1970 that it was risky business to rely on a combination of government and foundation funding for "Sesame Street," despite the fact that the series was, and is, one of the most successful projects ever launched by foundations and government. But the attention span of institutions supporting public activities is notoriously short in this country, a fact to be accepted. The Workshop prepared from the outset for the day, which came in the late 1970s, when it was no longer feasible to rely on foundation or government funding for the series.

The point is to try to anticipate the larger trends, even if particular projections of numbers prove to be off the mark.

Setting Specific Goals

The end result of the processes outlined above should be the development of specific goals for the organization to be accomplished in a given timeframe. As Kotler points out, an "objective" differs from a statement of "mission," in that the latter sets out the "basic purpose" of the institution, and the former constitutes the specific aims the institution will pursue over a given timeframe.[7] These aims, when restated in an operational and measurable form, become the institution's goals (i.e., an objective of the organization made specific with respect to magnitude, time, and who is responsible).

Kotler gives the following example of the different meanings of these planning terms: Beloit College, a small, private college in southern Wisconsin, defines its continuing mission as the "applied liberal arts education business," with emphasis on career preparation through the liberal arts. Its objective in a given year may be to "increase enrollment," and the ultimate goal will be "a 15 percent increase in next fall's entering class."

Of course, one can become overly enamored with subtleties of planning language and the degree of precision it is possible to obtain in defining mission, objectives, and goals. However, rarely is the effort to do so wasteful, for it will lead usually to new insights about the organization and its opportunities.

Establishment of a Financial Bottom Line

One end result of the planning process should be the adoption of specific financial as well as program goals. In essence, a nonprofit organization should have its own form of financial bottom line as an explicit institutional goal.

The adoption of a "bottom line" is an important way to express the connection between institutional financial viability and programmatic objectives. Further, it will serve as a source of constructive tension when pressure builds to increase expenditures.

---

[7] Kotler, *Marketing for Nonprofit Organizations,* pp. 91–93.

The bottom line simply may call for budgets to be balanced each year, or it may contemplate a planned, manageable deficit[8] or it may establish as a goal that a certain amount of resources will not be expended currently but saved for future needs, with a view towards accumulating a certain amount of capital. The point is to have a specific financial objective for the institution and to plan how the institution will achieve this aim.

Establishing Performance Standards and Feedback Mechanisms

The development of overall organizational goals should be built up from specific objectives for each department. A plan can thus serve as a reference point for assessing departments' progress in meeting their responsibilities.

The argument often is made that the objectives of many nonprofit institutions are inherently too vague to measure.[9] But such arguments assume that greater precision in stating the goals of a nonprofit organization is somehow impossible. The mere fact that a department is not a "profit center" in a financial sense does not mean that you cannot establish specific objectives and criteria for assessing whether these objectives have been achieved. It is a problem of definition. As Peter Drucker, a longtime commentator on organizational management, has pointed out:

> The most sophisticated and, at first glance, the most plausible explanation for the non-performance of service institutions is (that the) objectives of service institutions are 'intangible' and so are their results. This is at best a half-truth. The definition of what 'our business' is is always 'intangible' in a business as well as in a service institution . . . 'abolishing racial discrimination' is equally unamenable to clear operational definition, let alone measurement. But to increase the number of black apprentices in the building trades is a quantifiable goal, the attainment of which can be measured.[10]

Of course, some goals are easier to measure than others. The danger is that organizational attention will be focused on the measurable objectives at the expense of perhaps even more vital but less quantifiable goals. For example, the National Endowment for the Arts recently focused much of its managerial attention on reducing proposal processing time. As a result, the process is quicker, but the question remains whether it is more effective in identifying good projects. Transportation systems focus on on-time performance, but safety and cleanliness are harder to achieve and are often neglected.

[8] A planned deficit can be an appropriate way of providing a transitional period to adjust to an unanticipated economic shock (such as the 1974 explosion in oil prices) or to move an institution from a perpetual deficit to a balanced budget.

[9] Waks, in *Strategic Planning in Private Non-Profit Organizations*, p. 7.

[10] Peter Drucker, "Managing the Public Service Institution" (*The Public Interest,* fall issue, no. 3, 1973).

Still, the exercise of trying to set measurable goals for departments has an underlying value: to build a performance-oriented discipline within the organization. To establish such a discipline within the organization requires a process or structure that regularly clues people in as to what is expected of them. Thus, the planning process should be from the bottom up, with departmental objectives first drafted and discussed by various levels of working staff until major organizational goals emerge for top management and the board to consider. Therefore, every department within an organization should be asked to establish specific objectives it will seek to accomplish within specific time periods. At year's end, both senior management and the board should evaluate the extent to which goals were achieved as part of the process of setting compensation levels for the next year. This process closes the loop from employee goal-setting to employee rewards based on achieving goals.

The overall aim of the process is to establish, as part of the institutional culture, the idea of managing for results, with individuals accountable for achieving agreed-upon goals with a given level of resources.

Tax Planning

The tax laws applicable to a nonprofit organization are very different from those that govern a profit-making one, but they are equally complex and important. Careful planning of an activity can lead to sheltering certain kinds of income from taxation. It can also avoid a "public charity" from being classified as a "private foundation" with all of the attendant limitations or the loss of status as a 501(c)(3) organization. Tax planning is thus as important in the nonprofit sector as it is in the profit-making sector. (See chapter "Tax Planning: Forethought Rather Than Afterthought.")

SUMMING UP

Strategic planning is one of the critical tools available to shape the direction of an organization. In shaping direction through strategic planning, the starting point is defining the nature of an organization's mission—what the organization is to be, what services it is to offer, and to whom. The basic thrust must be to start on a course that will enable the organization to achieve its own distinctive niche among many enterprises seeking to serve society—for in the end, it is finding and adhering to that distinctive position, if you will, investing in areas of *comparative* advantage, that will enable an organization to find the opportunity both to better serve society and to do so as a lively, financially viable institution.

The search for a distinctive niche reflects the reality that whether business is profit-making or not-for-profit, it is in a competitive marketplace (unless it is among the few "fortunate enough" to be a monopoly).

This doesn't mean you cannot enter the same field as another enterprise: as in business, many fields will support multiple competitors. But this does mean defining very carefully your organization's comparative advantage. Be cautious, too, in assuming that expertise in one area is transferable to another. For instance, faculty expertise in undergraduate teaching with a research-based university does not necessarily mean the same faculty will be skilled in developing a program of adult education.

The point is that there is more merit than the behavior of modern business would lead you to believe in the ancient aphorism, "The shoemaker should stick to his last."

A central element in the planning exercise is to develop a sense of how the environment and opportunities of an organization are likely to change over time and to reshape directions accordingly. This is not a precise science but partially functions of disciplined analysis and informed intuition. (As Henry Kissinger once said, "Intuition is the principal difference between the statesman and the historian.") Leadership distinguishes itself in a major way by the quality of its informed intuition.

The strategic planning process also provides a convenient way of measuring the extent to which projected programmatic and financial goals are achieved. It becomes a standard reference to compare promise with performance—a way of incorporating into a nonprofit institution the ethic of managing for results.

Finally, in planning, an organization cannot focus on programming goals to the exclusion of financial objectives, nor can it concentrate on finance while overlooking programmatic aims. Program ambitions and resource availability have to be matched. Clearly defined financial goals—a "bottom line" if you will—must be established as well as programmatic goals.

Strategic planning is thus a useful and important process. But when all is said and done, don't be overly insistent on strict consistency between an enterprise's strategic plan and its day-to-day activities. Leave room for opportunism. If an organization is too rigid about planning, it will miss out on some excellent opportunities that will work even though they don't fit exactly into a neat master plan. Fletcher Byrom of Koppers recommends:

> As a discipline for a group of people, planning is very valuable . . . but once you've done your planning, put it on the shelf! Don't use it as a major input to the decision making process. Use it mainly to recognize change as it takes place.[11]

Peters and Waterman, after quoting Byrom, elaborate:

> The problem is not that companies ought not to plan. They damn well should plan. The problem is that the planning becomes an end in itself. It goes far beyond Byrom's sensible dictum to use it to enhance mental preparedness. Instead the plan becomes the truth and data that don't fit the preconceived plan are denigrated or blithely ignored.[12]

[11] Peters and Waterman, p. 40.
[12] Peters and Waterman, p. 41.

Kim McCann, a student in one of my classes, summed it up well when she wrote in an essay:

> Informed intuition as well as tough-minded business analysis are required of not-for-profit organizations in their entrepreneurial, risk-taking approach to the changing realities of their existence. This point is particularly key with respect to the role which quantifiable information should play in decision-making in the face of pressing financial conditions. Budget management and strategic planning are highly technical sciences, overreliance on the substance of which has skewed many private sector businesses' overall abilities to remain adaptive and successful as the economy creates serious challenges.

7

Marketing: An Undervalued Art

A MAJOR PRIVATE UNIVERSITY recently found that its yield of undergraduate women applicants had unexpectedly and precipitously declined from the prior year. ("Yield," in contrast to the number of admissions awarded, represents the number of applicants who are admitted and register at the school.) Women undergraduates were admitted to a separate college at the university, but as a practical matter, the program for women was fully integrated with that of men undergraduates. University officials had no inkling from prior years' results that a fall-off in women's yield might occur, no data which provided a clue as to why it had occurred, and no information as to why the drop-off was confined to women. The officials were completely in the dark as to whether the decline was a one-year aberration or signaled the beginning of a trend that might quickly engulf men's admissions as well.

The university, though it did not want to use the terminology, had a marketing problem. And like so many marketing issues, the first and often most difficult task was to assemble enough hard information to enable the university to identify the nature of its problem.

Some officials felt the university had erred in conveying the misleading impression, in some of its admissions literature and in its separate application form for admission to the women's college, that the women's program was a separate noncoeducational school. It would be easy enough to rephrase the references in the university brochures and to include the application for admission to the women's school as part of a single application form for admission to all parts of the university. But whether these actions would be responsive to the problem couldn't really be assessed because of the absence of marketing information.

Even after the university had spent a year researching the question, it was not able to pin down the problem with any precision. It simply did not have enough historical data to interpret current events; it had not built a continuous profile over time of consumer behavior, which would provide a basis on which changes could be intelligently analyzed. Like most nonprofit organizations, it had not been sufficiently "market-oriented."

Meanwhile, the university felt it had to act—in fact, it believed it had to mount some response before its initial research was anywhere near complete. Continued inaction followed by another such precipitous decline in admissions would wreak havoc with the university's tuition-dependent budget.

The university thus faced a classic nonprofit marketing dilemma: the need to act in a crisis without benefit of the marketing information required to define the problem, much less devise remedies. The university, like virtually all educational institutions, had not understood until this crisis the importance of marketing to its welfare. Simply put, it was "product-oriented," like so many nonprofit institutions, rather than "marketing-oriented."

A PLANNING TOOL

Marketing focuses first on informing an organization about consumer wants and needs and second, on stimulating consumers to utilize its output—whether to consume its services, to donate to its endowment, to subscribe to its philosophy, to volunteer for its programs, or otherwise to become involved with the organization. The planning phase of marketing is in reality a component part of the overall strategic planning process. A marketing approach first *positions* the enterprise's products or services relative to the products or services of other organizations in the same competitive universe. Then a *strategy* is devised to solidify and/or enhance this positioning, and in turn, the strategy is translated into specific marketing goals. *Research* importantly informs this process. Next, the specific tactics are devised to *implement* the strategy and to achieve the marketing goals. The strategic positioning, strategy and goals, and implementation tactics form the substance of a *marketing plan* which should also set forth a timetable for accomplishing specific results and a budget for the effort. Ideally, the entire marketing program will be *coordinated* from planning to implementation, and the results monitored by a single professional accountable for the outcome.[1]

Unfortunately, too many nonprofit organizations still dismiss marketing as mere slick salesmanship that seduces people to buy products they may not really want or need. (Marketing and sales are, of course, not the same thing.) As a consequence, little attention is paid by many such organizations to how a well-run marketing program can be instrumental in maintaining the vitality and responsiveness of an enterprise

---

[1] For a good discussion of marketing planning and control including model documents, see Kotler, *Marketing for Nonprofit Organizations,* pp. 174–191.

without disrupting its core values and mission. There is probably less professionalism in the field of nonprofit marketing than in any other area of its management.[2]

This chapter examines the component elements of marketing:

1. Research
2. Positioning
3. Strategy and Goals
4. Implementation
5. Coordination.

The chapter begins with "research" because without an analysis of an organization's customers, the potential and/or actual appeal of the organization's services to such customers, and the competitive environment, it is impossible to develop a sensible positioning of the organization. The chapter closes with an exploration of both the limitations and social value of marketing.

Research

Marketing decisions in well-run organizations are no longer made solely upon the basis of someone's gut feeling or anecdotal evidence (although intuition and even hunch will inevitably play a part). Today, a variety of sophisticated techniques are available to gather information and to evaluate consumer responses.

Market research serves four broad functions:

1. to inform the development of a marketing plan,
2. to help shape product development through pretesting models on potential consumers,
3. to inform decisions on the choice of communications messages and media,
4. to evaluate a product's acceptability following its introduction into the market place.

Information gathering systems include collection of publicly available data, observation of competitors' behavior, carefully structured analyses of consumer reaction to new products (e.g., focus group discussions, test mailings, etc.), and surveys of their actual response to a product (e.g., newspaper circulation audits, Nielsen radio and television ratings, polling of user attitudes). Each of these techniques has its advantages and disadvantages.

But underlying them all, in the best institutions, is the philosophy that the customer can contribute to product conception.[3]

---

[2] Raymond and Greyser observe in "The Business of Managing Arts Organizations": "In no area of arts management has the absence of professionalism been more evident than in marketing."

[3] As Peters and Waterman report (pp. 156, 198), "The excellent companies *really* are close to their customers. That's it. Other companies talk about it; the excellent companies do it. . . . The top 'better listeners' . . . pay especially close attention to their lead users. . . . The front-edge user (that is, the inventor rather than the average consumer), even in most consumer goods areas, is years ahead of the model consumer. . . . Listening or sleuthing of this class, at or near the edge of the state of the art, is a long way from commissioning polls or convening panels to discuss yesterday's tastes. . . ."

Children's Television Workshop is a model of a research-based nonprofit organization. It has always employed extensive and careful testing on target-age children of its proposed new television programs during their development phase. Such preintroduction research is valuable not only in forecasting acceptance, but even more important, in helping shape product design to accomplish the Workshop's program goals. As part of this research, both the appeal of various materials to children in the target-age range and their comprehension of content are tested. This feedback from children has measurably impacted the content and form of CTW's television series. For instance, in developing a series on science and technology for children between the ages of eight and twelve, formative research revealed that boys and girls in that age range have quite different tastes in subject matter. Care was then taken to find content which appealed to the tastes of both genders.

This preproduction "formative research" is followed up by postproduction studies typically conducted by independent research organizations to rule out "self-interest" influencing results. The aim of such "summative research" is to determine whether the series has attained its educational goals. In addition, direct audience research can illuminate the impact of a product on consumers. For example, a Yankelovich study documented that the "Sesame Street" series for preschoolers has achieved virtual saturation viewing in minority communities—one of the show's explicit social goals. The fruits of such summative research, coupled with close monitoring of the series' Nielsen ratings (measuring television viewership), are then employed by producers to keep the show fresh and lively and to develop new materials. Any sign of audience slippage leads to immediate reexamination of whether new approaches are needed. The fact that in its sixteenth season "Sesame Street" continues to maintain the same if not a greater hold on the preschool audience is a tribute both to the creative talents of the Workshop and to its extensive, thoughtful research effort.

Good, useful, and reliable research information is often available to nonprofit organizations if they look for it. However, while the search for market information must be conscientious, it can be overdone in the hope of finding *the* data which explain everything. Two analysts caution:

> In many non-profit industries data is often difficult to obtain and tends to lack the level of sophistication of data available in the private (profit) sector of the economy. . . . Most market analysts realize and accept the fact that inferences must often be made using data that are something less than "perfect information." . . . one can readily assume that perfect information on non-profit will be even further out of reach than it is for the analysis of private for-profit operations.[4]

---

[4] Philip D. Cooper and George E. McIlvain, "Factors Influencing Marketing's Ability to Assist Nonprofit Organizations" (Kotler, Ferrell, and Lamb, p. 12).

Positioning

With research in hand, marketing planning begins with positioning the organization's products with respect to the products of its competitors. The object is to find a particular niche where you are better at something than anybody else . . . to find the segment of the total potential market for which your product has its greatest appeal. The single most important decision in devising a marketing campaign is this positioning, argues marketing professional Edward Nash, in *Direct Marketing, Strategy, Planning, Execution.* Nash defines positioning as "the portrayal of a product in its proper status vis-à-vis other products." He adds:

> The essence of strategic product planning requires . . . a commitment about what your product or service is and how you want it perceived. You can't have it be all things to all people. It can be the best or the cheapest, traditional or innovative, entertaining or educational. To try to be everything at once is to be nothing.[5]

An essential first step to positioning is to develop a "product description." Kotler and Levy observe in "Broadening the Concept for Marketing":

> Business organizations have increasingly recognized the value of placing a broad definition on their product, one that emphasizes the basic customer need being served. . . . The same need for a broader definition is incumbent upon nonbusiness organizations if they are to survive and grow.[6]

Accordingly, a product description should not simply specify the characteristics of the product but also spell out what need the product fills and what benefits it will confer upon the customer. The product description is also the place to include relevant research on how the organization's product is presently perceived by the various groups which make up its market. As Edward L. Nash observes:

> What consumers think your product is can be just as important as what it really is. Perception is an aspect of reality.[7]

Accompanying the product description should be an analysis of the "marketing environment." Here, all the factors that may impact or influence marketing strategy should be reviewed. Among such factors are the competitive situation, including the behavior of competitors, government regulations (existing or potential), and economic trends.[8]

[5] Nash, p. 215.

[6] Kotler and Levy, "Broadening the Concept of Marketing" (Kotler, Ferrell, and Lamb, p. 7).

[7] Nash, p. 36.

[8] See Michael E. Porter, *Competitive Strategy, Techniques for Analyzing Industries and Competitors* (New York: Free Press, 1980).

In addition, the best available data on the number, demographics, and economic profile of the potential customers for the product should be set out. However, Nash warns:

> Your customer is not a statistic. . . . Logical reasoning will take you further than statistics in a . . . marketing plan."[9]

Hence, it is important to find out something about the target customer. What is his or her life like? What are his or her aspirations? What does he or she expect from the organization and its products?

With a fleshed-out product description and sense of the marketing environment in hand, you can approach the actual task of positioning the organization's product.

The task, then, is to define the organization's product relative to the product of competitive institutions. What strengths and weaknesses does the product have relative to the competition? What special appeal, in comparison to others, does it offer, and to which groups of consumers?

A college will not appeal to all students everywhere. It may define its target market by educational or other attainments, geographic location, family income, or other factors. The hope is that its market niche will be one to which the institution has strong appeal (e.g., as in appeal to residents within a nearby radius of the school). At the same time, no college can expect to satisfy all the selection criteria of every potential applicant, even within its target market. Its competitors will be stronger in some areas than it is. The tasks are to define its differential (or comparative) advantage and to identify those elements in its reputation or resources which can be exploited to create a special value in the minds of its target customers.

For example, a college may not insist that students take any required courses and may also allow students to create their own fields of study. Assume that at the same time the college's most formidable competitors are moving in the direction of more formalized, structured curricula. The college's curriculum design may thus appeal strongly to the niche of highly motivated, self-directed students, as well as to those with an aversion to being required to study fields that do not interest them. Its program will create a distinctive place for it in the market vis-à-vis its competitors.

In short, relating product appeal to the interest of target consumer groups, against the backdrop of competitors' behavior, serves to define an institution's market niche.

Strategy and Goals

Once a market niche has been identified, the next step is to devise a strategy for protecting and enhancing that position and then, as in the case of strategic planning, to translate that strategy into specific marketing objectives (e.g., to gain a 5 percent

[9] Nash, p. 48.

share of the market, to reduce enrollment by 10 percent over last year, to change the geographic distribution of the entering class, etc.). There are various means by which an organization can do so:

- Product modification
- Pricing policies
- Access
- Customer service.

Product modifications. Edward L. Nash observes:

> Originally, most businesses were based on the idea that a product is a fixed, inflexible entity. . . . Today, the emphasis has reversed with product development teams directed to find products or services to meet marketing opportunities.[10]

Without going as far as Nash's product development teams, it is possible for nonprofit organizations to take into account customer perceptions and responses in shaping a product, without sacrificing their basic aims.

Consider the hypothetical college whose market niche was identified above as highly motivated, self-directed students. To enhance its appeal to this group, the college might add to its flexible curriculum a work internship program which gives students credit both for employment related to their field of interest and for courses taken at other nearby schools. These refinements would add to the flexible character of the college program.

In some cases, refinements may add to an institution's costs. Careful market research and analysis can provide an index of whether such refinements are likely to have a positive impact on the target market.

Product pricing policy is a second ingredient in strategy formulation. There are various pricing options an organization can attempt to use in competition with its competitors, such as pricing its product at the same level or even below that of others. If it concludes its product is sufficiently unique, or consumers are sufficiently insensitive to price variances, it can offer its product at a higher price than the competition. The pricing strategy selected will be influenced by the organization's objective, whether to maximize immediate revenues or to build market shares by undercutting the competition on pricing.

In the case of the hypothetical college discussed above, it will check how its costs compare with those of its toughest competitors and then ask, "Can we attract more students by raising our charges next year less than those of our competitors?" Before making this decision, the college will identify where the students who decline to matriculate actually go to school. These schools are the college's major competitors. In

---

[10] Nash, p. 16.

addition, the college will try to learn the names of schools attended by students who had considered applying to the college. (Getting at the behavior of these potential consumers is not simple because of the difficulty of identifying them, although random surveys by telephone may be useful.)

The cost comparison will undoubtedly have to be supplemented by inquiries to students. The point of the research is to provide a basis for deciding whether a price differential may affect student choice of a college. Student aid policies must also be part of this analysis—pricing and credit analysis are part of the same equation. The college may find—as some already have—that their admissions are not price-sensitive relative to the competition. That is, a student's choice of the college may or may not be seriously impacted by a differential in the costs of attending one school compared to another. (In fact, Ivy League universities have found that students interested in admission are not deterred by the higher cost of attending such colleges, compared to schools perceived as less prestigious.) If this is the case, the college may charge higher fees than its competitors in the expectation its admissions yield will hold up, thereby increasing the college's net income. If admissions is price-sensitive, the college will have to keep its costs closely in line with those of its principal competitors in order to attract the desired number of students.

Pricing strategy will also involve reviewing how the product is priced: does the college announce one comprehensive student fee or separate fees for tuition, room, and board, and in the case of the latter, does it require all students to take a board contract? The separate fee approach assumes the impact of the total cost of the college's education can be masked by a separate fee structure. But consumer behavior has to be studied to see if such a strategy will work.

Access. In the case of a service-based institution like a college, formulation of a marketing strategy entails considerations of convenience and accessibility.[11] Student choice of colleges may be influenced by proximity; students may want to be able to travel between home and college without incurring substantial expenses, or they may want to go to school in the region where they plan to live. Schools may thus focus their primary marketing campaign on students who live within close geographic proximity to the institution.

Customer service. The relative quality of service offered by competitors can also be an important element in consumer choice. The more closely a basic product resembles other products (i.e., is a commodity product), the more likely quality of service will differentiate competitors. In the case of our hypothetical college, better student academic and personal counseling programs, better eating and social facilities, better dormitories, and better athletic facilities than those offered by the competition can be

---

[11] Cooper and McIlvain, in "Factors Influencing Marketing's Ability to Assist Non-profit Organizations" (Kotler, Ferrell, and Lamb, p. 15), note that such considerations replace the traditional distribution analysis in the case of service-based institutions.

significant factors in influencing students to choose one college over its competitors. In a real sense, investment in such services by the college is a marketing expenditure.

Implementation

Once an organization's strategy for maintaining or enhancing its market niche has been developed, specific tactics of implementation can be devised. A broad range of implementation techniques is available, including:

- advertising in different mass media (print, radio, broadcast television, cable television, etc.), including "telemarketing."
- direct response marketing (direct mail solicitation and certain types of direct media advertising).
- promotions (contests, drawings, special giveaways).
- public relations (e.g., efforts to influence media coverage).
- sales programs (brochures, catalogs, sales calls).

Each of these approaches will reach an audience of different size and composition at a different cost. The costs and benefits of each technique must be weighed in light of the marketing campaign's objectives and budget. For instance, advertising on national broadcast television is cost-effective where the very high cost of a commerical can be spread over a target audience reaching into the many millions. Where an attempt is being made to reach a mass audience, the cost per thousand of even expensive commercials becomes very efficient. However, if the target audience is smaller and narrower, commercial television, even local (or "spot") TV, becomes a costly and inefficient communications medium. For instance, a campaign of a national organization like the United Way may find national television commercials a cost-effective means of reaching its national audience. But a campaign for one of the local organizations supported by United Way may find it more efficient to advertise for funds in the local community newspaper or, if affordable, a local TV spot.

Each of these media for communicating with a target audience offers other advantages and disadvantages besides different cost efficiencies. For example, direct response marketing, whether by mail or coupon advertising permits close tracing of the extent to which an advertisement is generating sales inquiries. In turn, the percentage of such inquiries which are converted into a "sale," whether a product is involved or a drive to register volunteers or to disseminate information, etc., can be ascertained. A cost per inquiry and per sale of such a campaign can be calculated. In the case of a television commercial, it is more complicated to sort out the variables—apart from the commercial—which may be impacting sales.

Some alternative approaches may offer a quicker payoff than others, although efforts that produce results over a longer term may prove more fruitful. For example, a college may find the quickest way to improve its admissions yield is to have its officials visit as many high schools within its prime marketing region as is humanly possible. Such an all-out effort may boost admissions yield immediately. But over the long pull, such an effort is hard to sustain; building committees of local alumni, which takes time to do, may well enable the college to mount a sustained and thus more effective long-term effort at recruitment.

Advertising, direct marketing, promotion, and public relations campaigns have become such a complex art that firms providing such expertise now tend to be specialized. As a rule, most organizations turn to such outside experts to assist them in planning and executing such marketing implementation tactics.

A timetable has to be part of an implementation plan. A schedule of actions should be prepared and key decision points identified, i.e., what answers are required at what dates, in order to move the plan along.

Accompanying the timetable should be a budget which details the estimated costs of all the tasks and actions contemplated by the plan.

Sales Effort. A sound marketing program will make "selling" a product less difficult as it optimizes the product–consumer fit. But the level and quality of a sales campaign can influence consumer behavior. As economists sometimes bemoan, even good products are more often "sold" than "bought." A college may send representatives regularly to tour high schools, keep high school counselors up-to-date, organize active recruiting committees of local alumni, produce sophisticated print and audiovisual materials, and mount public relations efforts to keep its name before target groups. A college with these activities as part of its program to attract applicants, may gain a decided edge over competitors whose facilities and academic program are every bit as good, but who take a laissez-faire approach to attracting students.

Most schools now make some sort of formalized effort to recruit students. Their awareness of marketing has grown; as Kotler and Levy note:

> *Everything about an organization talks.* Customers form impressions of an organization from its physical facilities, employees, officers, stationery, and a hundred other company surrogates. Only when this is appreciated do the members of the organization recognize that they all are in marketing, whatever else they do.[12]

Coordination

Today, most business organizations place the management of phases of marketing under a single high-level officer. Activities that once might have been treated as semi-autonomous functions—sales, advertising, market research, and market planning—are now administered typically as part of a single management unit, reflecting the close

---

[12] Kotler and Levy, "Broadening the Concept of Marketing" (Kotler, Ferrell, and Lamb, p. 6).

coordination required to make sure the various facets of marketing are employed in support of each other.

To date, nonprofit organizations have rarely integrated their marketing activities; many still do not even have a person designated as a marketing executive. For instance, a university usually has a series of officers who have "marketing" responsibilities—such as the dean of student affairs, director of development, director of public relations, and the deans of various graduate and professional schools. Each has his or her own turf. Few, if any, would admit to being even in part engaged in marketing, and as a consequence, a coordinated approach to marketing in such an environment is difficult to achieve.

Perhaps the best way to ensure a coordinated marketing approach is to prepare a written marketing plan.

The argument for getting an organization's marketing plan down on paper is forcefully made by Edward L. Nash:

> Only a written plan makes it possible to obtain useful professional advice from co-workers and consultants. Without it, any expert is only reacting to the scanty information and predigested prejudices of his or her client.
>
> Only a written plan brings everyone involved into the total strategy. . . . Most important, only a written plan enables its preparer to fully think through every essential element which affects decision-making.[13]

A plan document will include a description of the product, the market, and the marketing environment (including the competitive situation, pertinent economic trends and relevant government regulations), an analysis of the marketing strategy, including alternatives to the proposed approaches, and an implementation section which outlines the proposed campaign, its timetable and budget.

VALUES AND LIMITATIONS OF A MARKET-DRIVEN APPROACH

Incorporating marketing consideration into product development is an important way for an institution to stay in touch with its customers, its competition, and the environment in which it operates. To be successful over the long term, an organization has to focus on the consumer's needs and desires. An entity must be consumer- as well as product-driven.[14]

Properly managed, marketing not only helps gain consumer acceptance of products, but also lends critical help in shaping the very nature of the products an institution develops. It also alerts management that the continued success of a product can never

---

[13] Nash, p. 33.

[14] See Peters and Waterman (pp. 150–198) and Kotler and Levy, "Broadening the Concept of Marketing" (Kotler, Ferrell, and Lamb, p. 9).

be taken for granted: consumers change behavior, basic conditions alter. Marketing is therefore an essential ingredient in maintaining the creative vitality of an organization and its sensitivity to the changing needs of the public it is intended to serve. A well-run marketing effort is an antidote to the development of a bureaucratic attitude in which preservation of employee positions and perquisites becomes more important than the service concept upon which the organization was founded.

Marketing is especially important to an organization under pressure to expand its revenue base. For most nonprofits this is the case, given the underlying economics of service enterprises (see The Economic Dilemma of Not-For-Profit Organizations, pp. 22–25). Such an expansion requires the organization to find new markets for its products. In this search, marketing can play a vital role in laying out a pathway to growth. Market-driven product development is thus an essential element in the management of modern nonprofits bent on finding new revenue sources.

But incorporating marketing considerations into product development does not mean that the nature of an organization's products should be determined solely on the basis of such input. Reasoned analysis, experience, other types of expertise and intuition, the organization's mission as well as policy objectives, should all play a role in product development.

For instance, in developing educational computer software, Children's Television Workshop discussed with consumer panels very early in the process, before products had been created, what parents' perceptions of educational software were. The panels indicated that parents had a very different idea of what "educational" software meant than the experts in child development who were working with the Workshop to create the software. The Workshop chose to follow the expert advice, as well as its own experience, in the creation of the product. What the early research indicated was not that the Workshop should abandon its well-founded notions of what was educational, but that it should take special care in its product promotion, packaging, and advertising to help parents recognize the educational aspects of the product.

Marketing, then, has its clear place in product development, but it must be balanced against other considerations and objectives. Essentially, this is the point of view advanced in the powerful criticism of contemporary American management by Robert Hayes and William Abernathy writing in the *Harvard Business Review:*

> The argument that no new product ought to be introduced without managers undertaking a market analysis is common sense. But the argument that consumer analysis and formal market surveys should dominate other considerations when allocating resources to product development is untenable.

The authors go on to point out that initial market estimates for computers in 1945 projected total worldwide sales of only ten units. They conclude:

Deferring to a market-driven strategy without paying attention to its limitations is quite possibly opting for customer satisfaction and lower risk in the short run at the expense of superior products in the future.[15]

---

[15] Robert Hayes and William Abernathy, "Managing Our Way to Economic Decline" (*Harvard Business Review,* July/August 1980).

8

Budgeting: Quantifying Priorities

ONCE UPON A TIME, the process of budgeting for most nonprofit organizations was very simple. My favorite illustration is the story of how one Ivy League university set its budget in the years right after World War II. The university was run by one vice-president and two deans, an administration size most faculty still wish prevailed. The vice-president and senior deans would meet with the president early in the summer at his summer home for a round of golf, followed by several rounds of cocktails. Somewhere between the first and second martini, the president and his two chief administrators would settle the budget for the year and decide on the amount of any tuition increase needed to keep the university happily in the black.

Times, of course, have changed.

Today, this university's budget process is a six-month undertaking involving not only a half-dozen vice-presidents and an equal number of deans, but also a committee of faculty, students, and employees who engage in a public participatory exercise to make recommendations to the president and trustees. In part, the current process is designed to give the university's various constituencies a sense of participation in setting financial priorities. But, in equal part, the process is designed to deal with the complications of setting priorities and managing an institution that has grown far more complex and faces far tougher financial constraints than it did in the days when its financial problems could be resolved over summer cocktails.

The genius of the university's current system is that it not only works politically with the university community, but also that it gives all of those working for the university an appreciation of the importance of carefully tracking the institution's financial condition. It is hard if not impossible, without this awareness, to develop accurate budgets for the university. Even the controller with the sharpest eye cannot overcome the indifference of operating staff to the importance of supplying accurate financial data. If, say, the engineers don't care about estimating fuel consumption with precision, or the athletic department about carefully projecting team travel expenses, the actual financial results for any year are going to invariably wind up as a surprise. Numerous universities and other nonprofit organizations that have proudly forecast balanced budgets, but wound up with unexpected deficits, have discovered this fact of organizational life.

OBJECT OF THE BUDGET PROCESS

The goal of the budget process is to identify the resource allocation choices open to a nonprofit organization. A budget should translate the aims and programs of an enterprise into numerically expressed priorities. A lot of jargon has been invented to describe the budgeting process—"zero-based budgeting," "planning, programming, and budgeting system (PPB)," and so forth. But the object of any budgeting process, however labeled, is a commonsense one: to enable an organization to relate its program ambitions to its available resources. The budget process should help identify and isolate for senior management the critical trade-offs facing the institution, and enable managers to monitor execution of the decisions that are made.

The object of the process is to achieve an equilibrium between the inevitable pressures to improve or expand programs and the organization's ability to generate the revenues needed to finance proposed activities. On one hand, timidity in setting revenue goals can become a self-fulfilling prophecy, unnecessarily limiting the scope of activities. On the other hand, unrealistic revenue expectations can get an organization into deep trouble. Certainly, an organization does not want to fall into the trap of letting its program aspirations drive the budget entirely; if it does it may quickly find itself facing program commitments it cannot fund, or worse, insolvency.

Anthony and Herzlinger argue in *Management Control in Nonprofit Organizations*:

> One great advantage of the policy of budgeting anticipated revenue first and then budgeting expenses to equal revenue is that this approach provides a bulwark against arguments, often made by highly articulate and persuasive people, for programs that the institution cannot in fact afford. (Especially pernicious is the argument: "We can't afford *not* to do this.")[1]

In the end it is not crucial that revenues necessarily be budgeted "first" and expenses then cut to match them. A planned deficit may make sense in certain circumstances. What never makes sense, however, is for an organization to kid itself about its financial

---

[1] Robert N. Anthony and Regina E. Herzlinger, *Management Control in Nonprofit Organizations*, rev. ed., p. 329 (© Richard D. Irwin, Inc., 1980, Homewood, Illinois).

prospects. In every case, revenues and expenses both must be estimated with as much realism and accuracy as possible.

Managerial Involvement

Active management of the process by which resources are allocated is one of the most powerful means of focusing an organization's priorities and shaping its operations. Management of the resource allocation (or budgeting) process is a way of ensuring that an organization puts its resources where its priorities are. In addition, the process should serve to create an environment within the organization that maximizes the chance for it to attain its aims.

Unfortunately, allocation decisions in nonprofit organizations too often reflect the influence of immediate pressures, with a heavy premium attached to pacifying competing claimants on the staff, rather than a carefully thought-out set of organizational priorities. Command of the budget process by top management is essential, therefore, if the direction of the organization is to be controlled by such executives. In "Why Data Systems in Non-Profit Organizations Fail," Regina Herzlinger underscores the importance of top management's understanding of and active participation in the design and utilization of an organization's financial systems and statements. In my personal experience, her observations are so perfectly on target that I quote her here at length:

> The state of control and information systems in most nonprofit organizations is dismal. Despite billions of dollars spent to provide relevant, accurate, and timely data, few nonprofit organizations possess systems whose quality equals those found in large, profit-oriented corporations. Nonprofit organizations do not lack data; if anything, they enjoy an overabundance of numbers and statistics. Rather, they lack *systematically* provided information, to help management do its job. Without good information, it is obviously difficult for managers to make reasoned and informed decisions, evaluate performance, motivate their employees, and protect the institution against fraud . . . .
>
> Many nonprofit organizations are deficient in the routinized internal control that ensures the integrity of the accounting for expenditures and services . . . yet the one factor accounting for most failures of information systems lies directly within the control of the organization: the characteristics and attitudes of top management.
>
> Rarely does one hear the executives of a nonprofit organization described as being "good with numbers." More frequently, the accolades are "creative," "innovative," "caring," or "great scholars." Being good with numbers may actually do the managerial image a disservice, for it implies the absence of such qualitative skills as creativity, courage, and humanitarianism. Indeed, some managers of nonprofits view their lack of quantitative skills as a rather endearing imperfection—like having freckles.
>
> Many of these managers were initially professionals who carry with them the culture and attitudes of the professional, including strong resistance to quantitative measures of their organizations' activities. They argue, sometimes persuasively, that professional work is too complex and diffuse in its impact to be easily accounted for and that naive at-

tempts to account for its outcome might undermine the credibility and integrity of the work itself . . . .

Many professionals-turned-managers do not command the technical skills required for the design and implementation of a good information system. When I have taught accounting to top executives of large nonprofit organizations, they have often told me that until then they had never been able to understand their own financial statements.

A lack of technical skills and an institutionalized aversion to measurement, when combined with the traditional definition of the role of manager in these organizations, lead many managers of nonprofit institutions to abdicate the task of designing and implementing a sound information system to their staffs, particularly to their accountants. A manager will say, "I don't know much about these numbers, but my accountant is a genius." It is doubtful that the manager has the capability to judge an accountant's genius. . . . Much depends on the quality of their managers, who, as I pointed out earlier, are often long on professional training experience but short on administrative skills and experience. The management component of most professional training is usually completely absent, limited to office practices such as billing, or covered through a quick survey course of administrative techniques—a week on accounting, a week on interpersonal behavior, and so on. This level of education is unlikely to develop people with the skills and attitudes of professional managers. . . . The top manager who remains uninvolved in the design of the content of the system negates the reason for its existence. Participation in the system design process ensures that the system is relevant and responsive to management's needs. An information system used regularly by top management for making such key decisions as budget allocation will eventually overcome any initial flaws of design and installation.[2]

Lest you think Herzlinger exaggerates, read the travails of National Public Radio, which "discovered" halfway through its fiscal year 1983 that instead of having a balanced budget, it would run a deficit of $2.8 million—only to find a month later that the deficit would be $5.8 million—and finally to learn a few weeks further on that the deficit for the one year was in fact to be $9 million. Frank Mankiewicz, then head of Public Radio, explained that a newly installed accounting system failed to warn of the mushrooming deficits.

He went on lamely, "As I now reconstruct it, from October to February, our finance department was not providing monthly budget tracking. I assumed the reporting system was still in place. No one was saying we were not raising the money we needed. I was relying on what our finance people were coming up with."[3]

---

[2] Reprinted by permission of the *Harvard Business Review*. Excerpts from "Why Data Systems in Non-Profit Organizations Fail" by Regina E. Herzlinger (January/February 1977). Copyright © 1977 by the President and Fellows of Harvard College; all rights reserved.

[3] Irvin Molotsky, "What Went Wrong at National Public Radio" (*The New York Times*, June 12, 1983, p. 27).

Budget Format

There are several forms of budgets, all of which should be part of the annual budgeting process: the *capital* budget, which lists and describes planned capital acquisitions and improvements, including expenditures to maintain physical plant; the *cash* budget, which shows projected cash receipts and disbursements; and the *operating* budget, which describes projected operating revenues and expenses. All three forms of budget cover a predetermined period of time—generally one year.

The format of the operating budget should provide a picture of the business of the organization highlighting the principle resource allocation choices open to the enterprise. The numbers should be organized to reveal the most crucial facts about the allocation choices facing an organization.

For example, the staff and other costs associated with the public relations efforts of a theater company can be lumped together with the costs of the individual productions to which they relate, or they can be stated separately as an individual line entry in the budget. There is no inherently right way to show such costs. It depends on whether it is more important at the time to show management the fully allocated costs for individual productions, or to focus on the scale of the company's public relations effort.

Hence, you begin to design a budget format for an organization by studying its business, identifying its most crucial operating problems, and outlining the financial choices it faces. When the issues have been identified, the format of the numbers will follow suit easily enough.

Traditionally, the individual lines in a budget, on the expense side, have reflected the organizational structure of the enterprise. The object has been to relate budget numbers to the organizational units which control the expenditures. Usually, income has been broken down into the classifications of the organization's official financial statements.

There has been a lot of useful focus in recent years on summarizing the financial data in a budget around program centers. The development of such program-based budgeting was prompted by the recognition that traditional budget categories did not enable decision-makers to assess the full dollar costs, including the costs of supporting services associated with particular programs. Such traditional budgeting also did not encourage the coordination of financial data with other data, which described programs under consideration and provided some indication of the "output." To overcome these drawbacks, program budgeting focuses on establishing categories defined in terms of the objectives of the organization and what are considered its final products.[4]

---

[4] For an excellent discussion of program budgeting versus more traditional approaches, see Paul Benacerraf, William G. Bowen, Thomas A. Davis, William W. Lewis, Linda K. Morse, and Carl W. Schafer, "Budgeting and Resource Allocation at Princeton University" (Report of a Demonstration Project Supported by the Ford Foundation, Princeton, New Jersey, June 1972, pp. 341–390).

Sometimes, the failure to group any related income and expenses around programs can obscure critical financial choices. For instance, the financial reports of a major U.S. symphony did not group the income from its overseas tour with even related direct expenses, to say nothing of appropriately allocating to the tours their fair share of indirect costs. Correlation of the income and direct expenses in a single budget center would have shown whether the tour generated a "profit" before indirect costs, or how much such income represented as a percentage of revenues, or the tour's gross margin. In fact, the tour's gross margin turned out to be only a tiny fraction of revenues—by far the lowest margin of any of the orchestra's program activities. Grouping revenues and related expenses for each program activity would have enabled the symphony's board to assess whether the tour was justified in light of the organization's overall financial condition, and to determine consciously the trade-off between artistic importance and financial risk.

As useful as the program-centered approach to budgeting is in many cases, a good many financial officers agree with the conclusions on its limitations reached by a team at Princeton University. The group, which installed the university's modern budgeting system, observed in a 1972 report to the Ford Foundation from which I quote at some length:

> Our last general comment concerning program categories per se is a negative one: the establishment of program categories in no way replaced the need for budget categories of the traditional kind, with entries corresponding to the location of operating responsibilities and the nature of the accounting system. At Princeton, we have continued to summarize our own financial conclusions in the traditional way, . . . and we have done so not just because of the necessity of working within an established accounting system. The more basic arguments for the traditional format are: (1) that it is useful in projecting certain sources of income (e.g., endowment, gifts and grants, and student fees), whatever activities or program they finance; and (2) that it is indispensable for controlling and monitoring the supporting services provided by a host of departments such as Purchasing, which has an identity of its own under the traditional format but not under a program budgeting format. Given the need for both formats, it is essential that methods be developed, appropriate to the accounting system of each organization, which will permit the ready translation of data from a program budget format to a traditional budget format and vice versa.
>
> Lest anyone think that the establishment of suitable sets of program categories will lead directly to strong conclusions concerning difficult questions of resource allocation, it should be emphasized that any such sweeping result is precluded by the enormous difficulties of measuring and comparing the "outputs" of separate program categories. How is one to measure, in any quantitative way, the output of research done by a Classics Department and then to express the result in a form commensurate with the value attached to the research done by the Physics Department or to the education offered by either department at graduate and undergraduate levels? The outputs of universities are basically people and knowledge, the qualitative dimension of each is extremely important, and no very satisfactory measures of performance exist.

Of course, these problems of finding quantitative measures of output are not unique to educational institutions. As Alice Rivlin has noted, the measurement of the benefits of many "people" programs is still in its rudimentary stage, and there is no assurance that convincing solutions will ever be obtained. Thus, she concludes that it is not possible to say whether it would do society more good to cure cancer than to teach poor children to read better; nor does she believe that this is a temporary situation.

The basic reason for our difficulty here is that education, like many other public activities (including, it should be noted, the activities of the Department of Defense where much of the early work on PPB was done) produces outputs which are not sold in competitive markets. As a result, the usual yardstick of the economist in measuring the value of, say, a ton of steel or a television set—market price—is inapplicable. Most research is not "sold" at all, at least through any market mechanism, and tuition can hardly be regarded as the "market price" of education at either undergraduate or graduate levels.

Our inability to express varying outputs in commensurate units (dollars or something else) generally makes it impossible to reach obvious and noncontroversial decisions when comparing programs with very different outputs. To refer to Alice Rivlin's general discussion of the same kinds of problems once more, she has noted: If any analyst thought it was going to be easy to make social action programs work better or to make more rational choices among programs, he is by now a sadder and wiser man. The choices are genuinely hard and the problems extraordinarily complex and difficult. Similar observations have been made by people with experience in other areas.

None of this is to say that analysis based on program categories is not useful. On the contrary, we believe that knowing the full resource costs of different programs can be extremely valuable, even when one is still forced to rely on judgments concerning the value of this or that program that are either largely intuitive or based on some consensus of professional opinion. . . . Moreover, there are instances when what we need to compare is not two different outputs, but two (or more) ways of performing essentially the same function, and in such cases it is comparisons of resource costs that matter most. In short, our purpose in stressing the problems of valuing outputs is not to scare people away from PPB as it may be applied to educational institutions, but to recognize one reason why such applications constitute an art form, not an exact science, and a difficult one at that.[5]

The point of this commentary seems clear enough: there is no one exactly right budget format. The choice depends on the analytical objectives management has in mind at any point in time. Whatever design is adopted however, it should be the one which most helps the intended audience for the budget document grasp the issues. The budget, in short, should be "user friendly," not just simply pleasing to its compilers.

---

[5] Benacerraf, Bowen, Davis, Lewis, Morse, Schafer, pp. 346–350.

Measuring Financial Performance

A crucial but difficult task in designing a budget for a nonprofit organization is to create a meaningful set of measures of the organization's financial well-being. Typically, nonprofit institutions think of financial success in terms of the growth in gross revenues rather than in terms of various possible "bottom-line" measures of the organization's financial viability. Moreover, very few organizations assess the efficiency with which they deliver their services, even though improved productivity is one key to coping with the constantly escalating costs of any service organization.

A budget for operations will, of course, disclose an organization's projected revenues less expenses, or net income. This is one financial performance measure. But a simple reference to net income will not suffice to give a complete picture of the enterprise's financial health (as, typically, net income alone does not suffice to measure the profitability of a profit-making company). Transactions that do not flow through the revenue and expense statement may be critical.

For instance, in the case of a university, capital gains earned by the endowment, unspent endowment income (e.g., a vacant endowed chair), and major gifts (gifts outside of annual giving) commonly are not included in the revenue and expense statement, but can be crucial.

Also, items like deferred maintenance of grounds and buildings will not show up in the revenue and expense statement, but they are critical factors in assessing the financial well-being of an institution. In addition, investments in wholly or partially owned subsidiaries are typically not included in the revenue and expense statement.

Of course, cash flow, or liquidity, is also not measured by the revenue and expense statement, even though it is cash flow rather than the accounting concept of "income" that determines the organization's ability to pay its bills.

For this reason, in addition to focusing on the operating budget, the budget process should include an examination of other pertinent indices of an organization's financial health. Typically, these other indices should include:

- the projected cash flow position for the coming year (including the portion of any debt that matures within the period and provision for uncollectable accounts receivable).

- the capital budget with focus on the condition of the physical plant and other tangible assets, and the extent to which adequate funds are being set aside to maintain the plant and such other assets properly, and to replace them as they wear out. In addition, the plans for the acquisition of new capital assets should be detailed.

The cash flow and capital budgets, together with the operating budget, will give a fuller, more instructive picture of an organization's financial condition than the operating statement taken by itself.

In addition to analyzing these three budgets, I have also found it useful, at least in the case of larger-scale institutions, to go one step further and determine year-to-year changes in the amount of "available liquid capital." The term refers to the amount of working capital, plus other funds, which the organization could raise quickly by converting assets into cash. For the purpose of this calculation, you include only those assets which have a readily determinable market value, such as publicly traded securities. Excluded are assets such as land and buildings, the actual value of which usually can be determined reliably only after they are actually sold. In calculating the amount of "available liquid capital," you should also exclude funds whose use is restricted by the terms under which the organization acquired them (e.g., restricted endowment).

The object of the calculation is to determine, after adequate provision for all liabilities, the amount of an organization's capital resources that are relatively liquid and can be readily drawn upon by management and the board for any purpose they may determine. In a sense, the measuring of "available liquid capital" is a way of projecting out the company's potential cash flow position over a longer time period than is normally covered by the cash flow statement. It is an effort, if you will, to assess the long-term liquidity of the organization.

A deterioration in an organization's "available liquid capital" position is a signal that the institution's financial flexibility is eroding. As such capital shrinks, the institution's ability to fund new initiatives or to finance a deficit in its operating budget diminishes.

More than one institution, after years of neglecting to make this kind of analysis, has discovered that it has spent all its unrestricted capital and is faced with operating deficits, a mountain of deferred maintenance which can no longer be postponed, and other underfunded liabilities. Organizations have no choice in such circumstances but to cut as many expenses as necessary to balance their budgets immediately. Whatever freedom of action they may have once had disappears with the exhaustion of their available capital. Close monitoring of year-to-year changes in "available liquid capital" would have enabled such institutions to take corrective steps before they were moved to the brink of insolvency.

In addition to the available capital analysis, it may also be useful to assess the value of the organization's assets not considered readily marketable or liquid, such as land, buildings, and shares in a privately owned business. One way to value such assets is at their original costs of acquisition. (If such assets are held in an independent subsidiary, it may be appropriate to write their original cost down or up, depending on whether the subsidiary has gained or lost money during the period under consideration.) One may also choose, if the assets are potentially of considerable value, to obtain an arms-length appraisal of their value. However valued, these nonmarketable assets—even if it takes time to dispose of them on fair terms—may represent an important source of resources to support an organization.

None of the foregoing financial indices, however, serve to measure how well an organization is accomplishing its mission. And it is here that the sharpest difference exists between profit-making and nonprofit organizations. In the case of the former, "profitability" is *the* measure of how well the enterprise is accomplishing its goals, even though companies may employ varied indices of "profitability." In the case of a nonprofit organization, it is a more subtle, complex task to assess how well its goals are being accomplished.

Identifying the Crucial Variables

As a whole, a budget should have an equal or 50–50 chance of proving right or wrong at the end of the year. That means, hopefully, forecasting errors that negatively impact the budget will be offset by better-than-expected results in the case of other entries. Still, there is always the possibility of significant changes between actual and budgeted results. Even great care in preparing a budget cannot avoid the impact of unforeseen events on the organization. Accordingly, it is useful in presenting a budget to identify for management:

- controllable and uncontrollable costs.
- contingencies: both potentially positive and negative developments that could alter the outcome.

In order to focus attention on the most crucial choices, the budget document should highlight a limited number of the major variables that could have the most powerful impact on the makeup of the budget.

What makes the budget process complex for institutions of any size is the large number of resource claims that arise during the course of even one budget year and, hence, the geometrically greater number of trade-off analyses that have to be made if every single resource claim is weighed against every other demand. For senior management to try to weigh every choice is impractical in an organization of any scale. There are limits to the number of intelligent, informed judgments decision-makers can handle, and for a budgeting system to be effective, the organization's top-ranking officials must concentrate their time and energy on the most critical discretionary choices.

I used to watch new members of the university-wide budget committee at Princeton invariably try during the first weeks of their participation in the budget process to compare every item in each departmental budget with every other. Soon, the new members became flooded with quite literally hundreds of choices among theoretically competing expenditures, and consequently lost in a morass of detail. Once they gave up trying to master every detail and focused their attention on a limited number of critical choices, the allocation process began to work.

A well-crafted system will shape a budget through a hierarchy of managerial decisions, with the more routine choices—those that are either nondiscretionary (expenditures over which the organization has little effective control) or those settled in prior years' determinations—made at the lowest managerial level, and those involving the most sensitive policy decisions, and usually affording the widest latitude of choice, being made by the highest level makers of policy.

For example, in the case of a university, the amount of expenditures required for regular maintenance of its boiler system is best decided by the organization's staff engineers. But the trade-offs between just three variables can be crucial:

1. Raising tuition, say $100 more than originally planned.
2. Increasing the salary pool for faculty and staff by 1 percent more than initially comtemplated.
3. Adding more money to the scholarship pool.

Making these sorts of policy level decisions by senior officials is the heart of any effective resource-allocation system.

Budget artistry in a complex organization lies in reducing countless potential allocation decisions to a limited number that senior management can effectively decide upon. Top management should work actively with its budget staff to identify just which decisions it wants to focus on itself, and which ones it is willing to delegate to staff personnel.

Tracking Variances

One of the virtues of drafting a budget is that management can monitor changes during the year in expected revenues and expenses. Typically, periodic updates of the original budget will be prepared—often on a monthly basis, but at least on a quarterly one— comparing for each line item in the budget the original projection with the most up-to-date estimate for the same item. The difference will be shown as a variance—positive if expenses are lower than originally estimated or revenues are higher than first forecast—or negative if the reverse is true.

The cause of substantial variances should then be explained—was the original estimate merely put together faultily (i.e., a forecasting error), or has some unforeseen circumstance or change occurred, and if so, is it merely an isolated incident or the foreshadowing of a trend? Or has the responsible operating unit either slipped up or, conversely, improved its performance in some fashion? If slippage is involved, what can be done to correct the error? If things are going better than planned, can the situation be further exploited?

By keeping close tabs in this fashion on budget variances—and their causes— management can gain important insight into how well the organization is being run.

Timing of the Budget Cycle

The budget process should be conducted at a time that best permits the maximum number of choices facing an organization to be evaluated together by top management.

For example, at Princeton I once got trapped by separate consideration of the operating and capital budgets. The operating budget determined faculty staffing, and the capital budget fixed laboratory expenditures. Traditionally, the two budgets were considered at separate points in time because certain decisions in the operating budget had to be made before it was possible to complete all the parts of the capital budget. Hence, the university determined new faculty hires as part of processing the operating budget, before it calculated into the capital budget the impact of new science faculty on laboratory costs. As a result, Princeton once got locked into a hiring program that was more expensive than anticipated, when it finally integrated the operating and capital budgets. On the basis of this experience, Princeton in subsequent years simultaneously evaluated the operating budget and related expenditures that would later be included in the capital budget.

Choosing Between Competing Budget Claims

Resource-allocation decisions in a nonprofit organization must be made without the availability of the single-minded decision-making framework that prevails in the profit-making environment. There, you usually have the benefit of the single-minded test for the "bottom line." In a nonprofit environment, you must choose on a qualitative basis between programs, *all* of which usually offer some relative benefit to society as well as to the institution. For example, think of the choice a university faces in cutting its budget between scaling back its philosophy department vs. scaling back the sociology department.

The key criterion in making such choices in the case of a nonprofit organization must be the relative contribution of competing claimants to the organization's core mission. Contribution to mission is *the* "return" to a nonprofit endeavor.

But any allocation decision involving competing claims for limited funds requires making a trade-off between both the projected returns of various alternatives *and* the probabilities of achieving such returns. Even where the projected returns are intangible, as they so often are in the case of nonprofit organizations, resource-allocation choices can be illuminated by analyzing competing claims in terms of their *respective contribution to organizational goals, taking into account the factor of risk*. The term "risk" here refers to the degree of likelihood of an activity achieving its stated goals. For instance, a university may be faced with the choice between providing increased support to an existing, traditional academic department and starting an innovative program, which could both enhance the university's reputation and attract new students. The odds are quite high that allocation of the resources in question to the existing department will achieve their intended objective. However, allocation of funds to starting an unconventional program is an uncertain business, even if the potential return is high.

This factor of "risk," as well as potential benefit, should be a part of resource-allocation decisions.

Full Disclosure

The chief failing that I have observed in budgeting by nonprofit enterprises is a tendency to bury unpleasant realities. Too often, organizations seem to take literally the cynical comment that nonprofit financial statements are designed to obfuscate rather than to educate. An institution should not kid itself about its true financial condition, but many do. They resort to unjustified optimism about future revenues, understate the vulnerability of their accounts receivable, or underfund the amount of plant maintenance required or other liabilities for which provision must be made. (Examples of other liabilities for which adequate provision is sometimes not made are the liability for severance payments and for earned but unused vacation leaves.)

Hiding liabilities leaves an organization open, not only to errant budget judgments, but also to the risk of a sudden, unmanageable jolt to its financial position when the day of reckoning arrives. The appropriate strategy is to make adequate provision for meeting *all* foreseeable obligations in a manner which smoothes out their impact on the budget.

For example, actual outlays for plant maintenance may vary considerably from year to year, according to the nature of the repairs to be made. Instead of simply booking the actual expenditures each year as they occur, the cost of such maintenance over, say, a five-year period can be funded by an annual charge to the budget equal to the average outlay over the period.

Balancing the Budget

For a good many organizations, the amount of revenue available in a year is fixed within relatively narrow limits, and the scaling back of proposed expenditures to fit within those limits is often an agonizing task. If current expenses are not cut back to the level of current revenues, the organization will run an operating deficit, which means the loss must be made up either out of future revenues or, if the organization has an endowment, out of its capital. In either case, the result is to service current needs at the expense of future needs.[6] This is the dilemma most nonprofit organizations face.

However, some nonprofit organizations are prosperous enough to have a choice whether to spend all their revenues in a current year or to husband some part of those revenues for future needs. Such organizations generate enough funds to provide a basic level of service. They can choose among either providing increased services currently,

[6] An operating deficit for budget purposes does not necessarily mean the organization also has incurred a cash deficit from operations. The booking of expenses and revenues for budget purposes may not parallel cash transactions. For example, cash from a sale may be in hand but not booked as revenue until the item sold is actually delivered some months later, after the end of the budget period. An organization may or may not have the working capital to absorb cash deficits—the operating budget will not disclose that; that is why it is important to prepare a cash budget.

putting aside some funds for future projects, or building up a pool of capital, the income from which will be used to support future activities.[7]

It is sometimes argued that if a nonprofit organization runs a surplus (i.e., revenue exceeds expenses), current clients are not receiving the services to which they are entitled. Indeed, the treasurer of Yale University once wrote:

> An operating surplus evidences lack of achievement rather than good management if educational quality can be improved.[3]

The difficulty with this approach is that it begs the question. The quality or volume of services an organization provides can always be improved or increased. (So often the argument in budget debates is made, "How can we afford *not* to do this?") Current efforts can always be expanded to consume available resources. The issue, however, is whether some investment should be made in the future. If an organization is committed to enduring, then should it try to husband some resources for future efforts?

Such investment, as noted above, can take the form of either allocating resources to the research and development of future programs and services, or to the building up of an endowment fund. In either case, the decision to "save" funds reflects a judgment that the organization's future programs will be every bit as valuable as its current efforts. This is not to say, however, that the decision must always be in favor of conserving some resources for the future. The wisest course in a given year may be to apply all available resources to current programs. Under certain circumstances, it may even make sense to run a planned deficit for a time.

For instance, a sudden, steep rise in certain costs may occur (as in the quadrupling of energy prices in 1974), and offsetting such increases in a single year may require too many damaging cutbacks. Spreading the burden of the increased costs over several years may be less harmful than a cutback all in one year. In most nonprofit organizations, cutting costs means cutting people. Instead of having to let able people go, it may be possible to reduce costs through attrition or other savings over time. In other cases, the deficit may be a short-term phenomenon, such as a temporary decline in a particular revenue stream. If it is reasonable to expect that this revenue flow will pick up again, then it may make sense to run a short-term deficit to avoid painful budget cuts.

In assessing whether to cut costs in order to bring a budget into balance, management should ask itself how fast it feels it must restore financial equilibrium and

---

[7] Such a fund is commonly referred to in the nonprofit world as "funds functioning as endowment," since the organization is free at any time to reverse its decision and spend the capital currently. In the case of true endowment funds, the institution is precluded by the terms of the donor's gift of the funds from using the principal for current expenses.

[8] Report of the Treasurer of Yale University, New Haven, 1967, p. 2.

what the "price" is of acting right away. For example, to achieve an immediate balance, will "irreversible reductions" have to be made? Will programs be eliminated that are hard to start up again if things improve later? Will people of scarce talents have to be let go who will be hard to replace later if the organization's financial condition improves at a future date? These are examples of what one means by "irreversible" reductions. You want to think carefully before making them.

These comments should not be read as suggesting organizations should take temporary steps in the face of painful financial realities. In fact, too many nonprofit institutions have done that, only to find that no windfall occurs to bail them out of facing up to hard choices. Too often, procrastination has only mortgaged the future more severely than if decisive action had been taken when the problems first emerged. In budgeting it makes sense to be conservative about predicting the future; after all, an organization can more readily adapt to unexpected good news than to unexpected disappointing results.

The sum of all this is that there is no one necessary response to all deficit situations. The point is to act in each case on the basis of an explicitly considered decision and to be very clear about the reasons for the action decided upon, whether it is to run a temporary deficit or to achieve an immediate balance.

IMPORTANCE OF PROCESS

As should be evident, the process of allocating resources is far more an art than a science. Allocation decisions inevitably involve largely qualitative judgments. There is no budget process that can quantify choices in such a way that they become self-evident. For example, whether a university should devote the $1 million expected increase in alumni gifts to hiring additional new faculty, to awarding an increased number of graduate fellowships, or to moderating the rate of increase in tuition charges, entails qualitative judgments. No system of budgeting can or should replace this judgmental factor in resource-allocation decision-making. This makes the *process* by which budget decisions are arrived at all the more important.

The nature of the process by which budget goals are set will have a critical bearing on the likelihood of securing organizational support for the objectives adopted. Since, as we have noted, qualitative judgments rather than quantitative criteria are going to govern most resource allocation choices, it is especially crucial that the organization have confidence that ultimate decisions have been arrived at fairly. Without a process which produces this sensibility, it will be impossible to gain acceptance of financial decisions. That is why the "process" of budget decision-making is virtually as important as the nature of the decisions being made.

To achieve this sense of fairness, it is important for senior management to give the employees who must make the budget work as much latitude as possible in determining the individual choices necessary to achieve a budget goal acceptable to top management and the board.

Different organizational structures call for different approaches to budgeting. Consider the structure of an organization with a group of specialized program professionals supported by an administrative staff. In this category would fall symphonies, dance companies, hospitals, universities, and museums. The specialized professional staff is considered the premier group within the organization. It is the group which implements the program of the institutions. In fact, in many institutions the program is seen as embodied in the persona of the specialized professional staff—viz., a symphony orchestra, a ballet, or university faculty.

In such an organization, each member of the specialized professional staff above the level of apprentice is often considered an equal with the same stake and voice in the affairs of the institution. Representation by such a group in the budgeting process is, therefore, a virtual necessity if the group's support is to be obtained. Decisions about budget resemble a political, rather than an executive, process.

In contrast, there are organizations that are more executive in their structure. In these organizations, there may also be a dichotomy between the backgrounds and goals of the professional and administrative staffs. However, the professional staffs are not thought of as embodying the program of the institution, although they may be its executors. Foundations and public television stations, for example, fall into this category. The staffs of such organizations are generally divided between program officers and administrative staff, but all are considered part of the executive group. Program officers are regarded equally with administrative staff as employees of the institution and subject to the direction of superiors in the hierarchical ladder. In such a structure, it may be possible to have a budget process staffed by executives from the finance area and managed without the benefit of a participatory committee of program professionals. However, whether that is the best strategy, even in such an environment, has to be evaluated on a case-by-case basis.

There are numerous models for structuring the participation of others besides the financial staff in the development of a budget in a political decision-making environment. One model used at Princeton provided for a "Priorities Committee," composed of administration officials and representatives of the faculty, staff, and students, to advise the president on the composition of the budget. Before the start of the budgeting process, the president, provost, and chief financial officer of the university met to assess whether the ultimate budget for the year should be balanced, or if a deficit was necessary and tolerable, or whether some kind of surplus should be achieved. Those who would manage the budget process were advised of the outcome the president initially favored. At most, one or two other guidelines might be established, such as: tuition increases should be part of the game plan for balancing the budget (although the amount of the increase would not be specified), faculty salaries had to be raised more this year than last (again without specifying how much), or that some expansion of the faculty was necessary. But within these limited guidelines, choices were left to be made by the committee established to advise the president on the budget.

In executive organizations, the budget is shaped primarily by the financial staff, but often with varying degrees of consultation with other organizational groups. Even in such an environment it makes sense to give as much latitude as possible to the people participating in the budget process, in terms of arriving at the budget goal that top management has set. If the staff and the executives managing the budget process are able to reach a consensus on how to achieve the budget goal, management should not intervene in the particular choices unless some totally unsatisfactory element has been part of the outcome.

For instance, in seeking budget reductions, make the department head first come up with his or her own suggestions. Choices will be better made by the person closest to the action, and also you will more likely have the person's cooperation if he or she is given an initial opportunity to devise his or her own budget reductions. At the same time as you invite employee participation, make sure that the key members of the board of trustees are also well-briefed. Give them a preview of the major issues at the outset and factor their concerns and questions into the budget review. Also preview with key trustees proposed budget recommendations before they are locked in.

Finally, remember the budget process will trigger as many emotional as rational responses. Hence, be sure that the nature of both the decision-making process and of the decisions made is effectively communicated to all constituencies.

In communicating with others in the organization about the budget:

1. Be sure to be candid. Explain negative developments. Be as specific as you can as to the causes of disappointing outcomes.

2. Don't claim more precision for projections than is possible. This will minimize negative reaction to an announcement that a prior year's forecast has proven to be off target. And be frank if you have made an avoidable forecasting error.

3. Put the report in a context (e.g., the impact on the budget of a changing business environment in which the organization operates). Help the audience to understand "why" things are happening as well as "what" is taking place.

4. Recognize from the outset that you will have to deliver the message to multiple audiences without drifting into inconsistencies. Accept that the tone and focus of the message may have to be varied according to the target audience.

In the case of the not-for-profit world, it is the program that attracts people to work for an organization and, therefore, people must feel they have a stake in the shape of that program. Put simply, people in a nonprofit organization care intensely about the substance of what the organization does; that's what motivates them to work for the institution, and it is just that kind of commitment and dedication that one needs to run a spirited not-for-profit organization. The budget process, which is so vital in setting the direction of an organization, must not only point the organization in an appropriate direction, but also gain support of the organization for that direction.

CUTTING THE BUDGET

Some time after developing this chapter, I participated in an expense-reduction exercise in a for-profit service organization that prompted several reflections on budget management: (1) the same managerial techniques and processes do indeed serve both for-profit and nonprofit businesses well, at least within the universe of service enterprises; (2) in both forms of organization there is generally little natural enthusiasm on the part of most managers for controlling or reducing expenses; it is not a process most of us find satisfying; (3) expenses will not be effectively reduced, regardless of the process employed, unless the enterprise's top executive establishes as a firm objective for the entire organization a specified level of cost reduction; (4) as important as the process adopted for identifying expenditure reduction is, equally critical is establishing a system to monitor whether promised cost-saving actions are in fact taken; (5) regardless of how effective such a monitoring program is, an organization will inevitably capture less than all promised expense reductions; accordingly, the target established for promised savings should be higher than necessary to achieve the desired financial goal; (6) expenses eliminated from the budget during a period of financial stringency will tend to creep back as soon as the budgetary heat is off and top management's attention is turned elsewhere; periodic cost-reduction exercises, supported by top management, are thus necessary to contain costs over time; and (7) one approach to soliciting proposed expense reductions is to ask managers how they would cut their budgets by certain percentages and to spell out the consequences attached to each level of reduction (i.e., a "top down" process); an alternative is for each organizational unit to analyze each activity it engages in to determine whether the costs are justified by the benefits (i.e., a "bottom up" approach). Whichever process is adopted, the key is to make all the officers responsible for managing organizational units understand they are personally responsible for achieving the savings target established by the top executive.

9

Tax Planning: Forethought Rather Than Afterthought

TAX PLANNING IS AS IMPORTANT to the successful operation of an exempt not-for-profit enterprise as it is to the success of a profit-making business. Exempt, nonprofit organizations must deal with a complex set of tax laws and regulations, many of which are peculiar to not-for-profit business while others are the same as those that affect profit-making companies. There are several benefits to paying attention to tax issues. Careful planning can shelter revenues which might otherwise be taxed or avoid nasty surprises on audit. Failure to comply with the tax law and IRS regulations can affect the very existence of a nonprofit entity as an exempt organization. Hence, tax planning for nonprofit organizations should not be left to chance.

In this chapter, as elsewhere throughout the text, our use of the term "nonprofit" refers to organizations which qualify under Section 501(c)(3) of the Federal Tax Code for exemption from federal income taxes and for gifts that are tax deductible by the donor. As we observed in "The Basics of the Exempt Organization," there are many nonprofit organizations which are exempt from income taxation, but what sets apart those which qualify under Section 501(c)(3) as a unique class is the deductibility of gifts to such organizations.

Nonprofit institutions once behaved as if they were ignored by tax authorities—this was in fact largely true in practice for many years. This is no longer a wise posture. The IRS, at the goading of Congress and taxable competitors of businesses operated by nonprofit entities, now has a staff section organized to deal with such organizations and the Service increasingly is scrutinizing the nonprofit world, especially in regard to unrelated business income tax. (IRS auditors typically are bent on finding revenue dollars for tax collection rather than reasons to lift organizations' exemptions.)

Moreover, Congress may one day insist on more stringent oversight. Remember, as was discussed in the chapter on the basics of not-for-profit organizations, abuse in the foundation world sparked the Tax Reform Act of 1969. Nonprofit organizations always must anticipate the possibility of even stricter tax oversight.

THREE TESTS UNDER 501(C)(3)

"The Basics of the Exempt Organization" reviewed briefly how the Federal Income Tax Code defines an exempt organization to which gifts are deductible on the donor's return.

You will recall that 501(c)(3) of the Tax Code exempts organizations:

1. organized and operated "exclusively for religious, charitable, scientific, educational purposes" (as well as a series of other socially useful purposes enumerated in the code).

2. no part of the net earnings of which inures to the benefit of any private shareholder or individual.

3. no substantial part of the activities of which is carrying on propaganda or otherwise attempting to influence legislation . . . .

Thus, there are three tests for exemption, each examined on the following pages.

Exclusively Operated for Specific Purposes

What does operated "exclusively" mean? It means that, under the IRS regulations, if more than an insubstantial part of an organization's activities is carried on for a purpose outside those defined as exempt in the code, the organization is not entitled to tax relief. Does this mean that no part of an organization's goals can be the generation of income?

The relevant IRS regulations provide that if the income-producing activities of a charitable organization further the organization's exempt purposes—i.e., if they are "related" to the exempt purpose—they will not jeopardize its exempt status. That is, the generation of such related income will not result in the organization being deemed to be operated for the primary purpose of carrying on a trade or business. On the other hand, if the income-producing activity is not related to the organization's exempt purpose, such activity can, if carried on with sufficient magnitude, threaten the exempt status of the organization. In other words, the organization's "primary purpose" can be held to be the carrying on of a "trade or business."

The fact that all of such unrelated income is applied ultimately to finance an exempt organization's activities doesn't protect its exempt status if generating unrelated income is deemed to be the organization's primary purpose. For instance, if 98 percent of an organization's time and effort is devoted to producing income and 2 percent to the writing of a check to the Red Cross in the amount of all its profits, the organization's primary purpose will be held to be the carrying-on of an unrelated trade or business.

Under IRS guidelines, an income-producing activity is "related" to the educational, charitable, or other exempt purposes of the organization if the production or distribution of the goods or the performance of the services from which the income is derived "contribute importantly" to the accomplishment of the exempt purpose, other than by producing income applied to its purposes. Under this test, a university's charging of tuition to its students would be "related," because educating the students contributes importantly to the university's exempt purposes. Conversely, the operation of a spaghetti factory by the university would not be "related," even though the income from the factory's operation is used for the university's exempt purposes. (This is an actual case—the factory earnings financed NYU Law School for many years.)

If the activity does contribute importantly to an exempt purpose, and its scale is related to carrying on an exempt activity, the profits it produces remain tax-free without any limitation on the size or extent of the activity. This principle was illustrated in Revenue Ruling 73–104, 1973–1 CB196. In this ruling, the IRS held that sale by an art museum of greeting cards displaying printed reproductions of art works contributed importantly to the achievement of the museum's educational purpose by stimulating and enhancing public awareness, interest, and appreciation of art. In reaching its conclusion, the IRS reasoned that the greeting cards encouraged a broader segment of the public to visit the museum and share in its educational programs and function. The IRS stated, *"The fact that the cards are promoted and sold in a clearly commercial manner and sold at a profit and in competition with commercial greeting card publishers does not alter the fact of the activities' relatedness to the museum's exempt purposes."* (Emphasis added.)

In reaching its conclusion on the relatedness of the greeting card activity to the museum's exempt purpose, the IRS expressed no concern with the size or extent of the business. Presumably, the more greeting cards sold, the more the public was informed about the museum's works of art and the more the public was made aware of the museum's programs and functions.

If an income-producing activity does *not* contribute importantly to exempt purposes except to raise funds, its profits constitute unrelated business taxable income, unless the income falls within the statutory exceptions for rental, royalty, dividend, or interest income. Such so-called passive investment income is exempted from unrelated business income tax.

As noted above, an organization's exempt status will be jeopardized when the magnitude of such unrelated business activity is so great that it raises the question of whether an organization is organized and operated for the *primary purpose* of carrying on unrelated business activity. The "primary purpose" test is essentially a proof requirement. The decisive issue is thus whether, in consideration of all the facts and circumstances in a given case, the organization's real purpose is charitable, or whether it is that of carrying on unrelated trade or business.

No Inurement of Income

The second test for exemption is that no part of the organization's net earnings may inure to the benefit of a private individual. Since an exempt entity by definition has no owners, how can income inure to the benefit of a private individual (apart from obvious abuses like "scholarships" awarded only to the donor's children)? Unreasonable compensation can be a disguised method of providing income to a private individual. Other forms of benefits can also mask the inurement of income to private individuals such as an advantageous interest rate loan. The issue is, where is the line drawn between reasonable and unreasonable compensation? Essentially, so long as the compensation payments adhere to arm's-length standards, comparable with similar salaries in the marketplace, they are permissible payments for an exempt organization.

However, where an exempt organization's compensation plan includes incentive arrangements, keying payments at least in part to percentages of revenue to be realized, the IRS has been inclined to apply special scrutiny. Traditionally, the IRS has approved such arrangements where there is a ceiling on the amount that can be paid under the percentage formula—and the organization demonstrates that both the formula and the amount meet the tests of marketplace comparability and reasonableness.

Accordingly, to ensure compliance with federal tax standards, a nonprofit organization's compensation policy should be governed by these principles:

1. The compensation paid to any individual should not be excessive when compared to amounts received by others similarly situated, having comparable responsibilities and handling similar tasks.

2. Any incentive compensation based on a percentage of the profits of the activity in which the individual participates should, in addition to meeting the above test, be subject to a ceiling limiting the total that can be paid under the formula to a dollar amount that can be shown to be reasonable compensation for the services rendered.

An IRS pronouncement on the subject of incentive plans (GCM 38905, June 11, 1982) seems to indicate a relaxing of its attitude toward such arrangements. The IRS declared in respect of incentive plans that:

> . . . so long as it [the plan] constitutes no more than reasonable compensation for services rendered, [it] is not necessarily incompatible or inconsistent with accomplishment of the exempt purposes of the employer, but may, indeed, be merely incidental thereto. Thus, we have come to believe the Service's effort should now be grounded in recognition of this fact, and concentrated on devising rules to assure that the benefit to the exempt function is realized. In short, we think an exempt organization should be permitted to establish and operate an incentive plan that devotes a portion of its receipts to reasonable

compensation of productive employees. The only concern of the Service should be that the plan is properly conceived and administered.

The underlying basis for this change was a recognition that:

> . . . benefits derived from incentive compensation plans generally accrue not only to employees, but also to charitable employers (e.g., increased productivity, cost stability) in aiding rather than detracting from the accomplishment of their exempt purposes.

The quoted pronouncement further suggests that in reviewing such plans, the IRS will focus on whether the plan is a reasonable and necessary means of attaining a benefit for the nonprofit enterprise (e.g., obtaining expert services traditionally not available except on an incentive basis), whether the plan makes provision to deal with any conflicts of interest that may develop between the benefited employee and the exempt organization, and above all, whether it can be shown that the arrangement could interfere with the accomplishment of the exempt organization's charitable purposes.

The inurement test can also pose an issue in the case of economic development activities by a nonprofit in cooperation with private interests (e.g., syndications of low- and moderate-income housing financing packages). In such cases, the nonprofit must show that the exempt activity could not have been undertaken but for the assistance of the private party.

Propaganda, Legislation, and Electioneering

The federal tax law withholds tax-exempt status from otherwise exempt organizations if their attempts to influence legislation go beyond acceptable limits or if they intervene in an election campaign. Note that in respect of attempts to influence legislation, the statute permits certain levels and kinds of activity, but in the case of elections it establishes an absolute test. Moreover, as we discussed in the section, "The Basics of the Exempt Organization," the statute imposes more stringent limitations on the political activities of private foundations.

One of the anomalies of the federal limitation on political activities is that it applies only to organizations seeking the benefits of Section 501(c)(3); other forms of nonprofit enterprise are not subject to such limitations on their political activities.

Suffice it to say that this section of the law is a thicket of complex legalisms peculiar to the Tax Code. For instance, the statute's restrictions on efforts by public charities to influence legislation actually leaves many openings for such activity. Among these are:

- The activity, although it involves influencing legislation, is permissable if it is an insubstantial part of the organization's activities. (There is now the option of escaping the statute by confining lobbying to certain amounts.)

- The activities are deemed to be a passive response to a legislative inquiry, or "technical assistance" to a legislative body.

- The activities are not directed at influencing legislation but at shaping executive branch actions or the actions of the judicial branch. Actions by an administrative agency are probably also open to lobbying by a public charity. Of course, if action is directed toward the executive or judicial branch in order to move them to influence legislation, then the statute applies. In other words, it is the nature of the governmental action that an organization seeks to influence, that counts under that statute.

- The activity may be deemed a permissable educational activity. Under IRS regulations an "educational" organization is specifically left free to advocate a political point of view so long as it presents a sufficiently full and fair exposition of the pertinent facts to permit an individual or the public to form an independent opinion or conclusion. Thus, study, research, and analysis of public policy questions are outside the reach of the statute as long as they are nonpartisan and the results are made available to the public.[1]

Once an organization has met the "exclusivity" and "inurement" tests—and provided it is not engaged in prohibited political activities—it qualifies as exempt under 501(c)(3). Of course, compliance is not determined only at the time exemption is applied for but must continue during the nonprofit's actual operations. Assuming the basic statutory criteria are met, the critical tax issue is then whether the exempt organization is classified as a "public charity" or "private foundation."

PUBLIC CHARITY VS. PRIVATE FOUNDATION

As noted in "The Basics of the Exempt Organization," the Internal Revenue Code divides section 501(c)(3) organizations into two categories: (1) public charities and (2) private foundations. A public charity is one that normally receives a substantial part of its support from governmental units or from direct or indirect contributions from the general public. Public charities are considered to have constituencies which oversee their activities, thus obviating the need for the type of legislative constraints imposed on private foundations.

Retention of public charity classification is highly important. Private foundations are subject to a number of special restrictive rules, applied to them by the Tax Reform Act of 1969. For example, a private foundation can generally hold no more than 20 percent interest in any business venture; it is subject to an excise tax on its investment income; and it qualifies to receive grants from other private foundations only where special requirements are met.[2]

---

[1] For those interested in a fuller understanding of this part of the tax code, see Treusch and Sugarman, pp. 177–206).

[2] If an organization receives more than a 20 percent interest by gift, the statute provides time for it to reduce its holdings to 20 percent.

Section 509 of the code enumerates special types of organizations that by definition qualify as publicly supported charities. In addition, there is the specially regulated type of publicly supported organization defined in code Section 170 (b)(1)(A)(vi). There are two ways in which organizations can qualify as publicly supported charities under that section of the code. One is the so-called "mechanical test." Under it, an organization must receive 33⅓ percent of its financial support from governmental units or through contributions from the general public.

Second, if an organization is unable to satisfy the mechanical test, it still may qualify as a publicly supported organization under a "facts and circumstances test" if (1) at least 10 percent of its support is normally derived from the general public or from governmental sources; (2) it carries on an active program of solicitation of public support; and (3) it possesses a combination of certain other factors indicative of public support.[2a] Both of these support tests are computed on the basis of an organization's sources of support over generally a four-year period immediately preceding its current tax year. (Under certain circumstances, this period may be varied.)

Under both the "mechanical" and "facts and circumstances" tests, it is necessary to review and classify the sources from which the organization derives its financial support. Certain quite technical rules govern this process. Generally, grants from governmental agencies and other public charities constitute public support without limitation.[3] That is to say, they are included in full, both in the numerator and in the denominator of the fraction used to determine whether an organization has derived 33⅓ percent, or 10 percent, of its support from public sources. Contributions from individuals, trusts or corporations, and grants from private foundations for particular projects count as "public" support (the numerator of the support fraction) to the extent that the contributions or grants from any one individual or entity do not exceed 2 percent of the organization's total support for the period. The total for such contributions and grants is included in the denominator of the support fraction without regard to the 2 percent limitation.

To the extent that income is derived from exempt functions, it is properly classifiable as income from exempt activities. As such, it is excluded by statute from both the numerator and denominator of the support fraction in the computation of public charity status. On the other hand, income from any activities that are unrelated to such purposes is included only in the denominator of the support fraction. (All investment income goes into the denominator.)

[2a] The most significant of these factors are the public nature of the organization's governing board and the extent to which its facilities or programs are available to the public.

[3] In this connection the fact that the agreement pursuant to which a payment is made is designated a "contract" or a "grant" is not determinative [Reg. 1.509(a)-3(g)]. A grant usually is made to encourage the grantee organization to carry on certain programs or activities in furtherance of its exempt purposes. However, the term "grant" does not include amounts received for a specific service or product that the payee provides to serve the direct and immediate needs of the payer.

The foregoing "technicalities" bearing on the classification of an organization as a "public charity" or "private foundation" will undoubtedly be quickly forgotten by most readers. What should be remembered is that there are significant consequences to each classification.

Tax Treatment of Different Forms of Income

Assuming an organization is determined to be a "public charity" for tax purposes, it may receive three different classes of income:

1. exempt,

2. unrelated but nontaxable,

3. unrelated and taxable.

Income which is related to an organization's exempt purposes is not subject to tax, regardless of the amount involved. This is the point of the museum ruling discussed a few pages earlier.

An activity, as noted earlier, will be "related" if it contributes importantly to the accomplishment of an exempt purpose—e.g., if it assists directly in the carrying-out of exempt objectives. In the case of Children's Television Workshop, for example, products such as magazines, books, puzzles, and games are "related" in that they directly supplement the Workshop's educational television programs, or they are educational in and of themselves. In such circumstances, no part of the income received would constitute income from unrelated trade or business which would be subject to tax. This conclusion would follow whether or not the income falls within the special exception to the unrelated business income tax for "royalties," "rents," "dividends," and "interest."

Income unrelated to exempt purposes (Sec. 513) is income from "any trade or business the conduct of which is not substantially related . . . to the exercise of [a] charitable, educational or other purpose or function constituting the basis for exemption."

In the case of CTW, for example, the making of commercial, purely entertaining movies would be an unrelated activity. If income is unrelated, it is subject to income tax at normal corporate rates *unless* it is "investment income" which is defined as "dividends, interest, rent and royalties." Investment income remains exempt from tax. This is the unrelated but nontaxable class of income referred to above.

A royalty is exempt as investment income, but defining what constitutes a "royalty" is not always a simple matter. For example, what distinguishes a "royalty" from a share of profits in a joint venture (in which case the income may be held to be unrelated trade or business income)?

Whether income is royalty or profits from a joint venture is a question of fact.

The key factors are the degree to which an exempt organization is active in the business from which the income is derived and the nature of such involvement. A limited amount of business activity by a nonprofit entity, designed to protect its name and ensure the quality of the product associated with that name is permissable—indeed, one is required by law to police the use of a trademark in order to maintain its validity. But a nonprofit organization's involvement in the running of the business—such as participation in marketing and promotion decisions to enhance sales—will rule out treatment as a royalty. The decisive test is whether the exempt organization's activities are related to quality control or to enhancing profitability; in effect, whether the exempt organization is a "passive" recipient rather than an active participant in the business from which the income is derived.

Good records can be important in determining whether or not income is classified as a royalty. The taxpayer, not the IRS, has the burden of proof in any challenge, and thus documenting one's practices can—assuming they are correct from a tax viewpoint—be helpful in any audit.

Planning Exempt Unrelated Income

Early tax planning can alert management to the possibility of structuring *unrelated income* so it is received in a tax-exempt form. For example, a nonprofit organization can negotiate a contract to receive revenues from a business as a license (rather than a joint venture), producing "royalties" that are exempt as investment income. But there is a trade-off. In licensing, the nonprofit organization gives up the possibility of acquiring an equity in the business and limits development of its business skills in the fields covered by its licensing program. Also, a nonprofit institution's right to review quality will still give it less influence in the design of a product than if it were actively involved in its creation. Accordingly, you always want to weigh tax vs. nontax business advantages carefully.

A nonprofit organization also can structure taxable, unrelated business income to minimize taxes, like offsetting the profits of unrelated business activities with certain losses of other unrelated business activities. This is the same kind of planning profit-making companies do (although losing money is the most costly form of tax shelter). Examples of more economic forms of shelter include the use of investment tax credits and accelerated depreciation to reduce the taxable gains of an unrelated business activity.

SUMMING UP

You have just taken a technical trip through the Kafkaesque world of the Internal Revenue Code, which has its own form of logic and language—a code that does not, to borrow a term from the computer world, speak in a natural language. Yet nonlawyers and nonaccountants can master it well enough to grasp its basic principles, speak comfortably with experts on the subject, and even challenge expert advice. Coping with tax problems is a mix of learning enough yourself to understand the issues and finding counsel on whom you can confidently rely for advice and education.

Nonprofit entities require the same expert advice on tax matters as profit-making companies and thus ought to have available to them an attorney who is expert in this field. At the same time, though, you should not simply treat everything tax counsel says as the "Sermon from the Mount." In fact, you never want to be at the mercy of such experts who may give you answers out of their own comfort rather than what serves you best. You have to understand the issue well enough to know which decision is yours to make and which should be left to counsel. Understand, therefore, where counsel is coming from . . . when his or her advice may be colored by what is the easiest or safest advice to give.

It is an oversimplification to talk of tax "law." The term "law" in the tax field often is used loosely to refer to statutes interpreted by court decisions, IRS regulations, rulings, technical advice, and private interpretations. Each of these has a different weight and importance in establishing the rules of appropriate tax behavior and treatment. Insist counsel be clear on just which of these sources his or her advice is based.

Look to counsel to distinguish when it is absolutely clear that an activity will be subject to taxation (and even to penalties) and when you are embarking on a course with uncertain and unclear tax consequences. Press counsel to assess the degree of risk to which you may be exposed, but reserve to yourself the business judgment whether to assume such exposure.

In some cases, obtaining a revenue ruling from the IRS can be a useful insurance policy against an individual agent later coming up with an adverse view of a transaction. In the end, whether to seek such a ruling is worth the costs is a business judgment. Some tax lawyers are prone to advise, "Let's get a ruling," since that does not expose their judgment to the risk of being wrong. But obtaining a ruling can be time-consuming—time you may not be able to afford from a business viewpoint—and sometimes it is unwise to ask certain questions of the IRS. They are not a judicial body charged with impartially administering the Tax Code but a collection agency seeking to maximize the flow of revenues to the government. Sometimes it is prudent not to put them on the spot. Whether one needs a ruling is a business decision as much as a legal one. The decision to seek a ruling must finally be made by the client and not the attorney.

Most tax decisions really involve dollars and cents—not outright prohibitions of a proposed course of action. You can engage in an unrelated trade or business: viz., there is no prohibition against it but you will pay taxes on the income unless it is in the form of dividends, rent, interest, or royalty. But the economic effect of paying the tax can be calculated, just as in a profit-making business context. Paying taxes is not a bar in and of itself to any action by a not-for-profit enterprise.

I have said *most* tax considerations translate into dollars and cents, but some may have implications beyond a simple financial calculus. In the case of a nonprofit institution, certain actions (e.g., distributing net earnings to individuals or, in an extreme case, engaging in prohibited political action) can cause an entity to lose its status as an exempt not-for-profit organization. And a loss of public charity status can subject it to operating restrictions and limitations.

In structuring activities, you must weigh tax considerations against business and programmatic considerations where the two are in conflict. As a manager, you cannot let tax considerations dictate automatically the form of the enterprise or the deal. On balance, nontax considerations may provide a more compelling rationale.

As the title of this chapter implies, in the tax area, the Boy Scouts and Girl Scouts have got it right: be prepared . . . plan ahead and not after the fact. That means consciously asking for tax considerations to be examined at the early planning stages and for documenting carefully in writing the decisions that are made. The outcome of any dispute in the tax field, like other areas subject to government oversight, will be affected by the quality of an organization's paper documentation. Good records and documentation are often the first and best line of defense in the case of an IRS audit. This is another reason why careful and early attention to tax issues is important.

More likely than not, as in the case of your personal return, many tax decisions will fall in the gray area. There will be no clearly right or wrong answer. You have to make decisions in such situations out of a sense of what is the best way to protect the organization's long-term interest. Think how many times you can push your luck in the tax field before you run the risk that an auditor will come down hard on you out of irritation that you are always trying to get away with something.

In the tax field it does not pay to be too greedy. Sooner or later you are going to be audited, and if you overreach in the search for short-term profitability, the long-term tax cost can be very great.

IV.
Professionalization of Management

10

Developing Human Resources

NONPROFIT ORGANIZATIONS ARE ENTERING AN ERA of professional management, some eagerly, some kicking and screaming, but the trend seems inexorable. There is essentially no alternative if they are to meet the complex managerial challenges facing them in a constantly changing world. The search for new revenues and the planning processes described earlier in this book cannot be carried out except by a superb professional staff supported by able boards of trustees playing their appropriate roles.

Any organization—for-profit or nonprofit—inevitably creates a set of expectations for employees. The range of possibilities is very broad: hard work, skilled execution, and individual initiative may be valued highly by the organization, or at the other extreme, it may be acceptable to work only the minimum specified hours, to do only exactly what one is told, and to expect promotions to be based strictly on seniority rather than merit. Compensation policy, as we discuss below—and how that policy is administered—plays a critical role in shaping such expectations. It provides one way of giving employees a stake in outstanding performance and initiative rather than leaving them content to be mediocre performers of a rigid routine. Certainly, you cannot expect employees to strive for outstanding results if the compensation system does not reward such effort. For example, at one major nonprofit institution where all employees were awarded the same-percentage annual salary increases, a proposal to increase the productivity of certain staff functions died because no senior manager was prepared to be its advocate; the system simply offered no reward for taking the risk of introducing change, and so the status quo prevailed.

There is also a whole range of nonfinancial means for shaping employee attitudes. For instance, the behavior modeled by senior officials, a superior's praise of a subordinate's initiative, the nature of the people included or excluded from important organizational decisions, and training to upgrade staff skills, are among the obvious nonfinancial ways of influencing employee performance.

Clarity in setting expectations, from the highest to the lowest level of management, also affects employee performance. At the highest level, the board needs to talk out with the CEO precisely what it expects him or her to accomplish, and to reach agreement on priorities. In turn, the CEO must spell out his or her expectations of senior managers, and so on down the line. Serious problems can result when this doesn't happen. For instance, assume some members of the board want the CEO to concentrate on raising funds and building the external image of the organization. Others, however, expect the focus to be on cutting costs and in improving day-to-day operations. No consensus is reached; perhaps, as is often the actual case, the agenda of the CEO is not even reviewed with the board. Under these circumstances, the CEO's performance very likely will disappoint some trustees and produce a tension which ultimately can undermine the chief executive's ability to perform his or her position effectively. Moreover, it is highly probable that the confused signals given to the CEO by the board will spill over to the directions passed on to the staff.

Lack of clarity in setting expectations can shape employee performance at the most elementary level of an organization. This anecdote illustrates the point: a central stenographic pool in an academic setting suffered from widespread complaints from users about the high error rate. Investigation uncovered that the only message given to typists was for more speed; apparently no attention was paid by superiors to work quality. When asked how she expected the errors to be caught, one typist said, "Oh, we all count on the authors to do that. We're only interested in getting out the work as fast as possible."

A whole range of factors affect employee performance: the role models created by senior management, the organization's financial and nonfinancial rewards system, and the policies communicated to employees. Managerial acts of omission, as well as of commission, will influence employee attitudes. The manager who makes no effort to shape employee performance reinforces prevailing behavior through neglect. Consequently, management that wants better employee performance has to work at getting it and not simply take employee attitudes and expectations for granted.

For years, not-for-profit organizations tended to be managed through a combination of low-paid employees and the pro bono help, from time to time, of individual members of their boards of trustees. A swing toward the professionalization of nonprofit management has brought about reliance on a full-time staff, adequate in number and qualification, to manage the organization, with the board of trustees appropriately focused on setting policy and evaluating managerial performance.

In turn, upgrading the caliber of professional staff has led to an increasing awareness of the role that well-conceived and administered compensation programs play in attracting, retaining, and motivating able personnel. Progressive nonprofit institutions, instead of pressing employees to accept low wages because of the asserted psychic compensation of working for a nonprofit, now offer a package of salary and benefits in line with market rates for employees bearing comparable responsibilities in other nonprofit and profit-making organizations. Increasingly, such compensation programs are designed to provide incentives for outstanding performance rather than to treat all employees equally regardless of the quality of their work. (See pp. 164–165 for the change in the IRS attitude toward such programs.)

As the value of qualified professional staff has become more evident, attention also has been directed toward improving the process for hiring personnel. It is no longer acceptable to say, as one CEO of a major nonprofit institution did in brushing aside a plan to search systematically for able young people, "Whenever I need somebody, I just take the résumés out of my desk drawer that have come in over the transom. I don't have to look for good people."

A high turnover of employees costs an organization severely. It clearly pays today to develop systems for attracting the best employees, systems which actively help them to develop their talents and find meaningful opportunities for them to apply their energies. The best inducement for good people to stay with an organization is the chance to expand their talents through challenging assignments.

This chapter delves into a broad range of topics centered around the theme of how to attract and motivate highly competent management. It addresses, in particular, how compensation and benefit programs can be designed and administered to recruit and to support talented personnel.

The chapter also explores the various methods for recruiting new talent and for discharging employees who do not work out. Despite its importance, the latter is a subject rarely talked about.

The chapter begins with a look at any organization's most fateful personnel choice—the selection of its chief executive officer. It closes with a discussion of the impact of managerial style on organizational morale and performance.

SELECTING A CEO ATTUNED TO BUSINESS AND PROGRAMMATIC CONSIDERATIONS

The internal environment and biases of any organization are strongly influenced by its chief executive officer. It often is said that an organization is but an extension of the personality and point of view of its CEO. The modern not-for-profit institution requires first-rate professional management in all phases of its operations, business as well as program. The starting point in bringing about such management is at the top.

A chief executive officer who has the capacity to run the *business* as well as the programs of the institution can alter the managerial style and focus of a not-for-profit organization. Staff who find that the CEO asks routinely about the financial aspects of problems, challenges them repeatedly to find more efficient and productive ways of doing things, and probes continually for opportunities to save resources or generate new income, will quickly perceive that financial and business concerns are an important part of the institution's operations. Without such focus from the top, the business management is likely to become distinctly second-rate.[1]

At the same time, the CEO must have a deep feeling for the purposes of the organization and, even more, a vision of what the organization can become.

The ability to devise organizational strategy in turn requires a personal capacity to act on informed intuition—to sense the direction to go in before the facts are so clear and overwhelming that the choice is self-evident to almost anyone. The heart of organizational vision is "foresight"; equally critical is the disposition to act decisively on it, to make decisions, sometimes without the comfort of all the evidence one might ideally want. (If you wait until then, you become a reactionary rather than a leader.) Such foresight, when combined with the talent to communicate to fellow workers— to reach them in their guts as well as in their minds—is the gift of superior leadership.

Traditionally, the typical criterion for selection of a chief executive officer of a nonprofit organization has been eminence in its program area. Of late, there has been some increased attention to the managerial talents of candidates, and this has often sparked heated debates on whether a nonprofit institution should be headed by a leading practitioner in the organization's program field or by a professional manager.

In the search a few years ago to find a president for the Metropolitan Museum of Art, great controversy was stirred up when the board of the cultural institution announced that it would seek in a president someone capable of overseeing all the far-flung interests of the museum, including relations with donors and its commercial ventures, which had become an important source of revenues. The art functions of the museum, the board decided, would be headed by an art professional who would be subordinate to the president.

The Metropolitan's professional staff was angered by this approach because it implied that activities other than the art functions of the museum would be given higher priority. The professional staff members also felt that somone who was not one of their group could not possibly understand their concerns. Moreover, the new alignment appeared to them to give inordinate importance to revenue-raising activities of the museum, which the professional staff felt were already consuming too much time and attention.

That the Metropolitan's program professionals wanted someone who could grasp and relate to their world is understandable. As noted above, the CEO of any organization, for-profit or nonprofit, ought to have a feel for the principal activities and purposes of the organization, to understand the philosophical concerns of the institution.

---

[1] The correlation between a CEO who is interested in and able to comprehend financial data and the establishment of good financial systems has also been described in some detail in the chapter "Budgeting: Quantifying Priorities."

For this reason, it is a clear advantage to select as president a person who has some experience practicing in the nonprofit entity's main field of activity. But actual experience as a practitioner in the field of the organization's interest is not an indispensable requirement for managerial leadership. For example, as a university executive, you can define educational objectives for the institution and give effective support to its scholars without having made your own mark as one;[2] or, as a museum executive, you can be sensitive to defining artistic goals and supporting artistic values without being an artist.[3]

My point is that the choice of a CEO should not turn on whether the candidate is or is not an eminent practitioner, but whether he or she can perform the traditional functions of a chief executive of an organization:

- Defining the organization's priorities and values.
- Outlining a strategy for achieving its objectives (including the means of generating the resources it requires to perform its mission).
- Identifying qualified personnel to run the organization and motivating them to do so.

In essence, this was the initial view of the museum's board of trustees. Interestingly enough, in actual fact, the museum has over the past five years moved away from the idea of a single CEO to a concept of "dual leadership," with the president and the director of the museum's artistic activities serving as its coequal senior officers.

Under this system, primary responsibility for the museum's curatorial, educational, and conservation programs rests with its professional staff under the leadership of the director as chief professional officer. The director also serves as the principal spokesman for the artistic and scholarly mission of the museum.

The president of the museum is regarded as its chief administrative officer with oversight of government relations, labor relations, the museum's expansive merchandising program, security, and other support functions. The president and the director are also viewed as sharing certain responsibilities, particularly public representation of the museum and fund raising.

Under the system of dual leadership, both the president and director report as equals to the chairman of the board. Part of the chairman's role is to work with the

---

2 Princeton University in 1956 appointed as its president an assistant professor of classics who had not yet taught long enough or produced enough scholarship to earn tenure on its faculty. During his 15 years as president, no one doubted his support for scholarship and other interests of the faculty, as he turned out to be one of Princeton's outstanding presidents.

3 Raymond and Greyser (p. 132) make this observation: "The need for professional operation of arts organizations, particularly in light of financial pressures, has never been greater. In 1975, the board of The Metropolitan Opera decided not to renew Schyler Chapin's contract as general manager. It named the executive director, Anthony Bliss, principal administrative officer as well. Chapin is reported to have said that it was wrong for a nonprofessional to be in a professional job. Which leads to the question, 'Professional *what?*' As we have said, the truly professional arts administrator combines managerial talents with artistic sensitivity."

two officers in areas where their responsibilities overlap, in effect, making the board chairman CEO of the museum.

Despite internal and external skepticism about the effectiveness of this approach, in the spring of 1985, the museum's board of trustees reviewed its experience with this system of dual leadership and concluded that it had served the Met quite well.

ATTRACTING A TOP-FLIGHT PROFESSIONAL STAFF

Nonprofit organizations no longer can rely on the timely pro bono help of trustees and friends from the business and professional world to supplement the capabilities of their permanent staffs. In addition to needing a superb executive as CEO, the modern nonprofit organization requires a staff with professional and business skills equal to those of persons performing comparable tasks in the profit-making world. In particular, nonprofit institutions need people with a flair for producing income; entrepreneurs as well as cool analysts are essential if nonprofit organizations are to build up their revenues.

At the same time, nonprofit professionals must have the sensitivity and finesse required to manage in an environment that does not operate with the single-minded discipline of a bottom-line, profit-making business.

However, it is not easy to attract able people with business and professional skills to nonprofit organizations. This stems in part from the "soft" image these institutions have in the business and professional communities. Good people, especially young people, are concerned that association with a nonprofit organization may make them less marketable later on with business and professional firms.

A senior financial officer of a major nonprofit institution explained that the most difficult part of recruiting financial personnel is to convince prospects that association with a nonprofit organization will not tarnish their career prospects. "The term nonprofit," she observed, "however inaccurately, is associated in many business people's views with inefficiency, lackadaisical work habits, and lack of interest in imaginative financial work. Prospects for financial positions are concerned that coming with us will cut down on their future career options and also that we will not value or reward the contributions they can make to improve the efficiency or productivity of the organization."

In a good many nonprofit industries, the recruiting problem is further complicated by the fact that the organizations pay significantly more modest compensation than the profit-making world. This leads us directly into the subject of compensation policy for nonprofit institutions.

Compensation Policy

An organization's compensation system has a major influence on the nature of its culture. The objectives established by the system, either explicitly or implicitly, as well as the manner in which it is administered, will do a great deal to shape the tone of an institution's working environment.

For example, at Princeton University, one of the paramount values the university communicates to its faculty is a sense of equitable treatment. Every salary increase is a product of a process which begins with departmental recommendations and then incorporates a review by a university committee composed of the university's president, deans, and elected faculty representatives of different disciplines. This time-consuming, elaborate process is designed to ensure individual members of the faculty that their compensation cannot be affected by whimsical or coincidental relationships with a departmental chairman but that their performance will be reviewed at arm's length by peers and others in the university.

In contrast, an organization wishing to promote more direct responsiveness to departmental management may vest its departmental managers with greater discretion in setting salary awards, thereby sending a signal that individual employees' compensation will be determined largely by how well they respond to the expectations of their departmental heads.

A professional consulting organization decided some years ago it wanted to foster greater cooperation among its partners, both in developing clientele for the firm and in working through teams to serve clients. Therefore, it added the concept of "cooperation" to its explicit list of criteria by which partner compensation is set. Now each partner is obliged in turn to demonstrate not only the business he or she brings into the firm and his or her reputation in his or her field, but also specific ways in which he or she has worked with others in the firm. The managing partner of that firm is convinced that his organization's greater deployment of partners as a team, relative to its competitors, is attributable to this change in the compensation system. In contrast, other professional service organizations place greater weight, sometimes almost single-minded emphasis, in awarding compensation based on the amount of new business a partner brings in. Characteristically, these firms see more individualistic behavior on the part of their partners.

Institutions which are engaged in revenue-producing activities may wish to provide very substantial rewards for outstanding results and, conversely, sharper cutbacks when results are disappointing. Other institutions may decide to provide lesser swings in the individual compensation of profit center managers. In such cases, awards in good years may be tempered by the sense that the firm as well as the individual helps create success. At the same time, during years when the market is not as favorable, the individual is insulated somewhat more on the downside. Such a system may emphasize association with the firm more than a system with greater swings, which tends to emphasize individual performance.

In sum, the form of compensation system adopted and its manner of administration will send important signals to individual employees about the values of the institution. A compensation system needs to be constructed carefully to be fully consistent with the ethos management is trying to create. This point sometimes seems to be poorly understood.

Market Rate Compensation for Nonprofit Employees

If not-for-profit organizations want talented employees, especially ones with managerial skills, they are going to have to compete with business and government, and that means paying competitive or market-rate compensation.

However, studies confirm that not-for-profit institutions pay lower wages than the government and business institutions they compete with for talent. The Filer Commission reported that "work for nonprofit organizations has traditionally been paid less than comparable work in business or government."[4]

A 1978 study comparing salaries of college and university administrators with comparable business positions in institutions of similar size found that the salaries of executives in higher education lagged behind those in the business world by 40 percent.[5] And if salaries alone lag by 40 percent, the gap in total compensation, which includes benefits, incentive compensation, and perquisites, would be even greater.[6]

Baumol and Bowen in their 1966 study of the performing arts also found that compensation in that industry lagged behind business and the professions for comparable work. The two economists noted:

> Performing arts organizations in financial difficulty have often managed to shift part of their financial burden back to performers and to the managements who also are often very poorly paid by commercial standards. The levels of income in this broad field must be considered remarkably low by any standards."[7]

The argument is that lower salaries in the not-for-profit world are justified by the psychic compensation of working for an organization that does worthy things. But

---

[4] *Filer Commission Report*, p. 84. One estimate is that in 1972, the average worker in nonprofit organizations earned $5,853 per year compared to $7,452 for the U.S. worker in general (p. 328).

[5] Howard R. Bowen, *Academic Compensation, Are Faculty and Staff in American Higher Education Adequately Paid* (Teachers Insurance and Annuity Association College Retirement and Equities Fund, 1978, pp. 54–57). Bowen, professor of economics and education at Claremont Graduate School, also analyzed in his study the salary situation of faculty members and general service workers at colleges and universities. He concluded that all three groups of campus employees—faculty members, administrators, and general service workers—are slowing, slipping behind in relation to trends in other industries and occupations (pp. 16–20).

[6] For instance, compensation based on profitability of the nonprofit enterprise in the form of equity or direct profit-sharing is not possible. The tax code provides that no part of the net earnings of a 501(c)(3) may inure to the benefit of an individual. This rules out direct profit-sharing though not a bonus based on achieving specified performance objectives. (The distinction, as explored more fully in the chapter on "Tax Planning," is whether the payment is structured as compensation for services or as profit-sharing.) The absence of equity or profit participations deprives small new nonprofit organizations of the most attractive form of compensation available to them in competing with larger, more established companies.

[7] Baumol and Bowen, pp. 102–104.

does it make sense to say that a person should get paid less because he or she enjoys his or her work? An argument can be made for paying less than market wages to persons with positions that grant them great latitude in deciding what they will work on. The freedom they enjoy may be a fair trade-off for accepting lower than market-rate compensation. Tenured faculty members of a university are a case in point.

But an accountant who works for a nonprofit enterprise enjoys no such latitude; he or she receives no trade-off for being paid less than an accountant who works for industry, unless you presume the accountant working for an exempt organization is not going to have to work as hard as his or her peer in industry. This is precisely the implicit presumption of many nonprofit enterprises in paying below-market cash compensation. It has too often resulted in inferior management for the not-for-profit world.

There is an argument that some not-for-profit organizations can't pay competitive wages because they can't afford to. Where true, it presents a real problem. Such organizations can't afford to compete in the marketplace even if they'd like to. But still, the appropriate policy is to aim to be as competitive as possible in the marketplace with respect to salary and benefits.

Many who accept the notion of paying competitive salaries still caution, however, that a nonprofit institution ought not to want to pay so extravagantly that "dedication" to an organization's purpose is not an important part of the motivation of the people who work for the enterprise. This caution needs to be given some weight. Remember, the underlying ethos of a nonprofit entity—its rationale for being—is to serve a public purpose. You need people who are "turned on" by such a goal to staff a nonprofit organization and extravagant compensation can make personal gain the overriding appeal. Any nonprofit wants to avoid making this the primary motivation of its employees.

Benefits and Perks

A package of benefits—and frequently perquisites as well—is now an important part of the total compensation arrangements offered to employees of an increasing number of nonprofit organizations. Of course, unlike profit-making organizations, the cost of such benefits is not a deductible expense to the employer, and so the cost impact of such programs is greater in the case of tax-exempt institutions.

Along with new approaches to salary, nonprofit organizations are revising their thinking about benefits, in part due to increased employee attention to these so-called "fringes." Employees are focusing more on this aspect of their compensation today because of:

- the entry of unions into the nonprofit arena and their traditional interest in benefits.
- the crossover of employees from business and government to the nonprofit sector.

• the flow of government money, during President Johnson's "Great Society," into non-profit benefits; government grants in this period funded benefits, many times in organizations that had never before offered such forms of compensation.

Today, employees generally expect such programs to be part of their compensation, especially the major components: vacation and sick leave, medical and life insurance, and retirement.

Benefit programs have indeed become so embedded in our organizational culture, just as social security and Medicare-Medicaid have become an integral part of our national social system, that their administration cannot be taken for granted. Casual mistakes in administration—or cases of hardship which develop because of a flaw in benefit design—can today disrupt the morale of any organization. In addition, benefit plans are now subject to complex, frequently changing federal regulation, and expert advice is invariably required to establish and administer such programs.

At the same time, the cost of providing benefits, especially medical insurance, has become one of the major burdens on most organizations' budgets and is thus also causing management to look at benefit programs with a fresh eye.

For many organizations, benefits now run as much as 30 percent or more of base compensation. Since for most nonprofit organizations salaries constitute by far the largest item in the budget (from 50 to 80 percent), a 30 percent cost for benefits becomes, in and of itself, a large item in the budget. This burden is compounded particularly by the sharply rising cost of medical insurance. Many employers have found that the costs of their medical insurance premiums have been increasing at 20–40 percent per year, far more than the rate of increases in base salary; this reflects the general national problem in containing medical costs. For all these reasons, care and attention must be paid by management to the design and administration of benefit programs.

As benefits have become more expensive, they have also grown more complicated. To design and administer a benefit program today requires specialized knowledge of law, finance, labor relations, and personnel. There is now even a program at the Wharton Business School which grants a "Certificate Benefit Specialist" degree. For a benefit program to be effective also requires management to think about each benefit as part of an overall compensation strategy, not just as a "given" required from the historical past.

Undoubtedly, benefits are not as closely scrutinized by potential new employees as the terms of a salary offer. If you want to attract someone to an organization, it will be the cash you offer in terms of salary, rather than non-cash benefits, that will most likely be the principal enticement. Benefits, if designed with a purpose in mind, can, however, be an important part of the overall compensation picture, particularly in retaining the services of valued employees who have the psychological determination to stay with the organization "if it treats me right." The availability of a good package of benefits, which increases in value with increasing service, will help to convince such employees that they are being well-served by staying on.

For example, at a good number of the larger foundations retirement contributions by the employer tend to be 20 percent of salary, or nearly three times the contribution in a typical profit-making company. Most universities' retirement programs also result in a 20 percent contribution to retirement, although about 6 percent may come from the employee. At the 20 percent level an employee with long service can look forward to retiring on more money than he or she earns while working—a powerful inducement to people getting on in years to stay with their present employer rather than move to an organization which may pay more currently but puts less into retirement.

Unlike salaries, nonprofit benefit programs tend to be more generous than those of business, despite the paradoxical fact that private firms can deduct the costs of such programs against their taxes, savings obviously not available to tax-exempt organizations. In part, the nonprofit benefit picture reflects that at one time the low salary structure of nonprofit institutions made it relatively inexpensive to offer generous benefits. (Sometimes guilt about low salaries prompted generous benefits.) Also, persons within and without the organization who may be critical of salaries have simply not tended to examine benefit programs. Thus, while there may be pressure on nonprofit salary levels, benefits have actually tended to escape scrutiny (though their increasing costs may change this), and this has encouraged some prosperous institutions to offer relatively more generous benefit programs even while keeping a tight lid on salaries.

Benefits today range from the fairly common provisions for vacations, medical insurance, life insurance, and retirement to the more unusual arrangements for thrift plans and other forms of deferred compensation, and for individual perquisites such as allowances for spouse travel and special subsidized financing for the acquisition of housing. Each benefit can be structured in a variety of ways which affects both its appeal to employees and its cost to employers.

Vacation

Most organizations provide a sliding scale of vacation periods according to the length of service of the employee. Some institutions also differentiate the length of vacations according to rank. The amount of vacation leave awarded, in addition to paid holidays, is a real cost to the organization. Moreover, an organization can build up a significant liability for the accrued vacation leave if it allows employees to carry forward from one year to the next the amount of vacation earned but not taken, and at the end of their employment to receive cash in lieu of unused vacation time.

A good number of nonprofit organizations have overlooked this potential liability until it mounted up to a very material exposure. Most organizations that have focused on the issue believe the sounder policy is to limit the amount of vacation that can be carried over from one year to the next—in order to preclude any employee from being away for a disruptively long period—and, in any event, to bar converting unused vacation into cash.

Life Insurance

Most nonprofit organizations provide some amount of life insurance coverage for their employees, but generally less than private business offers. Usually, the amount is some multiple of base salary (typically 1–1.5 times annual salary) up to a ceiling amount for very highly paid employees (foundations will generally provide somewhat higher multiples). However, most nonprofit institutions' retirement plans also provide for the payment of death benefits, which supplement an employee's life insurance.

Sick Leave and Total Disability

Life insurance protects an individual and his or her family in the event of death. Medical insurance reimburses a person for the costs of treating an illness. In addition, virtually all companies also agree to continue an employee's pay if he or she is absent because of illness—but only for some limited period of time. What happens then, if an employee is unable to work because of an illness that continues for a period longer than the sick leave provided by his or her employer? This is where total disability protection comes in. If a person is in fact *totally* unable to work, and has exhausted his or her sick leave, many organizations now provide insurance that pays the employee some percentage of his or her income as long as the disability continues.

Medical Insurance

There is a wide variety of alternative medical insurance plans with different provisions regarding how much of the cost of an illness must be first paid by the employee before the insurance takes over (the deductible); how much, if any, of the cost in excess of the deductible must be borne by the employee (coinsurer); whether to provide insurance for maternity expenses or outpatient psychiatric treatment (both are expensive forms of coverage); whether to cover dental expenses (very expensive); whether to cover dependents of the employee without additional charge to the employee (also expensive); and whether to limit the total amount the insurer must pay out for any single illness or within a specified time period. The choice for all these options importantly affects the organization's costs, as does its actual experience. That is, if in fact claims exceed the amount anticipated when the insurance premium was set, the insurer will subsequently raise premiums to reflect actual experience.

Employers are taking steps to contain the rise in medical insurance premiums; these include requiring larger coinsurance payments and deductibles, obtaining second surgical opinions, referring employees to groups of physicians which have agreed to preset fees ("preferred provider organizations") and implementing so-called "wellness" programs to reduce the demand for health services.

Retirement Plans

There are two basic kinds of pension plans: a defined benefit plan and a defined contribution plan. A defined benefit plan is a program in which retirement benefits are paid out in the form of monthly annuities according to a published and known formula, usually related to years of service. Under such a plan, the amount of payout is thus fixed, but what is not known is how much money the pension fund will have to earn in order to make such payments. The obligation of the fund is calculated annually by an actuary.

A defined contribution plan is the exact antithesis of a defined benefit plan. Under a defined contribution, the employer makes a known annual contribution to the plan, say 15 percent of each employee's salary, but no promise is made as to the final amount to be paid out to the employee at the end of the plan. The advantage of the defined contribution plan is that it allows the employer to know in advance how much to budget for pension fund contributions.

The cost of a pension plan will be affected importantly by whether the retirement plan is noncontributory on the part of the employee, or whether the employee must contribute something to his or her retirement as well as the employer. Cost will also be impacted by how much of a contribution the employer makes for each employee.

The biggest impact on pension cost by far, although few organizations seem alert to this point, is the effectiveness with which the pension funds are invested. The connection between investment performance and the cost of a defined benefit program is self-evident. But investment performance tends to be overlooked in the case of defined contribution plans because there is no promise to pay out a specific amount of income at retirement. However, better investment results may enable an organization either to provide more retirement benefits for the same employer contribution or to reduce the amount contributed to the plan without reducing the benefits to employees.

Many pension plans now provide an opportunity for an employee to make a contribution over and above the minimum required under the plan. Such contributions, under Section 403-B of the Internal Revenue Code, are treated as "salary reductions" and are not taxed as current income to the employee up to the amount allowed by the code. In effect, this feature offers an attractive deferred compensation program for nonprofit employees; indeed, for many years there was no comparable benefit available to employees of profit-making corporations.

The benefits available under qualified pension plans are subject to complex limits established by federal law. The law (Section 415 of the Internal Revenue Code) now (1) limits the amount of funds that can be contributed annually to the defined contri-

bution retirement plans to $30,000 per year and (2) limits the maximum annual re-
tirement benefits payable to a retiree to $90,000 per year. (Both limits are open to cost
of living adjustments beginning in 1988.) In addition, the law places limitations on the
extent to which a pension plan favors the more highly paid employees over the less
well-paid employees.

Some employers are offering employees who reach the "pension cap" the alternative of investing the excess amount in a nonqualified deferred compensation
agreement.

Vesting

Most pension benefit plans provide that an employee must serve a fixed period of time
with an organization before he or she becomes entitled to the benefits paid for by the
employer. The object, of course, is to provide some incentive for employees to stay
with the enterprise.

Colleges and many other tax-exempt not-for-profit organizations use Teachers
Insurance and Annuity Association/College Retirement Equities Fund (TIAA-CREF)
to invest pension funds and to administer the distribution of such funds. TIAA-CREF
was founded many years ago, at a time when the universities were beginning to struggle
to provide pensions for their faculties and staffs. TIAA-CREF, unlike most other pensions, is fully vested from the first contribution. That means that should the employee
leave an employer, even after one year of service, whatever has been contributed to
TIAA-CREF in the way of a pension fund contribution remains invested on behalf of
that employee and is paid out upon reaching retirement age. In contrast, most private
pension plans and many other not-for-profit plans require a significant period of service
before one's rights to pension contributions become vested, and even then the vesting
may be phased over a period of years. For example, no vesting may take place for five
years, but then, in stages, the contributions may become fully vested over an additional
five years.

The TIAA-CREF pension plan also provides accumulated contributions which are
paid out on the death of the employee by way of death benefit. This feature provides
an additional life insurance over and above whatever may be provided under the
organization's life insurance program.

In the pension area, federal law now establishes limits on how long vesting can
be deferred—a provision designed to deal with abuses in industry in which employees
worked for years with a company only to find, when they changed jobs, that they had
no rights to the pension they had built up over the years.

Thrift Plans

A special benefit offered by some institutions is the thrift plan. In this plan, under some
formula an employer matches the contributions of the employees to a savings program.

The employer's contributions are not taxable to the employee until he or she takes out those contributions. The thrift plan thus adds an employer's contribution to the employee's savings and provides for tax deferral as well. Usually, the employer also arranges for a number of investment options for the funds contributed by employees.

Some nonprofit institutions in very strong financial positions may offer both thrift and retirement programs. More commonly, one or the other is all an institution can afford. Unlike a pension program, a thrift plan will allow an employee access to money while employed. He or she doesn't have to wait until retirement to collect. This feature may make it possible to offer a thrift plan in place of a retirement program, and with lower employer contributions than under a pension plan.

Deferred Nonqualified Compensation Agreement

A deferred compensation agreement is a binding legal contract between employee and employer under which the latter promises to pay a certain sum of money to the employee at a certain time in the future, and in a certain manner. The terms of the payment are agreed to before contributions to the program are made. Funding can be either by direct contributions by the employer or by a salary reduction arrangement whereby the employee contributes his or her own money. Contributions can be structured to be automatic or contingent on the employee achieving certain performance goals (as in a bonus). The employee will be taxed only when he or she receives the money.

The great advantage is that the funds invested compound tax free until drawn down, thus enabling the ultimate fund to be much larger than it would have been if contributions were taxed when made. Moreover, the assumption is that an employee will not draw down the funds until he or she is ready to slow down professionally and the employee is in a lower tax bracket than at the time the contributions were made.

The nature of the investment the employer makes with the contributions is usually established by the deferred compensation agreement as well as the time and manner of payout. But for the tax deferral to work, the employee cannot have the right to the specific sum being invested on his or her behalf; the employee's right is limited to collecting certain sums from the employer at certain times. If the employer becomes insolvent before the payment is due, the employer's creditors as well as the employee can claim access to the funds invested for the employee.

The Cafeteria Approach

With the range of benefits now available, one of the most frequently pressed issues is whether employees may choose among different benefits and select those which are more valuable to them than others at that point in their lives. For example, some employees prefer to have dependent medical coverage without contribution and generous life insurance benefits in place of participation in a retirement program.

Later in life, when the children have grown up, the employee may want to shift to a more significant contribution towards his or her pension and reduce the scope of medical coverage. While it is ideal in theory to allow employees to select from a menu of benefits and to change their selections from time to time, administering such a flexible program is complicated and can be expensive.

Perquisites

Many organizations provide some form of benefits, other than by means of a cash transfer, to a select group of key executives. These benefits, commonly known as "perks," can be important financially to both employee and employer and, despite the bad press they have received, can be a useful part of a total compensation package. Perquisites can be:

- a tax efficient way to reward key employees since, typically, they are not treated for income tax purposes as the receipt of income by the employee.
- a form of compensation that does not need to be extended to all employees but can be limited to a select few, thus keeping the cost down.
- a good way to "individualize" compensation arrangements by tailoring the perk to an individual situation.

Among the range of such perks may be the granting of a below-market rate mortgage to a key executive to enable him or her to acquire a family home, or in some cases a vacation home, the rent free use of a house (a common provision for university presidents) together with a staff to run the house, free use of a car (sometimes with a chauffeur), supplemental life, medical, or disability insurance, or reimbursement for the cost of a spouse accompanying the executive on business trips.

Although the awarding of such perks can be a useful way of working out specialized arrangements with key employees, the limited awarding of such perks also makes recipients a potential source of envy among employees who do not receive them, as well as rendering recipients vulnerable to public criticism. The best protection is finding precedent for such perks in comparable organizations, and in all events, insisting on their careful review and approval by a trustee compensation committee.

GOVERNMENT REGULATION

As benefit programs became more widespread in both the nonprofit world and in private business, abuses began to develop especially in the business sector and among labor unions. These abuses, as well as recognition of the growing importance of benefits, led to the passage of ERISA (Employee Retirement Income Security Act) in 1974. This statute introduced a federal regulatory scheme over benefits requiring that benefits be made available to all employees of the same class on a nondiscriminatory basis. Certain other safeguards were provided against the abuses that Congress had found in benefit programs. In turn, the program provided for federal insurance of certain categories of private pension plans. At the same time, ERISA, which is administered by the Labor Department, added to the burden of paperwork and regulatory oversight imposed on not-for-profit organizations.

In addition to ERISA, there are important aspects of benefit programs which must comply with the Internal Revenue Code, and these must be checked carefully in developing any plan.

The business of providing benefits has become complex and costly enough so that most organizations of any size now employ, on a full-time basis, one or more staff experts to handle their administrations. They also often retain specialized outside consultants.

TRUSTEE COMPENSATION COMMITTEE

Given the sensitivity of compensation awards both to the morale of the organization and to public criticism, it is a vital necessity that an organization's policies and procedures in this area be reviewed and approved by a committee of its board of trustees who have no affiliation with management. Such a committee should examine: (1) the overall program of compensation for all employees, including both salaries and benefits, (2) the system by which raises and any bonus or incentive awards are granted, and (3) studies by outside consultants of how the organization's compensation compares to that of other comparable institutions. In addition, the committee should review and approve the compensation proposed to be awarded to the organization's most highly paid executives on a case-by-case basis and, of course, it should establish the compensation for the chief executive officer. Perks awarded to individual employees should also be approved specifically by such a committee.

Still, the basic point remains that nonprofit organizations have tended to undervalue the contribution that superior management can make. Talented management can pay for itself in the nonprofit world as well as in the business community. Of course, any organization wants to be very careful that the people it hires care about its purpose. But, at the same time, if nonprofit organizations want to avail themselves of the best managerial talent available in the marketplace, then they need to offer *reasonably* competitive compensation as measured by the market.

ADMINISTRATION OF COMPENSATION POLICY

One day, a friend, who is a senior officer of one of the nation's most important urban cultural institutions, was comparing notes with me about the approaches to compensation of various nonprofit organizations. I learned that what is considered elementary practice by compensation professionals was not followed at my friend's organization, and doubtless at many other nonprofit institutions. The cultural organization of which my friend was an officer:

- awarded all professional employees the same percentage salary increase every year, thereby equally rewarding stellar and lackluster performers.
- established no personal goals for employees from year to year as part of the compensation process, leaving employees without a clear sense of what specific accomplishments were expected of them.
- neither established salary ranges for each different professional position, nor conducted surveys to determine the salaries paid by other organizations for comparable positions.

The absence of such systems left salaries to be fixed by ad hoc determination.

In effect, the cultural organization failed to see compensation policy as an important tool for making employees accountable for the quality of their work and for motivating good performance. The organization's approach also failed to appreciate the importance of compensation policy in setting institutional priorities.

In setting compensation policy there are three overriding objectives:

- competition with the external market,
- provision of internal equity,
- provision of differentiated compensation increases based on performance (a performance-based compensation system).

All three are complex to administer, but, as in so many areas of management, a well-conceived and administered "process" holds the key to achieving managerial goals. And once again, "communication" lies at the heart of effective process. Compensation policy is one matter that you can't explain too often to staff (i.e., what policies are being followed and how they are being administered).

Following is an examination of each of these three objectives:

Pay competitive with the market. What is the relative competitive market? How do you, for example, judge someone who comes to a nonprofit organization from the academic world, but whose future well may lie with the profit-making world (a computer scientist, for example)? Or in the case of a Children's Television Workshop television producer, is the relevant competitive market commercial television or public broadcasting? Salaries are quite different in these two worlds.

How do you measure what the market is paying? The Workshop annually employs an outside consulting firm to assess the competitive external market for each job position at the Workshop. The review is done annually because the market changes from time to time. The firm surveys what people in similar positions are paid, but it is a very imprecise system. Positions in other organizations are hard to compare with positions within your own institution, and some positions simply are not comparable to positions in other organizations. Furthermore, good data on pay in other institutions is often hard to come by.

Nevertheless, as imprecise as the process may be, it is still important to use it in order to create a sense with your employees that you are trying to live up to your commitment to pay competitively in the marketplace, and that there is some objective basis for setting pay levels.

Internal Equity. This means that within an organization positions of comparable importance have comparable pay opportunities.

At Children's Television Workshop, the process for determining internal equity involved staff of the Workshop rating jobs by specific criteria (such as required knowledge, skills, complexity, scope, and impact). The job and not the occupant is rated. This can be done with an elaborate weighting formula or intuitively, but it is critical to have broad staff participation in establishing comparability of jobs. After all, the comparison will not be scientific, and the art lies in consensus and a sense of fair process.

When the two principles are in conflict, external market consideration should normally prevail. But, in any given case, if a sense of equity is critical, you may lean more heavily toward internal equity than market factors.

Performance-Based Compensation. Too often the policy in nonprofit institutions is to give everybody the same percentage raise, as the anecdote at the outset of this section illustrates. That rewards mediocrity and penalizes superior talent. The compensation structure in the not-for-profit world ought to reward performance.

A performance-oriented approach puts a real burden on management to make choices between ordinary and extraordinary effort, but that is indeed possible, particularly if one establishes clear performance objectives at the outset of the pay period that are understood and accepted by the employee and manager. The delineation of such performance goals also becomes a prime tool for setting the direction of the company.

To keep the heat on managers to make compensation recommendations based on performance, central management needs as a minimum to review the salary distribution pattern of departmental managers in giving increases and cross-examine a manager who does not show a reasonable spread between superior performance and ordinary performance in awarding salary increases. Another device is a bonus pool that is administered centrally upon application by particular managers to award specified employees.

The review of "performance relative to objectives" in connection with compensation awards is probably the most important management function any manager performs, and yet is generally the one done with the least care and attention. Central management needs to educate managers how to do this and to provide them with formats for executing personnel reviews without bogging staff down in tedious bureaucratic paperwork.

A genuine problem with all performance-based compensation systems in an inflationary period is the limited amount of real, after-tax money available for raises.

Typically, the salary increase pool will not be meaningful enough, after the bite for inflation and taxes, to provide *real* incentives to employees for superior performance. In many cases, the difference between a 6 percent increase and a 10 percent increase does not turn out to make a meaningful difference—after taxes and inflation—to the employees involved.

Nonprofit institutions ought to consider greater utilization of bonuses for truly outstanding performance—and rely much more on discretionary bonuses than formulas—to avoid the awarding of bonuses becoming regarded as a "given" by eligible employees.

THE RECRUITING PROCESS

Plainly, the key to an organization's future lies in the quality of the hiring it does and how well it nurtures good talent once it is recruited. Frequently in the not-for-profit world this is another of the least-considered aspects of management.

"Every person chosen right," the head of one of the nation's most efficient transportation companies once observed, "can have the most singular impact on productivity."

This has to be especially true of service industries, the nature of most nonprofit enterprises. Consequently, the recruiting process must be a critical concern of nonprofit management.

Ironically, in many nonprofit organizations the process of recruiting talent is done well for program employees and haphazardly in the case of administrative workers. Universities, for example, have relatively well-developed processes for recruiting new faculty, yet search in a random, casual way for administrative talent. The point is that a successful nonprofit enterprise must make a major investment in recruiting and nurturing all of its employees.

There are a number of mechanisms for recruiting people:

- advertisements,
- word of mouth,
- applicants who happen to appear at the door,
- recruiting by executive search firms,[8]
- search committees.

There is no one method that promises better results than the others. The most critical factors in making good choices are:

[8] An executive search firm is retained by management and recruits at its request. Regardless of who in the end finds the person selected to fill the job, the firm collects its fee. A standard fee of a search firm is about 30 percent of the first year's total compensation, so it is an expensive mechanism. An employment agency searches on behalf of employees and gets paid by the employer only if the employer hires a candidate of the firm.

- a clear sense of organizational purpose.

- a clear job description including a carefully drawn set of qualifications for candidates.

- a good internal screening process, so that both the candidate and the organization get a real chance to know each other. It is important to screen applicants for their psychological fit as well as their skill fit.

- a careful review of references in the employee's prior record (state laws relating to reference checks can now make this a more complex task).

There are no shortcuts to this process. Existing staff in the organization have to spend time interviewing candidates, checking with people who have worked with the candidates earlier in their careers (ideally these should be independent sources and not just the candidates' handpicked references), and where feasible, examining samples of their work. Based on my experience, in the case of at least important hires, it is worthwhile to have a skilled psychological interviewer see candidates to explore their emotional fit with both the organization and the particular position for which they are being considered.

Still, hiring is a percentage business and some poor choices will inevitably be made. Hence, you must have the nerve to fire as soon as you decide you've made a mistake.

HOW TO DISCHARGE EMPLOYEES HUMANELY

One of the skills that is very rarely discussed in business or management schools, but that is critical in managing an organization, is how to fire people. It's distasteful, unfortunate, and a very severe blow to an employee, but it is a necessary part of organizational life. Doing it well can be critical to the success of the organization and, certainly, to minimizing the damage and pain to the affected employee. In fact, firing people well is as critical as hiring people well.

From my own experience, the best way is to be as clinical and surgical about it as possible without being brusque or seeming unsympathetic. Being let go is a powerful form of rejection, and anyone being discharged is going to feel deeply hurt. Elaborate details, explanations, hesitation, indirection, and indecisiveness all make the situation worse. Don't beat around the bush. Get to the point quickly. Be sure to give a specific reason for your action. Be candid, too. In the long run, a discharged employee will handle the truth more easily than circumlocution. And make the explanation short, simple, and easily understood. Then, quickly get beyond the discharge to what's going to be done to cushion the blow to the employee. For example, spell out what the severance benefits are, what kind of out-placement counseling is available, and what other kinds of help you are willing to offer, including what you will say to people who might call for references about the person. These are the life and death questions that discharged employees face.

As an employer you have some obligation to help an employee you have let go make a transition to a new job. This is true even when the employee is being discharged because of unsatisfactory performance. After all, if the employee doesn't work out, it's at least 50 percent your mistake. You made the misjudgment to hire that employee in the first place, and you had a better idea than the employee of the kind of environment he or she was coming into, and what the expectations and the requirements of the position were. In a sense, it is as much your responsibility for misjudging the employee's capacity as it is the employee's responsibility for failing to perform up to expectations. (Obviously we're not talking here about the case in which the employee has engaged in wrongdoing or abused his or her position in some way.)

Accordingly, in discharging an employee, an employer should support the person in finding new work. Indeed, it is in any organization's self-interest to develop a reputation as a thoughtful and fair employer in the circumstances where a discharge is involved.

DEVELOPING TALENT

Beyond selecting good talent, there is a need to develop the talent once it is on board. The identification of such promising talent and its development is not something that can be done only by subordinate managers; it must be a prime concern of higher management. The critical factors in developing talent are:

- compensation policy that especially rewards outstanding performance rather than all employees equally.
- active identification by top management of the superior young personnel in the company and ensuring that they are being moved along a path that is interesting to them, and gives them an opportunity to develop.
- making sure such employees are aware they are considered outstanding prospects and know of their opportunities for growth.

A real problem in many nonprofit organizations is that there is not a great deal of room at the top. The organization that has only a very few jobs at senior levels can stifle opportunities for its younger staff. One antidote is to make sure that when good people reach a bottleneck, the organization assists such people in finding outside jobs. This will help the organization gain a reputation of being a good place to work because it gives a boost to an employee's career.

MANAGERIAL STYLE

Until now, this chapter has concentrated largely on certain of the explicit choices, tools, and processes by which a staff is built and motivated. But there is a more subtle aspect to leadership than our discussion has implied so far; it turns on the style by which one manages an enterprise. The manner in which one leads, as much as one's substantive skills, shapes the character of an enterprise.

Put another way, managers should be aware that they are instructors. Instruction may take place through explicit communication or role modeling. A manager is always a teacher and he or she constantly needs to focus on how managerial behavior is indeed instructing others.

I once asked the chief executive of a major corporation how he accounted for the turnaround of the company's fortunes under his leadership. He replied, "I selected very good people to work for us and then spent my time making them feel good."

Inherent in making people "feel good" is giving them a sense of recognition—that their contributions are known by their peers and valued—and that they are being treated fairly.

By definition, supporting people also means taking the time to be available to them—to listen to them and, more critically, to "hear" them. Perhaps this is the most vexing of all managerial tasks since it always seems that one is so pressed for time. Onetime CTW TV producer Ethel Winant claimed that CBS' William Paley, in contrast to me, had a clear desk and was always glad to have her visit him and fill up part of his day. It may be an apocryphal story, but creating the sense of personal accessibility is crucial to leadership.

Small touches can be critical, too. For instance, calling staff you do not come in contact with very often by their first name or returning phone calls, even a message to say you will call back later, are important gestures. President Jimmy Carter's reputation with Congress was badly undermined from the very outset when his legislative liaison developed a reputation for not returning phone calls.

Being supportive also means "letting go"—giving people a chance to exercise their talents, even though they may falter for a time. A meaningful degree of autonomy in pursuit of agreed-upon goals is required for individual executives to flourish and to produce the innovations any organization requires. It takes secure, intelligent leadership to accept the risk of imperfect performance by subordinates, and to know when to intervene and when to lay back.

Being supportive also means providing enough clear backing for managers that they are not easily subverted or circumvented in their decisions. Inevitably, change generates some organizational resistance. If top executives back down simply because a new policy is unpopular, staff resistance to change will intensify. Obvious as this may sound, more organizations than you may think place such a high premium on avoiding internal conflict that they often sacrifice change and innovation.

Above all, the character of any executive intervention with subordinates must be *consistent*. The most bitter complaint I heard against the CEO of one nonprofit organization was that he intervened capriciously, so you could never really tell when he was going to be interested in something or to ignore it. How he acted might turn on something as random as his dinner table conversation the night before or his contacts at social gatherings.

Management communication must avoid hidden agendas. "Clarity," "consistency," and "candor" are keys to effective communication. Deliberate camouflage of the real message can only breed confusion and, ultimately, distrust. On occasion, people may not like your message, but you will intensify their anger and breed distrust if they perceive that what you say is not always what you mean.

Finally, and perhaps paradoxically—making people feel good means at times not deferring to their views. If you are the senior person, your subordinates will expect, even if they don't say it aloud, that you will make choices out of your own knowledge and experience, and not always yield to the majority's view. As a leader, you are expected to have a personal point of view and to be able to articulate it in order to give direction and coherence to the work of an organization.

11

Managing Your Board: Building A Partnership

OVER THE YEARS I have found that professionals as well as students regard boards of trustees with a combination of awe and mystery. The regard stems from an appreciation of the position board members commonly hold in their professional lives. The mystery appears to stem from a limited sense of just what a board is supposed to do and how management is to relate to it.

THE ROLE OF THE BOARD

The board of trustees of a typical not-for-profit organization is its final governing body. Unlike profit-making enterprises where directors are chosen and removed by the business' owners, a board of most tax-exempt nonprofit institutions is, as a practical matter, responsible only unto itself. The exception to this rule, as pointed out in "The Basics of the Exempt Organization," are membership-based organizations. The trustees of most nonprofit institutions, however, select their own members, fix their own terms, and account only to themselves, subject only to such scrutiny as the IRS or state attorney general may exercise. Thus, trustees of an exempt organization have unusually broad latitude in governing the affairs of their organization.

It is difficult to characterize in general how boards behave in the nonprofit world—just as it is to do so for boards of profit-making enterprises. In my experience, board behavior ranges from passive and exceedingly deferential to the CEO to quite assertive and even interventionist. Miriam Wood, in a *Harvard Business Review* article,[1] suggests

---

[1] Miriam Wood, "What Role for College Trustees" (*Harvard Business Review*, May/June 1983, p. 52).

college boards follow one of three operating patterns: (1) ratifying style (or rubber stamp), in which the board sees its role as choosing a CEO for the institution and then putting itself as well as the enterprise in his or her hands; (2) corporate style, in which the board plays an active role in dealing with capital expenditures, property acquisitions, and asset management but expects the president to handle most other issues, with the board seeing itself as relating to the president rather than exercising direct oversight of the institution; and (3) participatory style, in which the board does not see the president as chief executive officer of the institution and is likely to establish direct relationships with various staffs and programs of the organization.

The appropriate role of an institution's board, profit-making or nonprofit, is primarily to set policy and to delegate execution of that policy to an able professional staff under the direction of the organization's president. It is the board's duty to ensure that competent staff is in place to manage the institution rather than to assume any managerial functions itself.

In practice, however, many nonprofit boards have accepted weak management or, in some cases and just as detrimentally, assumed staff functions themselves. For instance, a good number of the nation's foundations were at one time—and some still are—run by their boards, sometimes with no professional staff or a staff that was given no real authority. In some cases the small size of the foundations seemed to justify such an approach, but not always. For a time even some very large foundations have been managed by their boards. Rather than confining their role to the review and approval of grants developed by a professional staff in accordance with policy criteria established by the board, they have been actively involved in the development of individual grants.

You will also find the endowments of many universities are managed by the trustees, with a committee of the board actually picking the securities included in the endowment portfolio. For instance, Princeton employed this system until 1977 with good success, when after a two-year effort, the board was persuaded that its role was to establish investment policy for the endowment and delegate implementation of such policy to full-time managers.

The arguments in favor of separating the policy-making function from security selection in the case of endowment and management are set forth in the chapter "Endowment Management in the 1980s" and need not be repeated here. The point is: in every area of operations, trustees are best suited for and are most effective at setting broad policy. Carrying out that policy is the task of full-time management.

How Board Members Are Chosen

The process of selecting trustees varies according to the nature of the institution, its program, its age, the personality of the CEO, whether the CEO is the organization's founder, and other factors. For instance, most universities at one time employed a rather closed selection process in which the board members privately chose their own peers without outside consultation. Many such institutions have now evolved a process that combines elements of the old closed style with a new and more open participatory process. For example, at Princeton, some trustees are now selected by the board, some are nominated by the alumni organization and selected by alumni vote, and some are nominated and elected by the senior class.

Small organizations and most foundations (and some universities) still follow the more traditional selection model in which the president and chairman of the board, as a practical matter, nominate all new trustees and the full board approves their choices reflexively. This approach—also typical of most businesses—means trustees tend to be allies of the CEO.

In choosing board members, however, an amalgam of factors actually comes into play. The comfort level of the CEO with the nominee is always crucial. But CEOs as well as others tend to seek not just allies, but a board composed of varied skills and backgrounds related to the work of the enterprise.

Also weighed are the reputation and prestige of the candidate, as board selection still follows the star system for the most part. In recent years, membership in groups that have not historically had a major voice in this country has also become a criterion for board composition. The result is a blend of backgrounds on most boards. For example, in 1982 the board of Children's Television Workshop included:

- people from the three basic sectors of finance: investment banking, venture capital, and commercial banking.

- people in education (president of Columbia Teachers College and a professor from the Harvard Graduate School of Education).

- blacks and Hispanics who are successful professionals in their own right (university professor, lawyer, head of a mental health organization, and chief of an urban fellows program).

- a foundation CEO.

- a cable TV CEO and former Corporation for Public Broadcasting board member.

Independence of Trustees

What degree of critical detachment from management is appropriate for a member of a board? How much loyalty should a trustee give a CEO? What other ties are appropriate between a trustee and his or her organization?

All of these questions relate to the issue of what constitutes an appropriate degree of "independence" for trustees. An article Burt Malkiel and I—who serve together on a mutual fund board—wrote in 1982 could just as well have been written about nonprofit organizations as profit-making ones.[2] In the piece we approached the concept of "independence" this way:

> For a board to be effective, the atmosphere at meetings should be collegial rather than antagonistic, and there should be a disposition on the part of directors to seek a consensus. "A director" should disagree when disagreement is justified. In particular, a board should never yield to management when management's self-interest is at variance with corporate interests. In other words, the appropriate posture for a board should be one of loyal independence.
>
> The SEC and other proponents of reform in corporate governance regard an independent director as a person who is neither an employee of the corporation nor an outsider who has a significant relationship as a lawyer, banker, supplier, or customer with the company. But any attempt to define independence is elusive. For instance, is a lawyer who renders no current service to the company independent if he or she hopes to obtain future legal business from the company? Is a retired employee independent of his or her former colleagues? Is a friend of a corporate officer who has no business ties to the company in fact independent?
>
> Independence is really a state of mind, and since we cannot discern the psyches of board members, we prefer to replace the word "independent" with "unaffiliated." An unaffiliated director may be defined as a person who has no material business or economic relationship (other than shareholdings) to the company or familiar ties to management.
>
> One might think management would welcome outsiders, who have no material business ties to the company, to their boards for one simple reason: It is hard to discharge a firm that has a significant service relationship to your company if a senior member of that firm is on your board.

In the article, we took the position that the key to director independence lies in board control of the nomination process and influence over the agenda of the board. In support of this view, we observed:

> Most unaffiliated directors of corporations are now selected by the company's CEO. A recent study by Korn-Ferry, a management recruiting firm, showed that the great majority of new directors had been previously known by the companies' CEO's.[3] The fact that a director is an acquaintance of or is recommended by the CEO does not, of course, preclude the director from acting in a manner independent of the officer's wishes. The point at issue is who determines the makeup, the point of view, the spirit of the board.
>
> A board with full responsibility for selecting its own members and for assessing the quality and experience necessary to membership will likely develop a posture of independence from management. The board will see itself as an entity in its own right rather

---

[2] Paul Firstenberg and Burton Malkiel, "Why Corporate Boards Need Independent Directors" (*Management Review*, April 1980, pp. 26–38).

[3] At the same time, 70 percent of the nation's 1,000 largest companies have boards composed of a majority of outside directors. (*Business Week*, September 10, 1979, p. 72).

than as an extension of management and will develop a cohesion of its own, quite apart from the company's management.

For the board to exercise independence from management, the board also needs to participate in shaping the agenda of board discussions. There is no easier way to silence even the most vociferously independent board than for the CEO to bog it down in listening to reports that require no action and to act on the minutiae of corporate business so that it has no time to examine vital issues.

An independent-minded, unaffiliated, and competent board of trustees is not going to be a pushover for management. It is going to insist on a strong voice in setting directions. Such a board should be welcomed by management, but some unfortunately fear a sharing of power with a board. Such managements fail to appreciate how an appropriate sharing of responsibility will benefit the organization as well as be a significant help to themselves.

Contributions An Effective Board Can Make

What special contribution can a group of supportive but nevertheless independent-minded trustees make to the governance of a nonprofit organization? There are at least five ways in which a board can be of special value:

1. It can continuously evaluate management's effectiveness in accomplishing objectives approved by the board and reflect that evaluation in the compensation awarded management. To be effective in evaluating management, the board must be prepared to translate its judgment of performance into judgments about the compensation of executives. If the board grumbles about management but then goes ahead and awards the CEO and other key executives the maximum possible compensation permitted by existing policy, its concerns will probably be ignored. There has to be a financial bite to the trustee's bark. Overseeing compensation gives the board a uniquely effective opportunity for criticizing or complimenting management.

2. It can identify and frame policy issues that for one reason or another may not be receiving the degree of attention they deserve from management. Trustees have the advantage of not being caught up in the everyday affairs of the organization. This detachment gives them a vantage point from which to see issues in a way denied to management. Independent trustees can have a clear advantage over insiders in identifying issues management may have incorrectly formulated or overlooked.

3. The board can evaluate—and improve where necessary—the quality of management's decision-making processes. Under the pressure of day-to-day events, some managers may be inclined to move too quickly; others may stall and avoid tough choices. Without necessarily trying to second-guess management, boards should be satisfied that critical decisions are being reached through sound processes. By questioning decisions, the board can force management to prepare more thorough analyses and think more carefully; it can request that management consult outside experts; and, to expedite matters where necessary, it can establish strict deadlines for decisions.

4. The board can provide an independent check on the effectiveness of controls against such perils of organizational life as misappropriation of funds, conflict of interest, inaccurate internal reporting, and inappropriate behavior by management.

5. The board can support specific corporate policies and objectives before public and governmental authorities. Trustees who are able to speak out on behalf of the enterprise can be a valuable asset.

Given all that a board can contribute, a good, strong board—fully aware of what its role is and what it is not—is a major asset to any enterprise and a source of unique support for management.

Limitations on Board Effectiveness

Boards of trustees are essentially reactive—they work best when they can respond to presentations by management and are called upon to concur or disagree with quite specific proposals by the organization's executives. The strength of a board lies in large measure in its detachment. Boards—by definition a loose grouping of individuals—do not function best when they must initiate action; for instance, when the board is put in a position where it must develop its own set of proposals. In a sense, a board functions in an adjudicatory capacity, much like a judicial tribunal. Executive actions are not comfortable for a board (or for a court), and therefore are best carried out by management.

Boards also are more effective when they deal with a unified management. Divisions and controversies within management are hard for the board to arbitrate. Divisive controversies within management draw boards into highly charged emotional issues which trustees may find themselves lacking the time or familiarity with the personalities involved to handle well. In the face of management division, particularly among the most senior executives of the company, boards naturally tend to try to find compromises that will placate all the factions. In the face of controversy, it is almost in the nature of a group of individuals who must negotiate compromises in their own position in order to reach a consensus, to try to find an arrangement that will offer something to all of the competing factions.

For instance, the chief executive of a nonprofit institution was confronted with false accusations about his professional conduct by a subordinate member of his staff, who made the charges of misfeasance directly to the board. While the board quickly came to understand that the charges were unfounded, it was unwilling to discharge the employee. Fearing a public counterattack or lawsuit by the disgruntled employee, the board allowed her to continue in the organization's employ. It sought to placate the head of the organization by downgrading the accusing employee's job.

In the not-for-profit area, you sometimes come across boards in which at least a number of members lack experience in the direction of institutions and have some difficulty in contributing to the resolution of the management issues relating to the institution. This lack of sophistication is a handicap. As Burt Malkiel and I observed:

> If the board is uninformed and unsophisticated about the company's business, it is going to be a patsy for the CEO. The crucial base of director independence is competence—not just general wisdom but a capacity to understand the company's business. A director need not (and really cannot) be expert in all the operations of a business; indeed a variety of specialized expertise is necessary to the creation of a strong board. But you cannot stand up to management as a director if you do not know what you are talking about.[4]

The board of a not-for-profit institution, with its traditional business membership, ought to be well-positioned to press management to think and act in a businesslike fashion as well as to insist that the staff of the organization has the professional competence to conduct the business of the enterprise. But business executives serving on such boards are often hesitant in their roles as trustees to be assertive in suggesting that business practices have a place in the management of not-for-profit organizations. As the general manager of a major public broadcasting station put it, "When my business trustees come to a board meeting, they seem to check all their business expertise at the door."

Thomas J. C. Raymond and Stephen A. Greyser observe pointedly:

> ... the board is obligated to make many decisions that are businesslike in nature—but often are not treated in a businesslike way. Otherwise hardheaded businessmen serving as trustees often seem to lose their objective powers of appraisal ... All too often trustees are intimidated by artistic directors who cry, "This is not a business!" The frequency of complaints over alleged interference with artistic freedom, coupled with the board's artistic inferiority complex, are usually sufficient to cause it to retreat from its proper devil's advocacy position—and to perpetuate inefficient and sometimes disastrous practices.[5]

Managing the Board

For a board to be of maximum value, it must be supported intelligently and indeed "managed" by the organization's staff. It is impossible in this chapter to distill all the lessons I've learned about managing a board—both as an executive and as a board member in a varied set of nonprofit and profit-making institutions—but let me at least offer some points:

- The size of the board affects the quality of board discussion and decision-making. If a large board is required to represent diverse constituencies, then committees of the board must be formed to deal with specific subjects—e.g., finance, compensation, in-

[4] Firstenberg and Malkiel, "Why Corporate Boards Need Independent Directors," p. 37.
[5] Raymond and Greyser, "The Business of Managing Arts Organizations," pp. 126–127.

vestments, audit, substantive programs, and so forth—in order to create a reasonably sized forum in which to discuss issues. And the full board must be encouraged to give weight to the recommendations of such committees in their areas of jurisdiction.

- Board meetings should be scheduled for a year in advance in order to allow busy trustees to plan their affairs so they can attend.

- More frequent, rather than less frequent, board meetings are useful in keeping a board educated about an organization's business. A board that is up to speed will come to a point of decision on major issues more readily than one that is poorly informed.

- Don't over-present to a board. Avoid excessively long presentations by management that leave too little time for board members to ask questions and talk among themselves. Let board members have a chance to discuss and debate with each other. Management should not unnecessarily interrupt exchanges between board members. At the same time, if presentations to the board should not be overly long, they should be well-organized and well-presented. If the issue is important, don't wing it.

- Assume the board members are very pressed for time—they may not even have time to think about your affairs until they are on their way to your meeting. So in any paper or oral presentation you prepare, "short" is far better than "long." At the top of any presentation, state the issue you want considered and follow up with your recommendation. Then elaborate on your reasoning but make sure the trustee who has had but a few minutes to look at the paper or is hearing your proposal for the first time, is presented up front with the issue and your recommendations for handling it.

- In your decision-making timetable, allow plenty of time for the board to assimilate issues. Remember, while you may be living daily with a problem, board members come in and out of your organization's affairs. The more important the issue, the more time you should allow for the board to deliberate. Wherever possible, plan to have the board consider especially crucial or complex issues over several meetings and don't press them for an immediate response. One CEO I know inflames his board by constantly bringing up the most critical issues at the end of a meeting, often as directors are getting ready to leave.

- As CEO, get to know your board members on a one-on-one basis. Treat each member as personally important to you. Give them a chance to express their concerns and to ask their questions of you, alone and outside the board room. You will learn things about your board members you could not discover in a board room setting, and will build personal relationships that will be important when crises arise.

- On tough, controversial issues, find individual members to champion management's position. Pre-bicker members whom you think can be persuaded to support management's viewpoint and who will be effective in persuading their fellow board members. (I have a saying, "Never go before the board and ask for a decision on a critical issue unless you have the necessary votes lined up beforehand.") At the same time, don't pre-bicker every issue. Pick and choose your shots.

- Encourage the board to make some decisions management may not agree with, but with which it can live. You want a board that feels it can act independently of management without causing a crisis. If the board feels it is independent, it will be less prone to assert its independence for the sake of asserting it. Hence, it is important to build an atmosphere in which the board feels it can decide issues without its every decision being regarded as tantamount to a vote of confidence or no confidence in management.

- Do not press for a decision on an extremely controversial issue if you expect to win only by a narrow margin. Retreat, regroup, and develop a formula that finds a wider consensus. A narrow margin can create hard feelings on the board among the losing minority, and they may not feel committed fully to a decision made by only a slim majority. This can leave you open to second-guessing if the operating results following the board decision are not immediately positive. In addition, pushing forward on the basis of a very narrow margin of support may lead dissenting board members—indeed, even your supporters—to feel management is inflexible, perhaps even arrogant, eroding its support within the board.

- When the going gets hot and heavy in the board room, look for ways to modify aspects of your proposal to accommodate board views while preserving the core of your recommendation. If you try to win it all, you may come up empty-handed. Sometimes, to gain support, you have to make a gesture to the opposition to show that you are flexible and that you respect the views of others.

- Let a trustee preside as chairman of the meeting. One of the most critical functions at board meetings is to keep the discussion on track or to end it when it has gone on too long. It is much better that this moderating function be performed by a fellow board member than by the CEO. Board leadership by a board member is also an important symbolic way of reinforcing members' feelings that they, and not the management, are in control of the board.

- Don't be defensive in answering questions or comments by a board member. If you're wrong, admit it. If you disagree, do so without apologizing. If you are defensive in the give-and-take with board members, they will soon regard you as insecure.

- Provide opportunities for board members to educate themselves about your operations in depth without over-imposing on their limited time. Provide opportunities for the board to visit projects and see the organization in action.

- Another way to educate board members is to allow various management team members to make presentations to the board and seek decisions from it. Presentations by subordinate managers are good training for the executives involved. They give the board a chance to know the management team better and allow the CEO to appear more confident and more in control than if he or she were to present every issue to the board. After all, one of the CEO's critical responsibilities is to build a team. Letting other executives perform before the board is one way to demonstrate this has been done.

- If it is an executive's first time to make a presentation, you'd be advised to review it with him or her beforehand and coach him or her a bit; once he or she is before the board, do not intervene unless you feel the executive is making a very damaging error. Intervention will not only undermine the executive's confidence but will also create the appearance of an excessively controlling and insecure CEO. You can also structure the process so the board chairman will ask you as CEO for your comments after an executive's presentation—that's an easy, nondestructive way to pick up any ball the executive may have dropped.

- Allow the board to develop a sense of itself as an independent entity. Encourage board members to meet and talk among themselves informally outside your presence. This also will show your confidence in yourself as CEO by saying, "I'm secure enough in how well I'm doing to allow you to talk without me present."

- Arrange for some purely social occasions for the board—this will reinforce the sense that you regard members as important, and the socializing opportunities will improve communication between board members which will benefit management in the long run.

In the end, the long-term usefulness of even an able board will depend largely on the degree to which management wants to play a shared role in governing the company. Management must invite the board to play an active role in areas where it can be useful if it wants the best that able people can bring to the enterprise.

V.
Superior Entrepreneurial Management

12

The Entrepreneurial Organization

PROFOUND AND ACCELERATING CHANGE is a fact of modern life. New technologies, new economic forces and conditions, new political monuments, and new social and moral values have altered all of our institutional arrangements, all of our personal structures. As John W. Gardner has observed:

> No sensible person would assert that earlier centuries experienced change as the twentieth-century has experienced it. A radical speeding up of the tempo of change is at the heart of the twentieth century experience and has gained a powerful grip on the modern mind.[1]

Consequently, adaptation to a constantly changing environment is a modern organizational imperative. This means a disposition for taking risks is essential to the continued vitality of nonprofit institutions. As Peter Drucker has pointed out, in a world buffeted by change, the only way to conserve is by innovation.[2]

Entrepreneurial management—or risk-taking management—is the process of motivating an institution to grow as it encounters change. In the world of finance, the term "risk" is defined as "the chance that expected returns from securities or other assets will not materialize and, in particular, that one's investments will fall in value."[3] I label certain organizations "entrepreneurial" because, in order to reap the benefits

---

[1] John Gardner, *Self-Renewal, The Individual and The Innovative Society* (New York: W. W. Norton and Company, 1981, p. 6).

[2] Peter Drucker, *Landmarks of Tomorrow* (New York: Harper and Brothers, 1952, chs. 1 and 2).

[3] Malkiel and Firstenberg, *Managing Risk in An Uncertain Era: An Analysis for Endowed Institutions*, p. 10.

that flow from innovative change, they are willing to accept the uncertainty inherent in new endeavors and the possibility of disappointing results.

This readiness to take risks alters the dynamics of the institution from "reactive" to "active," from being potentially resistant to change, or even hardened against it, to becoming an affirmative and enthusiastic pursuer of new opportunities.

An entrepreneurial organization, then, has an institutionalized bent for risk and innovation. The organization is energized by acts of imagination and motivated by an innate optimism that its visions can be successfully translated into viable programs, even in the face of formidable obstacles. However developed its capacity for analysis, the organization also has an intuitive daring and overriding confidence that its future will be even more creative and productive than its present.

BARRIERS TO NONPROFIT RISK-TAKING

In the nonprofit sector, as for organizations generally, there are a series of obstacles to risk and innovation. Philip Kotler, in *Marketing for Nonprofit Organizations,* after citing a series of examples of entrepreneurship in the nonprofit world, nevertheless maintains:

> Nonprofit organizations typically do not have an entrepreneurial view of themselves. Colleges, hospitals, museums, symphonies, and government agencies tend to operate in the same way year after year. Colleges will add some new courses and drop some old courses but remain the same in their basic operating characteristics.[4]

He goes on to explain:

> Nonprofit organizations tend to be noninnovative for a number of reasons:
>
> 1. Nonprofit organizations have typically not faced or recognized competition and therefore lack a spur to do better.
> 2. Nonprofits usually lack the budgets to experiment with new products or methods. Further, their boards and/or legislators often refuse to support innovation.
> 3. Nonprofit managers are typically not entrepreneurial. Their training consists of a specialty (e.g., social work, art history, etc.) or administration with an emphasis on running existing organizations rather than creating new ones.
> 4. Nonprofit organizations see their services as necessary and not requiring justification or marketing.

Kotler's list points up that there are indeed impediments to taking risks in the nonprofit world. My own list, however, differs from his. It includes:

---

[4] Kotler, *Marketing for Nonprofit Organizations,* p. 113.

- the absence of established incentives and rewards for successful entrepreneurship. In the private sector, there is extraordinary financial compensation for an act of entrepreneurism. A person willing to take the risks of initiating an entrepreneurial venture can anticipate the character of the payoff for a successful effort. No such clearly understood reward system—financial or nonfinancial—exists in the nonprofit world.

- the concept of entrepreneurship is not typically part of the vocabulary or ethos of nonprofit organizations; entrepreneurship is usually thought of as a concept relevant only to profit-making businesses. In part this reflects the nonprofit focus on program content. In part it reflects the sector's reluctance to use terminology or concepts commonly associated with business. Many of those who staff nonprofit organizations consider it an important personal self-definition to separate themselves from the values of the commercial world, and they do not embrace easily the vocabulary or concepts associated with the business sector. It is not so much that the nonprofit managers are trained in a "specialty" or "administration," or as Kotler puts it, "boards often refuse to support innovation," but that the culture of nonprofit enterprise does not view itself in terms of entrepreneurship.

- a tendency of nonprofit organizations to state their aims so vaguely as to defy assessment of whether goals are being attained. Most individual risk-takers tend to be goal-oriented personalities. In the business world, "profits" serve as a scorecard for measuring achievements. The absence of readily perceived organizational objectives in the nonprofit sector tends to deprive such individuals of an important stimulus to their creative energies. Well-defined and understood goals provide a performance yardstick.

- the relative scarcity of capital available for the nonprofit sector. The fact is that few nonprofit activities enjoy enough economic success to build up a fund to plow into new ventures. But even fewer nonprofit organizations think in terms of accumulating capital from their current activities to underwrite the development of future ventures. It is not just that "nonprofits usually lack the budgets to experiment with," as Kotler expresses it, but that such organizations, even those with strong earning potential, do not tend to plan for future investment but spend currently whatever they earn in a given year.

These are all quite real barriers to nonprofit entrepreneurship. Nevertheless, they can be overcome and a risk-taking environment developed within a nonprofit institution.

THE CHARACTERISTICS OF AN ENTREPRENEURIAL ORGANIZATION

What are the elements of organizational management which overcome resistance to innovation and unleash the creativity that flourishes in a period of entrepreneurial change? My catalog of characteristics numbers ten:

- A coherent set of aims and values
- Energies focused on comparative advantage
- Being light and intuitive on one's decision-making feet

- An adaptive environment
- Excellence of execution
- Staying power
- Marshaling and nurturing exceptional talent
- Finesse with diverse constituencies
- A sense of where the action of our times is and how to impact it
- Active-positive leadership.

Not every superbly run nonprofit entity will necessarily exhibit all of these qualities. But the kind of organizational environment of any entrepreneurial nonprofit enterprise will very likely be consistent with the institutional portrait that emerges from this list.

In my view, a first-rate entrepreneurial organization will incorporate as part of its culture certain qualities and attitudes. They are described on the following pages.

A Coherent Set of Aims and Values

In large measure, people in an organization take their cues on how to behave from their perception of the institution's values and beliefs. The nature of the initiatives staffs pursue, the kind of people to hire and reward, the style of internal communication, the latitude given people and groups to innovate, and a whole host of other actions are largely influenced by people's expectations of whether the institution they work for approves or disapproves of such behavior.

In some instances an explicit set of rules governing certain kinds of action will exist. But in most circumstances, people deduce what is expected of them from the institution's goals and values.

For example, on one hand, a university that makes it clear that serving the interests of the faculty is its primary concern can expect its administrators, in allocating its resources, to give priority to programs which benefit the academic interests of the university. A health care facility located in a lower income area is likely to attract a staff concerned with servicing the poor. On the other hand, a foundation that indicates that it places a premium on avoiding politically and socially controversial grants is not likely to see its staff urging support for programs that run counter to accepted mores.

The clearer the evocation of values and goals, the easier it is for the organization's members to understand what is expected of them. Mixed signals will confuse people in an organization. Clarity, consistency, and conviction are essential in institutional communication.

A sharply defined sense of what the institution aims to be—and what it does not want to be—serves as a powerful sorting device, enabling the organization to better evaluate which new proposed endeavor builds on some central strength or competence of the institution (i.e., its comparative advantage), which one is an unrelated adjunct that the organization has no special skill to undertake, and which would conflict with its value structure or basic purposes.

Without this sense of coherence, an organization can flounder, unable to determine whether a proposed new direction will complement and fit with the basics of the institution or merely involve change for the sake of change.

Energies Focused on Comparative Advantage

For an institution to perform well, it must focus its energies. No institution can expect to do everything well; over the years it will acquire more skill at some tasks than others as it accumulates specialized experience and expertise ("know-how") in certain areas. Experience shows that if you stray from your area of competence, you are likely to stumble and falter in execution, and that the range of an organization's expertise is often narrower than it would like to admit. Thus, sharply defining what an organization's genuine skills are is a crucial business.

For instance, Children's Television Workshop's unique edge lies in blending entertainment and education in television programming for young children. Over the years CTW has built up a body of "know-how" about such programming. But the Workshop has also discovered it is not as expert in devising television programming for adults as it is for children. The lessons learned from children's programming and the skills and experience of its staff did not prove to be readily transferable to adult shows. When CTW undertook adult programming it found it had to start out largely from scratch, as if it were a new venture, and could not draw on its reservoir of specialized talent. The result was that in the area of adult programming its product was not as admired as a competitive product, and the ability to raise continued funding support for such efforts diminished. In contrast, in the children's field, the Workshop continues to be the leader in educational programming with an ongoing ability to attract support for its new endeavors.

Of course in a competitive, Darwinian economic world it is an organization's relative rather than absolute expertise that counts. That is why an organization's "comparative advantage" is spoken of. Even in the nonprofit sector, all enterprises face some form of competition—if not direct competitors in the same line of enterprise, at least competitors for the best talent, for resources, and for public support and attention. To attract better staff and more resources and support than your competition, you need to outperform them. This means you need to concentrate on what you do best as an organization relative to others.

The authors of *In Search of Excellence* have come to a similar conclusion about the excellently run large private companies. One of their eight criteria for excellence is "stick to the knitting." In this connection they write:

Our principal finding is clear and simple: organizations that do branch out (either by acquisition or internal diversification) but stick very close to their knitting outperform the others. The most successful of all are those diversified around a single skill.[5]

Concentration on an entity's comparative edge is thus a guiding strategy for any successful enterprise . . . private or public.

Being Light and Intuitive on One's Decision-Making Feet

Modern research underscores that there is as much "logic" to our intuition as to our powers of analysis. Intuition is not simply quixotic hunch, but the intelligent application of remembered past patterns to future uncertainties. Informed intuition plays a large part, therefore, in guiding the destinies of an entrepreneurial organization.

Do not misunderstand my point. I am not trying to discourage analysis of organizational choices. There is plenty of room for analytical work in making a decision on a future course of action. The proponents of a new endeavor ought to know how things will work at the "nuts and bolts" level. They ought to take a "bath" in the operational details and assess the capacity of the institution to deal with such operational facts of life. Whether an organization brings some unique value or competence to the field that will give it an edge in operating in the area should be examined, too. The risks in the endeavor must also be identified and an analysis made, if they can be avoided or minimized by some structure or arrangement. In other words, at least as much emphasis should be placed on identifying the sources of risk, and whether the organization can cope with them, as trying to measure risk. When it comes to measuring the potential returns vs. risks, quantification techniques can be useful as expressions of the relationship between benefit and risk.

Remember, however, that our ability to place a quantitative overlay over projected events diminishes rapidly as such events occur more than a few months from the present. Hence, the greater the risk—and therefore the greater the prospect for significant returns—the harder it is to forecast in advance through the projection of numbers what the outcome will be. In such a case, the assumptions on which the analysis turns become highly speculative. And the more volatile the arena, the harder it is to predict the future.

Thus, an overdependence on numeric projections of future events can provide a false comfort and divert decision-makers from examining the hard realities involved in the choice.

---

[5] Peters and Waterman, p. 293. *Business Week* ("Do Mergers Really Work," June 3, 1985, p. 89) reports a similar finding by the management consulting firm, McKinsey & Co. The magazine reports the consulting firm "put 58 major acquisition programs undertaken between 1972 and 1983 to two tests: Did the return on the total amount invested in the acquisitions exceed the cost of capital, and did they help their parents outperform the competition in the stock market? The finding: 28 of the 58 clearly failed both tests and six others failed one. Most likely to fail: the megamergers, especially those involving companies in unrelated businesses."

Such quantitative projections of risk and reward are at best metaphors for our intuitions about uncertain future events. Whether to go ahead in the end is a judgment call and inevitably involves a leap of faith of some kind.

Rosabeth Moss Kanter states it well in *The Change Masters*:

> Blueprints and forecasts are important tools and should be provided as much and as frequently as possible. But they are only approximations, and they may be modified dramatically as events unfold.[6]

A well-run organization will thus make judgments about new initiatives through a *balanced* process of tough-minded analysis and informed intuition played out against a sharply defined sense of the organization's mission and goals. And it will make its choices within a timeframe that does not exhaust the energies of the proponents of change or allow windows of opportunity to shut before the institution has acted. Planning and opportunism have to be balanced in a fast moving world.

An Adaptive Environment

Innovation is best stimulated by an environment of open, uninhibited communication between superiors and subordinates in which new and especially unconventional ideas receive a supportive hearing. New ideas in their first stages are vulnerable to attack. It is easy enough to choke off a new concept by subjecting it to withering cross-examination before the idea has been fleshed out and there has been time to develop a response to the tough questions.

A supportive response seeks to build on fragile new ideas rather than to dissect their flaws. It resists excessive demands for coordination, review, and endorsement from collateral branches of the organization . . . cries often from the least flexible wings of the organization that everyone be promptly informed and have an early opportunity to comment on all developments. Such pressure tends to produce unduly layered reviews of new ideas and stifle the development of new concepts.

Innovators need to be insulated from such unduly structured processes and procedures. They must be given some breathing room to work according to their lights and to experiment. The proponents of new ideas must acquire a powerful champion within the organization who sees it as his or her task to nurture and protect new concepts and to wring out from the organization the necessary support for their development.

In particular, to help talented teams of people access the information they need to propose new ideas, to encourage them to collaborate with other talented people, and to come forward with new concepts, the organization must offer a fluid system

[6] Rosabeth Moss Kanter, *The Change Masters* (New York: Simon and Schuster, 1983, pp. 304–305).

of communication without rigidly compartmentalized boundaries. Rosabeth Moss Kanter observes:

> Where integrative connections help information flow freely and people talk across organizational boundaries, the more potential entrepreneurs are likely to see opportunities or to get information to move beyond an assignment to propose a new option for the organization. Ideas for innovations begin to take shape in companies in which information . . . is available and exchange of ideas is encouraged.[7]

An organization that seeks to encourage innovation must also be tolerant of mistakes made in the pursuit of new concepts. To try something new is to risk mistakes and failure. If error is ruled out, so will innovation be killed off. Indeed, there is no more certain way to discourage new ideas than to criticize and shunt aside those who have developed imaginative new concepts because some of those concepts have not been successful. To do so will create a climate in which the rise to the top is achieved by never being on the "wrong side" of an issue, a climate inhospitable for invention and innovation.

The organization must be adaptive to different personality styles. Insistence that all personalities be cut from one mold will inevitably drive out talented persons who are "different" from the organization's prevailing personality model. An environment conducive to risk-taking will be tolerant of personalities who disturb the status quo as they pursue initiatives. Innovators, by definition, challenge prevailing organizational views and norms.

For example, a university replaced its retiring athletic director who had held sway for over twenty years. His successor was brought in from outside the university. One day the president complained to a colleague, "What's wrong with our new AD? He always seems at the center of controversy." The colleague replied to the president, "If after twenty years of rule by one man, his successor doesn't create a great deal of static, he isn't bringing about any real change."

Static, tension, and conflict are thus the expected by-products of the lively pursuit of new directions by imaginative innovators.

At the same time, there must be some "checks" and "balances" on individual initiative. The autonomy given talent must be circumscribed at some point by the lessons of experience and institutional judgment. An organization is like a family system. If parents raise children strictly in their own image, if they do not grant enough autonomy, allow them to experiment and make mistakes, and support their aspirations even if they vary from their parents' values, then the children are likely to grow up as dependent children without the self-confidence to strike out on their own as independent adults. But if the children are given no guidance, none of the benefits of their parents'

---

[7] Kanter, p. 220.

experience, or no sense of their values, they are likely to feel lost . . . without a sense of sufficient support and structure to pursue their own independent visions.

Thus, at the center of the art of managing risk-takers is a seeming paradox, that of granting the risk-taker the autonomy he or she requires on one hand, and at the same time providing enough security and support so that he or she does not feel alone or isolated on the other.

The art of organizational building, then, is to appreciate this seeming paradox of human needs and to provide within the organization a balance between structure (a secure sense of place) and flexibility (the opportunity for individual self-expression) and, above all, to create a set of values which gives the individual a sense of higher purpose for his or her daily efforts.

Excellence of Execution

In class one day, students were acting out their notions of an entrepreneur within an organizational setting. One student, playing the role of the entrepreneur, conveyed the impression that he was not concerned with how to make operational the program he was espousing. To listen to him tell it, the idea was enough. Somehow it would get done. I was sharply critical of the portrait he developed.

"An entrepreneur," I said, "*does* have a strong sense of how to execute his or her idea. Entrepreneurs are not hip-shooters. They have well-developed instincts and trust their intuitions. But they are equally brilliant executors. They have visionary ideas, but what truly sets them apart is the ability to turn a concept into an operational reality."

Ultimately, every nonprofit organization's effectiveness in achieving its mission turns on how well it executes its activities. Since most such organizations depend on external sources to provide necessary revenues (be they funding providers or purchasers of products), executing well enough to satisfy a market test is a matter of survival. Even foundations, whose endowments assure their continued existence, are judged largely by whether they are effective in performing their missions.

To be a first-rate institution, then, there must be an intensive focus on producing a superb product. The commitment to quality will be critical in motivating the best people to work for the institution. Talented people invariably want the chance to do their best at the work they love. Moreover, it is the quality of the performance that will ultimately distinguish the product in the marketplace and gain it the respect of the public.

For instance, the private universities that offer the highest quality educational environment can charge higher prices and still not lose students to lower-priced institutions that are perceived to offer a less effective product. Factors such as ancient prestige and entrenched tradition may account for part of such institutions' power in the marketplace, but product excellence is a singularly important reason.[8]

---

[8] See Richard Spies, *The Future of Private Colleges: The Effect of Rising Costs on College Choice* (Research Report Series No. 117, Industrial Relations Section, Princeton University, 1973).

An institution that executes well usually has an intense, outspoken commitment to quality. Doing superb work is a self-evident part of the ethos of the place . . . people at all levels care about doing their tasks well, quality efforts are recognized and rewarded (and the converse is also true; poor work draws negative forms of attention). Standards of quality are at the forefront of concern and rigorously enforced.

Quality must be achieved within the limit of the resources the institution can afford to devote to a given task. This is often the hardest point for nonprofit staffs to accept— such institutions are not dedicated to making money. But every institution deals with some form of financial constraint, and the art is to achieve outstanding performance within the level of resources available.

Staying Power

An organization embarked on a new course, like an individual entrepreneur, must be so convinced of the importance and feasibility of the idea that it stays with the endeavor long enough to test it fairly, even in the absence of initially confirming results.

New ideas cannot be expected to take hold right away. It inevitably takes more time and resources to achieve results than envisioned when plans for a new endeavor are drawn up. Few innovators are clever enough to devise a foolproof plan; it takes experience in a field to know how to operate in it; it takes time to find the right people to execute a concept. It takes a while to overcome unanticipated obstacles and to identify and override mistakes.

The March of Dimes, following its success in finding a vaccine to prevent polio, shifted its mission to funding research on birth defects.

It took ten years after the start of the new program to arrest the decline of public contributions and begin the climb to historic high levels of public support.

MacGeorge Bundy, former head of the Ford Foundation, has observed about foundation efforts:

> Serious program work takes time, so it requires a firm decision to enter a field and stay with it for a period of years. A problem that is important enough to deserve a major commitment is one that will very seldom be resolved in a year or two. Moreover time is needed, in most cases, to know whom to work with, and to be known in turn, so that people who have better ideas than yours will know where to find you. Time is needed, most of all, to be able to give staying power to those whose work may make a difference.[9]

The importance of staying power is hardly unique to the nonprofit world. The business sector is filled with examples of ventures that were not initially successful but that eventually made it big when their backers stayed with the endeavor despite initial losses.

[9] MacGeorge Bundy, "C³I in Foundation Work" (A Ford Foundation Report, Series 71, 1979).

In sum, a genuine commitment to innovation requires the steadfast patience to allow the new endeavor a fair chance to succeed.

Marshaling and Nurturing Exceptional Talent

Producing a workable new idea is most often going to be the result of the interdependent output of a team of talented individuals rather than the result of a single person's extraordinary efforts. Today, the process of product innovation is often too complex, involving too many skills and tasks, for mastery by a single individual.

To encourage innovation and risk-taking among a broad range of employees, the organization's leadership must model such behavior itself, being comfortable with recognizing and rewarding the successes of subordinates (even when a breakthrough created by another may eclipse any personal achievement of the leadership). This means that mentorship and the nurturing of talent must be as important an institutional priority as the accomplishment of the organization's day-to-day business.

David L. Bradford and Allan R. Cohen, in *Managing for Excellence*, have crisply described the importance of managing to develop talent. It is worth summarizing their views at some length:

> What happens when modern, complex organizations are managed with a traditional, heroic leadership style? The heroic response from the leader who is responsible for "managing, motivating, controlling and coordinating subordinates" cuts into the needs of the subordinates for job challenge and control. . . . Managers demand so much for themselves that they do not demand enough from their subordinates. They do not make full use of the talents of their expensive employees.
>
> Since [such] styles emphasize the manager having the answers and being in control, they overuse the task abilities of the leader and underutilize the competences of subordinates.
>
> Heroic overconcentration of responsibility reduces the organization's chances to tap subordinates' talent fully.
>
> Rather than depending on heroic rides to the rescue—with the answers and the total responsibility—[the manager as developer] has sought the far greater power and potential for excellence available in the commitment and abilities of the whole group. These managers have in mind a developmental, collaborative, galvanizing but subordinate-centered image. . . . [The manager as developer has] the dual goal of getting the job done while engaging subordinates in a way that helps them.[10]

Talented innovators within an organization also need to be rewarded for the value of their contributions to an enterprise. When risk-taking brings extraordinary returns to the institution, so should unusual rewards be made available to the responsible

[10] David L. Bradford and Allan R. Cohen, *Managing for Excellence* (New York: John Wiley and Sons, © 1984, pp. 11, 21, 55, 56, 61, 63).

innovator or innovators. And this should be the case whether the innovation is a nonfinancial contribution that advances the program of a not-for-profit organization or a contribution to the profitability of the enterprise.

Financial rewards, especially in the form of bonuses or incentive compensation pegged to specific achievements, carry a powerful message. Rewards for risk-takers, however, need not always be financial. Important nonfinancial compensation can be offered in the form of a high degree of autonomy (or the latitude one has to choose his or her particular task). People are typically willing to trade freedom in their choice of work for financial compensation. Often simple praise and recognition are reward enough.

Support for risk-takers (or, if you prefer, "innovators" or "entrepreneurs") also entails designing a reward system that compensates risk-takers for their work as such and does not require them to shift to a different track in order to reap rewards. The reward ladder of most organizations is usually one-dimensional: the highest rewards come with moving into administration or general management, thereby channeling highly differentiated ambitions into a single career path. As Bartolome and Evans point out in a *Harvard Business Review* article:

> People come to equate success with the managerial ladder, which would be appropriate if skilled managerial people were the only skilled people we need. But this is far from the case. Most organizations have relatively few general managerial positions and while these are important posts, the life blood of the company is provided by people who fit with their jobs in other ways. To encourage these people, reward ladders need to be far more differentiated than they are at present."[11]

Finesse with Diverse Constituencies

Few nonprofit organizations possess sufficiently large endowments to support all of their activities (foundations are the notable class of exception). Most nonprofit entities have to obtain financial assistance from external groups like government and foundation funders, private benefactors, or purchasers of their services. In most cases, a nonprofit organization will raise funds from more than one class of supporter, and thus must be able to deal with constituencies as diverse in character and expectations as government bureaucracies, endowed foundations, and wealthy patrons, as well as the media which translates the institution's message and image to the public.

Soliciting support can be as varied as organizing to influence a legislator who oversees a crucial government funding source, writing elaborate grant proposals, impressing evaluators sent to recommend whether or not an agency or foundation should fund a project, courting potential individual donors, and dealing with the press, which

---

[11] Bartolome and Evans, "Must Success Cost So Much" (*Harvard Business Review*, March/April 1980).

may or may not be neutral in its approach to an organization. Each of an institution's diverse constituencies often requires a different approach, a different expression of the institution's message, and a different set of skills in managing the contracts.

Wealthy patrons of an institution will expect to be given a forum in which to express their views about the conduct of the organization they support. You reject giving them such an opportunity at your peril. Even if you give them a voice, however, they may become disenchanted and become harsh critics. (No person, as numerous nonprofit organizations have learned, is as harsh a critic as a onetime donor who feels his or her beneficiary has strayed from an acceptable course.)

In other circumstances a nonprofit institution must develop the muscle and finesse to fend off adversaries among its constituents. The staff of government agencies may become restless with supporting even a very popular program. Feeling they lack the influence within their own agency to terminate the flow of funds, they may seek to end support by feeding criticisms of the program and its administrators to the press and to legislators or by launching a sweeping audit of the recipient's affairs. To rebut such criticisms, and mount enough pressure to secure continuation of such funding, the nonprofit organization needs political allies and the skill to mobilize them.

Management of internal staff can also require political finesse. The internal staff of a nonprofit organization may be split into rival camps, reflecting the dual objectives of such organizations—mission and financial well-being. This duality generates within the culture of a nonprofit entity a tension between providing maximum support for programmatic ambitions on one hand, and policies designed to assure financial viability on the other. These seemingly contradictory objectives are often reflected in acute jurisdictional conflicts between program and business staffs, and between financial and program goals.

In almost any type of institution, jurisdictional tensions exist—but in a nonprofit institution these conflicts are intensified by the different professional backgrounds and consequent different outlooks and vocabularies of business and program personnel.

When an institution's varied constituencies take opposite positions on the same issue, matters can become especially complicated and heated. For instance, the allocation of funds in an organization with scarce resources—characteristic of most nonprofit institutions—will inevitably produce such a conflict. Where there aren't enough funds to support everyone's interests, someone's ox has to be gored. In such situations, management is confronted in organizational terms with a "zero sum game"—one constituency can only be pacified at the expense of another. The trick is to move to a decision by means of a process which maintains the cohesiveness of the institution. To accomplish this requires that management provide all interests with the opportunity to be heard. They must also be convinced that the decision will finally be made by people who are objective and not biased. More than this, gaining acceptance for an outcome entails painstaking education by management. This in turn means officers have to be skilled at exposition—at explaining issues and rationalizing decisions.

A Sense of Where the Action of Our Times Is and How To Impact It

The purpose and indeed the justification for the existence of any tax-exempt nonprofit organization is to meet a societal need. Not just any need, of course, but a need that the private business sector cannot be expected to fulfill and that government, by its very nature, can respond to only on a political basis. (See chapter, "The Nature of a Nonprofit Organization.") Support will flow to those organizations that are successful in identifying such a need. The degree of enthusiasm for their work will largely reflect the extent to which they touch on an area that the public regards as calling for urgent attention. In other words, the magnetism of the nonprofit entity's mission attracts talent to work for the organization and funds to carry out the organization's program.

The urge to be part of the "action of our times" is thus the essential catalyst for an entrepreneurial nonprofit organization. It is a drive unique to the nonprofit form of enterprise; it reflects the zest to make the connection between one's work and the larger currents of society. Entrepreneurially minded institutions are not content with the status quo; they seek to live on the cutting edge of the nation's ever-changing social and cultural agenda.

Of course, merely identifying a societal need is not enough. The ultimate test will be how effectively the organization impacts that need. Performance as well as concept are critical in gaining support.

The good business entrepreneur has a sixth sense of what the marketplace will buy and how to produce a product for such a market. The nonprofit entrepreneur must also design a "product" for which there is a demand and devise a cost-effective means for delivering it to the consumer.

MacGeorge Bundy, as head of the Ford Foundation, sensed in the 1960s that the nation's foremost domestic issue was "racism." He made it the foundation's number one priority, encouraging his staff to devise a whole array of innovative approaches to impact American society in this area. Robert Goheen, as president of Princeton in the late 1960s, correctly perceived the women's revolution in this country and led Princeton into becoming coeducational over the virulent dissent of a large number of alumni. Lloyd Morrisett and Joan Cooney in 1969 felt that preschool children could be educated by television and designed "Sesame Street" to teach and inform young children. Tony Panepinto, in the mid-1970s, understood the need to provide mental health services within the community for those who could not afford to pay for private treatment and built an organization to respond to this need. Ruth Maxwell in 1980 identified that chemical dependency was a family disease and established a center to treat the family as well as the dependent person.

All these leaders, in connecting their organization's mission to the social and cultural problems of our time, made them lively and exciting places to work and elicited backing for their efforts. Even in the case of initially controversial programs—such as Ford tackling racism or Princeton moving into coeducation—the institutions, despite flak, kept abreast if not ahead of the social movements in this country. In so doing, they reaffirmed their utility and value. In looking back, there seems little doubt now that if the Ford Foundation had ignored questions of race, or if Princeton had tried to sidestep the feminist revolution, they would be less important institutions today.

Kotler and Levy write:

> All organizations are formed to serve the interest of particular groups. . . . In the course of evolving, many organizations lose sight of their original mandate, grow hard, and become self-serving. The bureaucratic mentality begins to dominate the original service mentality. . . . All these actions tend to build frustration in the consuming groups. . . . Many organizations have been stunned into recognizing they have lost touch with their constituencies. They have grown unresponsive.[12]

In sum, nonprofit organizations must provide service to consumers. They must be responsive to the needs of others. For a nonprofit institution to thrive, it must be in touch with the ever-changing nature of society's unmet needs and must continually demonstrate its responsiveness to them.

Active-Positive Leadership

Finally, the building of an entrepreneurial organization is heavily dependent on the presence of an active, positive-minded spirit at the helm of the organization.

To borrow from James David Barber's book, *Presidential Character*:

> We are speaking of the personality who has a conviction that the future is not set, not inevitably either for good or ill . . . who has a flexible style which employs a variety of tactics as the situation requires . . . who has the capacity to become engaged in the enterprise without becoming so immersed in it as to lose detachment, objectivity and perspective . . . and finally has the capacity to communicate excitement, moving from a base of internal strength, connecting with other people, stimulating their interest, invigorating their positive imaginations, imparting to all around a sense that they are at the center of fascinating events and that the center is moving.[13]

In characterizing such leadership as "active-positive," I do not mean to imply the personality must be charismatic or magnetic. In fact, Peters' and Waterman's colleagues, Phillips and Kennedy, point out:

> Success in instilling values appears to have had little to do with charismatic personality. Rather, it derived from obvious, sincere, sustained personal commitment to the values the

---

[12] Kotler and Levy, "Broadening the Concept of Marketing" (Kotler, Ferrell, and Lamb, pp 9–10).

[13] James David Barber, *Presidential Character* (Englewood Cliffs, NJ: Prentice-Hall, 1972, pp. 12, 210–211).

leaders sought to implant, coupled with extraordinary persistence in reinforcing those values. None of the men we studied relied on personal magnetism. All made themselves into effective leaders.[14]

In a broader sense, I have been talking about leadership with a capability to develop a purposeful vision of the future and to instill that sense of purpose in others.

In sum, I am talking about combinations of logic and emotion, intellectual power and emotional force, calculation and intuition, and vision and risk-taking, all essential elements of character and personality that motivate people and institutions to change. When these elements fuse in one person we have the quintessential entrepreneurial leader in action.

Such leadership creates within an organization the motivation that energizes individuals to avoid the path of least resistance and inspires them to stretch and grow. The talent to so inspire others is, Peters and Waterman maintain, the hallmark of the leadership of our excellent business corporations.[15] It is equally the mark of our best not-for-profit organizations.

THE IMPERATIVE OF SELF-DEFINITION

Before I end, a small note of qualification is in order. In the focus on change, let it not be said that all forms of change are necessarily an advance. Indeed, the high velocity of change in the modern world may account for the pervasive sense of anxiety many seem to feel in contemporary life. For change to be genuinely productive it must spring out of a strong sense of coherence. Without a sense of who you are—and who you are not—there is the danger that, rather than being a calculated adaptation to new circumstances or opportunities, change will be a misplaced search for identity. Without a sharply defined sense of what you do uniquely well, there is the danger that you will dilute your strength and your quality by extending yourself into areas that are not fields of your comparative advantage.

Thus, in this chapter I have talked about the imperative of self-definition and a strong belief structure as a central frame of reference for sorting through choices. For institutions as well as individuals, a strong sense of identity allows people to see the constancy of change in human affairs as an opportunity for liberating growth and personal self-renewal.

[14] Peters and Waterman, pp. 287–288.
[15] Peters and Waterman, pp. 81–86.

VI.

Profiles of Nonprofit Entrepreneurs

Profile of an Entrepreneur: Ruth Maxwell

HER ENTERPRISE is housed on the second floor of a church annex, above a nursery school. To get to it, you have to pass by the three- and four-year-olds in the nursery, and a mix of their gleeful and tearful voices follows you up the stairs. Her office is dominated by two chintz-covered couches set perpendicular to each other around a coffee table. A desk is pushed into an alcove on the other side of the room, out of sight. She greets you warmly, without any weariness, and leads you to one of the couches. She offers you coffee, and when you decline, seats herself opposite you, maintaining eye contact all the time. The setting is far more that of a sitting room than a business office, so it seems an altogether unlikely place in which to find a hard-driving entrepreneur building a growing organization.

But Ruth Maxwell is very much an entrepreneur in the mode of the driving personalities who found and build an innovative enterprise. The organization she is building has grown from the $57,000 gross revenues it earned in its first year of operation to the $250,000 that it generated in its third year (1983).

Certainly, her vocabulary is classically entrepreneurial. Her speech is filled with energy and with a passion for her venture. Plans of her next projects come tumbling out one after the other, and she obviously has more ambitions than there are hours in the day to execute them. She talks eagerly of the increased returns the new activities will bring and how she intends to acquire all of the space in the church annex. She adds, "We're going to make an offer for all the space on a long-term basis. The nursery school can't make that kind of commitment, and so we are hoping to get the entire building."

When you press her to tell you what problems she agonizes about as she falls asleep at night, she dismisses your question with, "I don't agonize." When you rephrase your inquiry to ask what her concerns are for the future of her enterprise, she replies, "As I go to sleep, I think of immediate things to be done . . . the trouble I'm having with your question is that it never occurs to me that things won't work out. Failure never enters my thinking."

What sets Ruth Maxwell apart from typical business entrepreneurs is that she has founded and operates a tax-exempt, nonprofit enterprise. The institute, which bears her name, provides an array of services and training in the field of chemical dependency and family therapy. Modeled after the successful Johnson Institute of Minneapolis, the Maxwell Institute is the first of its kind in the Northeast.

If Ruth Maxwell talks and acts like an entrepreneur, she operates in a sector that rarely employs such idioms or thinks in such terms. She is one of the under-recognized members of the not-for-profit world: the breed of entrepreneurs who found and build new institutions.

How did Ruth get started as a not-for-profit entrepreneur? She began her career as a psychiatric nurse and then became a chemical dependency therapist at the Alcoholism Rehabilitation Center of Roosevelt Hospital in New York City. During this period of her career, she authored a book, *The Booze Battle*. Then she founded her own private management consulting firm, which designed and helped operate treatment programs for alcoholics and other psychologically disabled employees in industry. Although she was making a good living from her firm, at the end of the 1970s she found herself bored and lonely.

My interview with Ruth Maxwell went on for more than an hour.

Sitting in her warm and easy office, she recalled, "I was working alone, making money, but the employee-assistance field was dull and not challenging, and I was not working with the families of the alcoholics. In addition, I was commuting from the suburbs to an office in midtown New York and clients located on Wall Street. . . . Most days, I had to go right to Wall Street and I didn't even get to my office. . . . I don't like the Wall Street area. The buildings block out the sunshine. I was perpetually depressed down there . . . and every year I went to Minneapolis to update my training, and I knew what they were doing out there . . . ."

Like many entrepreneurs, the decision to move in a new direction, while it had been growing within her for some time, was actually made on the spur of the moment. She recalled, "I went to dinner at a friend's house and there I ran into Rick Hernandez, now my partner at the institute. I had known Rick from earlier in my career and he was head of a detoxification unit in the Bronx at the time we ran into each other again. He hated his work. Both our spouses had some income and we had put some money away. I found myself saying to Rick, 'Let's form a Johnson Institute,' and he replied without a moment's hesitation, 'Let's do it.' And so we were on our way."

The Maxwell Institute, in the mode of many new enterprises, was started on a shoestring and a lot of high hopes. In the beginning of 1980, Ruth Maxwell approached a wealthy friend who gave her $10,000 to start the institute and Ruth then loaned the new organization $8,000 of her own money. With these funds, the institute was launched.

The first year the institute earned $19,460 in fees and $37,640 in contributions, including $8,000 from Ruth and $10,000 from an unsolicited gift after the institute helped a family member of the donor. Another $3,000 came from IBM, following treatment of an employee, and the rest were small contributions solicited through countless calls on prospects.

Revenues rose to $116,000 in the institute's second year ($70,000 in fees) and then zoomed to the more than $250,000 the institute earned in 1983.

The scope and volume of services offered by Maxwell has also grown rapidly. In its first year—actually a ten-month period—the institute treated some 155 new clients and began holding about three group sessions by the second half of the year. In its third year (1983), the institute serviced:

- 30 new clients a month
- 11 group sessions on an ongoing basis
- 8 week-long seminars per month (this number will have increased to 12 by 1984)
- A number of offsite, short training sessions for health care and other professionals.

Other new services—such as a six-week evening course for parents—began in early 1984.

Asked why she chose to organize the institute as a not-for-profit enterprise, Ruth explained, "It is modeled after the Johnson Institute in Minneapolis, which is a not-for-profit organization. There was no model of a for-profit enterprise for us to follow, but we did have a not-for-profit model."

In addition, she pointed out that both she and her cofounder, Rick Hernandez, had worked in the not-for-profit sector, and they felt more comfortable in that environment than in the profit-making world. They both also felt that the not-for-profit form was "more acceptable at the time."

When I picked up on "at the time," she explained, "Well, now I see the development of private hospitals and they are doing a good job. So I am not sure what I would do today if I were starting over."

Ruth went on to tick off some of the special benefits of the not-for-profit form for her institute:

- The tax deduction to donors helped attract money from families grateful for the service that she provides and from other individuals with a special interest in the field of alcoholism and chemical dependency.
- The church where her institute is located charges a very low rental fee, but the church is willing only to rent to a not-for-profit organization. (Ruth seemed surprised to learn that the church's unwillingness to rent to a profit-making organization was a policy decision of the church, rather than a requirement of the Internal Revenue Code for

exempt organizations. Exempt organizations may indeed rent to profit-making organizations.)

The institute is organized as a Connecticut corporation and licensed as an educational facility by the State University of New York. When I asked Ruth why she formed the institute as a Connecticut corporation, she replied that when the institute was put together, she did not know where it actually would be located. A friend who was a Connecticut lawyer, as a favor, did the paperwork of organizing the institute.

Not surprisingly, Ruth thinks of the institute as "hers." She seemed a little taken aback when I pointed out that the control of the institute rested with its board. I explained that if she had formed a profit-making corporation, as its owner she could remove the board at any time it failed to do her bidding. But in the case of the nonprofit institute, the board is self-perpetuating, and has the right to hire or fire her at any time. If they disagreed with her, she could not remove them.

"You know, Ruth," I said, "right now you and the institute are perceived undoubtedly by the board as inseparable, and the board is going to do your bidding. But boards have a way of changing over time and acting up. You might want to think about having an employment contract and also making it clear that you have only licensed your name to the institute."

Ruth looked at me reflectively for a moment and said, "I should think about a contract. Just a few months ago we had our first real conflict with the board, and it was over salaries. I put into the budget salaries based on what people are paid for this kind of work in the for-profit world, and that shook up two of our board members—ironically, the two wealthiest members of the board. They got quite upset with our new salaries and ultimately resigned in some anger over the matter."

I then pressed her as to whether she had ever wondered how she could reap the benefits of any financial success the institute might enjoy if someday she got tired of working. Again, she was reflective for a moment and said, "No, I have never really thought about that. But the institute could be successful financially. The Johnson Institute has reached that stage and Mr. Johnson, who founded it, has retired and is just fading away without benefiting from what he built."

We then went on to talk about the mission of the institute. The Maxwell Institute sees its field as encompassing not only alcoholism but all forms of chemical dependency, and it focuses not just on the dependent person but that person's entire family. The premise is that a family is a delicate ecological system, and when one of its members or parts is out of balance, the equilibrium of the entire family or system is disturbed. Therefore, treatment must embrace not only the dependent person, but all of those within his or her family system.

The institute provides an array of services, which are all but unmatched in the field of chemical dependency treatment. The services include:

- intervention with the dependent person. Persons suffering from alcoholism and other chemical dependencies rarely are able to recognize their own illnesses. This service mobilizes the family and other friends of the chemically dependent person to confront him or her, and at that confrontation to insist that the dependent person seek treatment immediately. The aim is to motivate dependent persons to accept treatment earlier in the disease process when recovery rates are higher.

- recovery support therapy for families of persons who are undergoing treatment. Since chemical dependency affects all members of the dependent person's family, support for the family, as well as the dependent person, is integral to recovery of both the person and his or her family.

- training for teachers and health care professionals in the treatment of chemical dependency. Not surprisingly, teachers in today's schools know virtually nothing about chemical dependency illness. But it is a startling truth that almost none of our country's medical schools offer any training in the disease.

- assessments of adolescents. In these evaluations, the institute tries to determine whether a teenager is dependent chemically. The assessments involve work with both adolescents and their families, since not only will the dependent adolescent inevitably deny being ill, but parents will tend also to deny the presence of the illness, frequently dismissing warning signs as merely "typical adolescent behavior."

- programs to deal with alcohol and drug abuse in schools and communities. The first such program was established by the Institute in Tarrytown, New York, and a grant now is being sought from a foundation to extend the program to four additional communities.

At present, the institute's $250,000-plus in revenues are evenly divided between its self-generated revenues and donations. The largest "donation" was in fact the product of a lot of management time and effort—a theater benefit planned and organized by the institute for the first time in March 1983. It netted $49,000 for the institute. Of the $125,000 in self-generated revenues, about $53,000 comes from training programs and consultations, while $72,000 comes from client services (interventions and assessments).

Ruth is concentrating on expansion of the institute's training program as the chief means of increasing the institute's revenues. She sees a ripe opportunity to provide training in the treatment of chemical dependency to health care professionals. With some irritation in her voice, she noted that such professionals receive virtually no such training despite the fact that alcoholism and other forms of chemical dependency are among the nation's most widespread illnesses, behind only heart disease and cancer. Her margin of profit on such training programs is good, she said, because she uses volunteers to prepare the core materials, and part-time training consultants, who do not charge the institute for their services, to run the seminars. "They want the publicity of working with us," she observed proudly.

I asked why, in light of her experience prior to organizing the institute, Ruth had not pushed the institute more into developing employee assistance programs for corporations. She replied that most large corporations already had such programs. She added that developing such opportunities is a multi-year process and to search for employee assistance business among smaller-sized corporations did not seem as good an opportunity as founding training and school programs. No other agency in the Northeast, she noted, was providing such services; and besides, she concluded, "I love working with kids."

The institute is a small enterprise. Its full-time staff consists of just three professionals, including Ruth, and one secretary. The institute also employs two part-time persons and a consulting medical director. This staff personally does the assessments and interventions, runs the family support therapy sessions, sets up the training programs, handles the day-to-day business of the enterprise, and plans its new endeavors. Working in such an environment is both exhilarating and a relentless grind.

"The first year," Ruth related, "it was a full day and then out every night to another church dinner to tell people about our services. It's still days, weekends, and evenings, and this past year I got very tired. This July I took my first vacation in years. . . ."

The ten-member board of the institute is a hard-working group, of which Ruth by her own admission asks a great deal. The board members are all people Ruth knows or has identified and selected for membership. The board meets monthly and typically is given specific assignments to work on between meetings. For example, the board was asked to develop the options for the installation of a pension plan for the institute's employees. In character with many smaller nonprofit organizations, some board members perform functions that would be undertaken in large organizations by staff or outside paid professionals. Such functions include legal and accounting work or help with the organization of the institute's first theater benefit.

The interview's most revealing moments came near the end when Ruth and I talked about the chemically dependent teenager of a family we both know. Ruth talked reflectively about the case, and of how difficult it is to break through the denial of everyone in a dependency situation, including family members as well as the addicted person. She spoke of the lengths to which such a person will go to hide the illness from family, friends, and themselves. Denial is made easier because there is no objective test, as science has uncovered for so many other diseases, which will diagnose whether a person is suffering from chemical dependency. Only knowledge of the disease and experience in dealing with it can enable detection of the illness in someone. But as Ruth observed almost wistfully, "Until you get a person into treatment, you can't be sure if they are in fact addicted."

As she spoke, it was apparent that Ruth Maxwell was totally caught up in the work of healing and had virtually a limitless store of loving concern for those who so desperately needed her help. She is indeed one of a rare breed—a person who combines in her daily work both entrepreneurship and humanism.

Profile of an Artisan of Institutional Change: MacGeorge Bundy

IT HAD BEEN MORE THAN TEN YEARS since I had last seen MacGeorge Bundy. It was now December 1983, and Bundy was working in the converted apartment building on lower Fifth Avenue in Manhattan that serves as his faculty office at NYU. His secretary Alice, who had been with him in Washington and at the Ford Foundation, was at a desk in a cramped outer office. Mac was in a room littered with books and files, where he was at work on a long-promised book on nuclear policy. He wore a sport shirt open at the neck and his tweed jacket was slung over the back of his chair. He had to move aside a pile of books to make room for me to sit down. The setting was a far cry from the elegant, polished surroundings from which he ran the Ford Foundation.

For 13 years (1966–79) Bundy had presided over the affairs of the foundation, the nation's largest with some $3.7 billion in assets and an annual budget of over $200 million in the 1960s. At the time he became president, the Ford Foundation's assets were equal to one-sixth of the total resources of all the nation's 25,000 foundations.

Bundy directed the foundation from a spacious, rectangular-shaped office on the tenth floor of the foundation building. The office was lined with books and utterly quiet, as if it were a library. At one end was a floor-to-ceiling picture window which looked out on the 11-story atrium within the foundation building. At the base of the cavernous atrium was a lush garden.[1] No shades covered his office window, so Bundy was always visible to anyone on the outside.

---

[1] The dramatic and elegant building was completed in 1967 at a cost of $17.5 million. Intended as an esthetic addition to New York City, it has been a subject of continuing controversy both as to its appropriateness and to its architectural merits.

The president's office at the foundation was an altogether fitting setting for the former dean of the Harvard Faculty of Arts and Sciences and national security adviser to Presidents Kennedy and Johnson. Indeed, Bundy was one of the shimmering jewels of Kennedy's "New Frontier," with an almost legendary reputation for a cool style and a lucid, finely honed intelligence. (Kennedy once said admiringly of Bundy, "You can't beat brains.")[2]

During 1970–71, I was a program director at the Ford Foundation. There I knew Bundy as a man who matched his Washington reputation. He had a brilliant, versatile mind and the ability to express *the* issue at the center of a problem with astonishing quickness, clarity, and conviction. He would draft a policy paper with just the right balance of simplicity and depth to enable its readers to plunge into a lively debate. His audience would feel sufficiently informed to express its reactions, and also anxious to learn more, rather than intimidated into silence and confusion by too much information.

This skill was coupled with an extraordinary breadth of information and knowledge, not to mention contacts, in fields as diverse as the arts, the popular media, and public policy. Bundy also enjoyed a deserved reputation for being a decision-maker who comes to judgments quickly and who does not waver even under fire. These qualities enabled him to exercise strong leadership of the Ford Foundation (although by his own admission, he gave great latitude to his division heads within the broad policies he formulated).

To some, his manner has always seemed to border on the autocratic, and he indeed has the gift for the sharp put-down one might expect of a Harvard dean. But his manner is infused with an element of gaiety as if he knows the role people expect him to play and so he plays it with relish lest he disappoint them.

He is, however, an emotional man. Roger Wilkins, who served as an officer of the Ford Foundation in the Bundy era, offers this insight in his autobiography: Wilkins was having dinner at Bundy's home one night when the subject came up of the controversial Ford grants to Kennedy's staff following the senator's assassination. Wilkins said to Bundy:

> I know why you made those grants. You were at the White House when John Kennedy was killed and you saw how devastated and distraught all those people left were. You figured that those guys could pull themselves together if they were given some projects to do and some time to do them in.

Wilkins looked over at Bundy who had his face in his hands. When Bundy looked up, tears were brimming behind his clear-rimmed glasses. "Yes," Bundy said softly, "Yes."[3]

---

[2] David Halberstam, *The Best and the Brightest* (New York: Random House, 1969, p. 44).
[3] Roger Wilkins, *A Man's Life* (New York: Simon and Schuster, 1982, p. 258).

Bundy has strong instincts and is given to listening to his hunches. One day in 1971, I reported to him on a request from the Children's Television Workshop, which Ford helped to launch, that the foundation now finance CTW's development of a cable television system in Washington. I told Mac I thought the particular project was beyond their capabilities, but I added how impressed I was with the energy and potential of this then three-year-old organization which had startled the television world by producing "Sesame Street" and then "The Electric Company." I suggested we find a way, other than by the cable project, to help CTW build its self-generated revenues and reduce its dependence on government funds. Bundy leaned back in his chair, tilting it slightly as he put his hands behind his head, reflected for a few moments, and then asked, "Do you think we'd lose our money if we invested in the Workshop?" he asked. "No," I replied. "Okay," he went on, "then let's give CTW $10 million as unrestricted support."

The whole conversation had taken no longer than five minutes. But Bundy never wavered from the decision of that moment during the next nearly 12 months as he and I and others in the Ford Foundation negotiated to overcome the initially strong objections of the foundation board of trustees towards providing capital to enable CTW to launch business enterprises.

Bundy is also a sensitive, caring man, although that side of his nature is not often revealed in public. If he does not vacillate, he is not all-indifferent to criticism. Shortly after *The Pentagon Papers* were published in the spring of 1971, he announced at one of his customary staff briefings following a trustee's meeting, "The publication of the papers raised in the minds of some questions about my fitness to lead the foundation." He announced he would shortly hold an open meeting for the entire Ford Foundation to discuss the subject. He did hold such a meeting and though he gave no ground, he also set no boundaries on the questions asked of him.

MacGeorge Bundy took over as the Ford Foundation's fourth president on March 1, 1966. The man he succeeded, Henry Heald, former president of NYU, had been the foundation's chief executive for nine years. His tenure had been marked by increasing tensions between himself and the foundation's board of trustees. Heald had sought to build a professionally managed foundation with staff and trustees each playing their appropriate roles. Before Heald's arrival there was a history at the foundation of presidents who acted without trustee consent on crucial matters and board intervention into the foundation's operations.

The board, in the pre-Heald era, had also reacted nervously to criticisms of various foundation projects, especially from the political right.[4] Heald succeeded in persuading

---

[4] See Waldemar A. Nielsen, *The Big Foundations* (New York: Twentieth Century Fund, 1972, pp. 78–93).

the Ford board to give up its review of any individual grants to focus instead on setting policy parameters for programs.

During Heald's tenure, the foundation expanded its support of individual artists and cultural institutions. It accelerated its support of international affairs programs and launched an effort to improve conditions in a number of large cities. But its largest grant program was aimed at helping a select group of universities and colleges further "their overall development as regional and national centers of excellence." In simple, nonbureaucratic language, the program's goal was to enable a group of second-class institutions to become first-class.

The program reflected Heald's concept of the foundation as a kind of banking partner to higher education. While the grants required the recipients to raise matching funds, they were open to the criticism that they only made it marginally easier for the institutions to do what they could on their own. Moreover, the amounts of money required to sustain the program were soon beyond even the foundation's means as the real value of its endowment began to erode in the 1960s.

By 1965, strains between Heald and the board had increased. The board found him "increasingly a stiff and uninspiring man, inadequate both intellectually and in social outlook to lead the world's largest private Foundation."[5] By the summer of 1965 the search was on for a new president, and the choice was Bundy.

"The foundation trustees," Bundy related, sitting with me in his NYU office, "wanted the foundation to be strongly led . . . they were ready for active leadership . . . .

"I had expected to go back to Harvard, but Mary [his wife] wanted to go to New York. I had reached the conclusion that I wasn't doing a good job of communicating with LBJ, and the foundation appointment seemed a good way to separate without giving him a hard time."

One of Bundy's first actions as president was to establish a major redirection in the Ford Foundation's program priorities. He recalled, "The foundation was only marginally engaged in the most important domestic issue of 1966—the race issue. [I myself was to learn it was also American Indians, Hispanics, women, and other disadvantaged groups.] Getting the foundation trustees on board went very quickly. They agreed I could state this was our most important interest, and I announced it in a speech to the Urban League."

The new program direction was launched with a series of unrestricted grants to the Urban League and the NAACP, the first such form of support the foundation had ever given to a black organization.

Bundy followed up by naming as head of the Ford Foundation's National Affairs Division a man of his own choice, Mitchell Sviridoff, a former trade union leader who had never attended college. Bundy recruited Sviridoff from the Lindsay administration

---

[5] Nielsen, *The Big Foundations*, p. 92.

and then, in January of 1967, brought in Roger Wilkins, a black official in the Kennedy and Johnson administrations, to run National Affairs' Office of Social Development, which was to be the spearhead of the foundation's efforts to support minority groups and communities. A year later the first black was added to the foundation's board: Dr. Vivian Henderson, president of Clark College in Atlanta. Very quickly, the percentage of the foundation's outlays allocated to National Affairs more than doubled, many of them grants for minority voter registration, community economic development, and other politically sensitive objectives.

Bundy's recounting to me of the change in foundation priorities made it sound very simple: the trustees wanted a man with fresh ideas, and Bundy supplied them. One former foundation colleague and admirer of Bundy speculates, however, that a business-dominated board of trustees did not necessarily buy Bundy's idea of making the racial issue the foundation's number one priority out of commitment to social innovation. In his view, the board had probably anticipated Bundy would make his move in the international area. He observed:

> The support for Bundy's racial initiative reflected less conviction that Bundy was right than the corporate tradition of deference to a new chief executive and of giving him initial latitude to initiate his new ideas. Bundy was effective because he had grown up as part of the establishment, was always regarded as part of it, and was sensitive to the psychology he confronted . . . Bundy also helped himself by bringing some of his friends on board from government (Robert McNamara and Kermit Gordon), and, of course, having the CEO name some board members is also part of the corporate tradition.[6]

The impact of Ford's focus on the nation's racial concerns may have reached beyond the organizations it supported. The Ford Foundation, as the nation's largest philanthropic institution, attracted widespread attention, especially with the well-known Mac Bundy at its helm. The foundation had the capacity to put its imprimatur on things, to make activities and endeavors acceptable for business and government to support. Eamon Kelly, now president of Tulane University and a former Ford official who was deeply involved in the foundation's support of minorities, has aptly observed, "What the Ford Foundation said was an acceptable endeavor became so . . . it made the notion of a programmatic response to the civil rights revolution acceptable for business and government."

The foundation's international programs, which some had thought might be Bundy's primary interest, were given a lower priority than domestic programs. And within the international field, the program focus shifted from Europe to the third world

[6] Bundy, when I read him the above quote, responded, "I doubt the judgment that the board made when I arrived was business-dominated. I don't have the list in front of me, but the strong men on the board as I remember it were people like Webster and Black and Cowles and Wysanski—Henry Ford held back, I think quite deliberately, in my early years. But this is a matter of nuance, and anyway you are quoting somebody else."

under the direction of David Bell, whom the trustees had recruited from his position as director of the U.S. Foreign Aid Program to become executive vice-president of the foundation.

Bundy also took a major plunge into noncommercial television, giving the electronic medium a higher budget priority than the foundation's traditional support of the arts. To spearhead this effort, Bundy recruited Fred Friendly, former head of CBS News. "Walter Lippmann called me," Bundy recalled, "and said 'Mac, you're going up to the Ford Foundation and you ought to talk to Fred Friendly.' The foundation had then a commitment to educational broadcasting, but with Fred we got into being the private banker and counselor to public broadcasting . . . we were heavily involved . . . that was Fred's style."

This active, interventionist style to grant-making also characterized much of the work of National Affairs. In the pre-Bundy era, Ford, like most other foundations, received applications for grants, reviewed them without extensively scrutinizing the operations or management of potential recipients, and wrote a check for those it approved with few strings attached. By and large, recipients were limited to well-established institutions with national reputations.

Under Bundy, the foundation began asking tough questions and making tough demands on its grant recipients. It got into the details of the recipient's program design and the quality of the people who would be running the programs it financed. And it was by no means shy in insisting, as a condition of its support, that grantees make changes in their programs and their personnel and meet performance tests. Foundation officers and their consultants began digging into the nuts and bolts of grantees' operations, especially their financial management.

Our discussion about the foundation's more interventionist style led me to ask Bundy to draw some generalizations about the elements of effective foundation grant-making. He responded:

> The process begins with a quality staff which can identify the problem and a means of attacking it. And, crucially, there must be something in the environment that makes people ready to respond, a ripeness or readiness for change . . . someone must be interested besides the foundation. . . .

Bundy continued:

> I came to believe in "knowing issues" and "staying with the problem." . . . It is very rare that the best thing to do is to make a single grant and go away. . . .

For amplification of this point Bundy directed me to a speech he gave near the end of his tenure as foundation president. In these remarks, delivered in May 1979, he observed:

Serious program work takes time. . . . Time is needed . . . to know whom to work with, and to be known in turn, so that people who have better ideas than yours will know where to find you. Time is needed, most of all, to be able to give staying power to those whose work may make a difference.

In support of his view Bundy cited the foundation's controversial decision to fund public interest law firms, a decision, especially in the area of environmental law, which some of the foundation's trustees opposed vociferously. "It took years," Bundy noted, "to build relationships with the bar."

I asked Bundy how a foundation ought to choose its program objectives. He offered:

There are a lot of good things to do. . . . You have to look at who you are . . . what you know . . . what skills you have . . . what you are personally interested in . . . one could never say one idea is better than anything else . . . one only could say it's worth doing and we know how to do it. . . .

In the same speech quoted earlier, Bundy enlarged on this theme, saying:

The foundation that wants to make a difference by a sustained program effort has to have a clear understanding of its reasons for choosing a given program area. It must be able to answer the question: Why pick this field? It must believe in its decision hard enough to put up with failure and, sometimes, controversy. It must also be willing to ignore shifting fashion . . . what is visible right now. True commitment implies an opposite way of deciding what matters.

Bundy reflected that there were few cases in which the Ford Foundation made a major investment in an institution where it did not get involved with management. He pointed to the foundation's program to improve the viability of theater groups. "We were not trying to meet the immediate crisis in theater companies," he observed, "but to help them position themselves to be able to cope continually with their financial needs. We used the carrot of grants to induce their managements to act in a money-conscious manner and so we developed a roster of consultants who would get into their financial nuts and bolts."

Bundy quickly pointed out that the Ford approach was not necessarily typical of the foundation world. At the other pole, he observed, are foundations which "agree on a purpose with a first-class institution and then let the institution execute the grant without much oversight."

"But this style," he quickly added, "won't work where the institutions are not yet fully matured."

One of the very few innovations in foundation techniques for funding programs was developed early in the Bundy regime. It was consistent with the more interventionist approach taken by Ford toward those it supported under his leadership. The new technique involved "investing" Ford Foundation funds in an organization instead of making a grant. The investment, either in the form of loan or equity, was not only to be repaid, but the foundation was to earn at least a modest return on its funds.

The object was twofold: first, by expressing support in the form of an "investment," the financial viability of the recipient organization and the economic feasibility of its proposed program were subject to review. Second: the fact that recipients were obliged to pay back the foundation investment meant those repayments could be recycled to support new activities. In times of scarcer foundation resources, recovery and recycling of funds was an important consideration.

The significant shifts in the foundation's priorities under Bundy were quickly reflected in the foundation's budget. The following table, drawn from Nielsen's *The Big Foundations* (New York: Twentieth Century Fund, 1972), summarizes the major changes in program priorities between 1966, Heald's last year, and 1969.

Table 6. FORD FOUNDATION GRANT BREAKDOWN BY PROGRAM DIVISIONS, 1966 AND 1969 (in millions)

	1966		1969	
	$	*% of total*	*$*	*% of total*
National affairs	29.0	8.3	42.	20.6
Education	72.6	20.8	46.	22.5
Humanities and arts	88.0*	25.2	20.	9.8
Noncommercial TV	15.9	4.5	16.5	8.1
International	118.4	34.0	51.5†	25.2
Population	21.3	6.1	8.	3.9
Nonprogram	2.7	.7	20.	9.8
Total	347.9	100.0	204.0	100.0
		(99.6)‡		(99.9)‡

* This figure was unusually high for the year because of $80 million of special grants to symphony orchestras.

† The reduction is largely due to the elimination of the international training and research program, which had supported extensive fellowships and grants to United States institutions dealing with international affairs.

‡ Figures supplied by the Office of Reports of the Ford Foundation. Because of rounding, figures do not add to 100 percent.

The table reveals another major change initiated by Bundy: a sharp cutback of the Ford Foundation's budget. Under Heald, the outlays of the foundation had risen rapidly from a level of $162 million in 1957 to $365 million in 1966. But the foundation's endowment was not growing at a pace near the rate of the increase in its program outlays, and capital was being used to finance programs. Shortly after his appointment, Bundy and the board decided to cut the budget to roughly the level of the foundation's annual income at the time, about $200 million. (Note: the foundation then treated as income only dividends and interest received; in those years, it did not follow a total return spending formula.)

Later on, the Ford Foundation found it impossible to sustain even this reduced level of spending as the turbulence in the capital markets cut into its endowment performance. "I was optimistic about the capital markets," Bundy observed, "but I wasn't right."

Bundy then added:

> I think the key point is simply that we cut back as much as the board would let us, and that initiatives for budget reductions always came from me until the very last year or two, when the brethren got even gloomier than I—and thank goodness they have turned out to be wrong. I think the foundation's budget is well above $100 million now. And the corpus has recovered very well on the basis of the strategic dispositions laid out in Roger Kennedy's time. [Roger Kennedy was Bundy's vice-president for finance.]

If Bundy's intuition about the behavior of capital markets was not clairvoyant, he still seemed clearly the right man at the right time for the Ford Foundation. He had a keen instinct for new foundation priorities that were in tune with the changing agenda of the country, and he had the skills to articulate new directions and persuade trustees to support them.

He clearly changed the foundation's priorities, as well as its operating style, from a primarily passive supporter of mostly elite educational and cultural institutions to an interventionist financier of new, less mature organizations bent on achieving racial justice, social change, and providing alternatives to powerful commercial interests.

His tenure at Ford suggests there is a ripe moment for change—when the powers that have to be moved are ready to move and there is a constituency for a new initiative. Bundy properly sensed he had such a moment and seized it with relish and imagination.

Works Cited in the Text

Anthony, Robert N., and Regina E. Herzlinger. *Management Control in Nonprofit Organizations,* rev. ed. Homewood, IL: Richard D. Irwin, Inc., 1980.

Barber, James David. *Presidential Character.* Englewood Cliffs, NJ: Prentice-Hall, 1972.

Bartolome and Evans. "Must Success Cost So Much?" *Harvard Business Review,* March/April 1980.

Baum, Claude. *The System Builders: The History of SDC.* Santa Monica: System Development Corporation, 1981.

Baumol, William, and William G. Bowen. *The Performing Arts: The Economic Dilemma.* New York: Twentieth Century Fund, 1966.

Benacerraf, Paul, William G. Bowen, Thomas A. Davis, William W. Lewis, Linda K. Morse, and Carl W. Schafer. "Budgeting and Resource Allocation at Princeton University." Report of a Demonstration Project Supported by the Ford Foundation. Princeton, 1972.

Bittker and Rahdent. "The Exemption of Non Profit Organizations from Federal Income Taxation." *The Yale Law Journal,* January 1976.

Bowen, Howard R. *Academic Compensation, Are Faculty and Staff in American Higher Education Adequately Paid?* Teachers Insurance and Annuity Association/College Retirement and Equities Fund, 1978.

Bowen, William G. *The Economics of Major Private Universities.* Carnegie Commission on Higher Education, 1966.

Bowen, William G. "The Effects of Inflation/Recession on Higher Education." *Educational Record,* Summer 1975.

Bradford, David L., and Allan R. Cohen. *Managing for Excellence.* New York: John Wiley and Sons, 1984.

Bundy, MacGeorge. "C^{3}I in Foundation Work." Ford Foundation Report, Series 71, 1979.

Carey, William L., and Craig B. Bright. "The Developing Law of Endowment Funds" in *The Law and the Lore Revisited*. Report to the Ford Foundation, 1974.

"College Funds Taking Steps to Raise Yields." *The Wall Street Journal*, August 10, 1983.

Cooper, Philip D., and George E. McIlvain. "Factors Influencing Marketing's Ability to Assist Nonprofit Organizations" in *Cases and Readings for Marketing for Nonprofit Organizations*. Philip Kotler, O. C. Ferrell, and Charles Lamb, eds. Englewood Cliffs, NJ: Prentice-Hall, 1983.

Crimmins, James C., and Mary Keil. *Enterprise in the Nonprofit Sector*. Partners for Livable Places and The Rockefeller Brothers Fund, 1983.

"Do Mergers Really Work?" *Business Week*, June 3, 1985.

Drucker, Peter. *Landmarks of Tomorrow*. New York: Harper and Brothers, 1952.

Drucker, Peter. "Managing the Public Service Institution." *The Public Interest*, Fall 1983.

Firstenberg, Paul, and Burton Malkiel. *Managing Risk in an Uncertain Era: An Analysis for Endowed Institutions*. Princeton: Princeton University, 1976.

Firstenberg, Paul, and Burton Malkiel. "Why Corporate Boards Need Independent Directors." *Management Review*, April 1980.

"Foundations fail to live up to their potential, critic says in new book." *The Chronicle of Higher Education*, November 20, 1985.

Freedman. "Financial Problems Are Compromising Nonprofit Theaters." *The New York Times*, March 14, 1984.

Gardner, John. *Self-Renewal, The Individual, and The Innovative Society*. New York: W. W. Norton and Company, 1981.

Giving and Getting. New York: Chemical Bank, 1981, updated 1984.

Giving in America: Toward a Stronger Voluntary Sector, Report of the Commission on Private Philanthropy and Public Needs (Filer Commission Report). Washington, D.C., 1975.

Halberstam, David. *The Best and the Brightest*. New York: Random House, 1969.

Hayes, Robert, and William Abernathy. "Managing Our Way to Economic Decline." *Harvard Business Review*, July/August 1980.

Herzlinger, Regina E. "Why Data Systems in Non-Profit Organizations Fail." *Harvard Business Review*, January/February 1977.

Ibbotson, Roger G., and Laurence B. Siegel. "The World Wealth Portfolio." *The Journal of Portfolio Management,* Spring 1983.

Kanter, Rosabeth Moss. *The Change Masters.* New York: Simon and Schuster, 1983.

Kotler, Philip. *Marketing for Nonprofit Organizations,* 2nd ed. Englewood Cliffs, NJ: Prentice-Hall, 1982.

Kotler, Philip, and Sidney J. Levy. "Broadening the Concept of Marketing" in *Cases and Readings for Marketing for Nonprofit Organizations,* Philip Kotler, O. C. Ferrell, and Charles Lamb, eds. Englewood Cliffs, NJ: Prentice-Hall, 1983.

Lazer and Cully. *Marketing Management.* Boston: Houghton Mifflin, 1983.

Levi, Julian H., and Sheldon Elliot Steinbach. *An Analysis of Voluntary Support of American Colleges and Universities, 1973–1974.* American Council on Education.

Lorie, James H., and Mary T. Hamilton. *The Stock Market.* Homewood, IL: Richard D. Irwin, Inc., 1973.

Lovelock, Christopher H., and Charles B. Weinberg. "Public and Nonprofit Marketing Comes of Age" in *Review of Marketing 1978,* Zoltman and Bonoma, eds. Chicago: American Marketing Association, 1978.

Malkiel, Burton. *A Random Walk Down Wall Street,* 4th ed. New York: W. W. Norton and Company, 1985.

Malkiel, Burton. *Risk and Return, A New Look.* National Bureau of Economic Research, Inc. NBER Reprint No. 291.

Managing Educational Endowments (The Barker Report). New York: The Ford Foundation, 1969.

Molotsky, Irvin. "What Went Wrong at National Public Radio." *The New York Times,* June 12, 1983.

Morrisett, Lloyd. "Corporate Planning for Foundations" in *Strategic Planning in Private Non-Profit Organizations.* Bedford, MA: MITRE Corporation, 1979.

Nash, Edward L. *Direct Marketing, Strategy, Planning, Execution.* New York: McGraw-Hill, 1982.

Nielsen, Waldemar A. *The Big Foundations.* New York: Twentieth Century Fund, 1972.

Peters, Thomas J., and Robert H. Waterman, Jr. *In Search of Excellence.* New York: Harper & Row, 1982.

Porter, Michael E. *Competitive Strategy, Techniques for Analyzing Industries and Competitors.* New York: Free Press, 1980.

Raymond, Thomas J. C., and Stephen A. Greyser. "The Business of Managing Arts Organizations." *Harvard Business Review,* July/August 1978.

"Real Estate Transaction" in *The Buck Starts Here: Enterprise on the Arts.* A Conference for Nonprofit Organizations on the Legal Aspects of Making Money. Volunteer Lawyers for the Arts, 1984.

Rudney, Gabriel. "A Quantitative Profile of the Nonprofit Sector." New Haven: Institution for Social and Policy Studies Program on Non-Profit Organizations, 1981.

Silk, Leonard. "The Origins of Stagflation." *The New York Times,* June 20, 1978.

Spies, Richard. *The Future of Private Colleges: The Effect of Rising Costs on College Choice.* Research Report Series No. 117, Industrial Relations Section, Princeton University, 1973.

Strategic Planning in Private Non-Profit Organizations. Bedford, MA: MITRE Corporation, 1979.

Sturz, Elizabeth. *Widening Circles.* New York: Harper & Row, 1983.

Tregoe, Benjamin B., and John W. Zimmerman. *Top Management Strategy: What It Is and How to Make It Work.* New York: Simon and Schuster, 1983.

Treusch, Paul E., and Norman A. Sugarman. *Tax-Exempt Charitable Organizations,* 2nd ed. Philadelphia: American Law Institute, American Bar Association Committee on Continuing Education, 1983.

Wall, Wendy L. "Helping Hands, Companies Change the Ways They Make Charitable Contributions." *The Wall Street Journal,* June 21, 1984.

"When Should the Profits of Nonprofits Be Taxed?" *Business Week,* December 5, 1983.

Wilkins, Roger. *A Man's Life.* New York: Simon and Schuster, 1982.

Wood, Miriam. "What Role for College Trustees." *Harvard Business Review,* May/June 1983.

Yankelovich, Skelly, and White, Inc. *Business Planning in the Eighties: The New Competitiveness of American Corporations.* New York: Coopers and Lybrand, 1983.

Index